PYTHON
for
MBAs

MATTAN GRIFFEL
and DANIEL GUETTA

Columbia University Press
Publishers Since 1893
New York   Chichester, West Sussex
cup.columbia.edu
Copyright © 2021 Mattan Griffel and Daniel Guetta

Library of Congress Cataloging-in-Publication Data
Names: Griffel, Mattan, author. | Guetta, Daniel, author.
Title: Python for MBAs / Mattan Griffel and Daniel Guetta.
Description: New York : Columbia University Press, [2021] | Includes index.
Identifiers: LCCN 2020032750 (print) | LCCN 2020032751 (ebook) | ISBN
    9780231193924 (hardback) | ISBN 9780231193931 (trade paperback) | ISBN
    9780231550574 (ebook)
Subjects: LCSH: Python (Computer program language) | Business--Data
    processing.
Classification: LCC QA76.73.P98 G77 2021 (print) | LCC QA76.73.P98
    (ebook) | DDC 005.13/3—dc23
LC record available at https://lccn.loc.gov/2020032750
LC ebook record available at https://lccn.loc.gov/2020032751

Columbia University Press books are printed on permanent
    and durable acid-free paper.
Printed in the United States of America

Cover design: Noah Arlow

PYTHON FOR MBAs

CONTENTS

PART 2

PYTHON FOR MBAs

INTRODUCTION

HELLO! We are Mattan Griffel and Daniel Guetta, and we're going to teach you about Python. Before we introduce ourselves, we want to tell you a little bit about the intended audience for this book, what we'll be learning together, and some tips on how you can get the most out of reading this book.

This book is designed for people who have never coded before; so if you're feeling intimidated, don't be. In fact, even if the only kind of Python you've heard of is a snake, or if you're not sure exactly what coding *is*, you'll feel right at home—we'll discuss both in chapter 1. Businesspeople without a technical background decide to start learning how to code for a lot of different reasons. Some want an introduction to a different way of thinking—they realize the world runs on code, and they don't want to be left out. Some are looking for ways to write simple scripts to streamline or automate their work. Others work with coders and technical teams on a day-to-day basis and want to better understand what those teams do. Some are tired of relying on overworked business intelligence teams to get answers from their data and want to be more self-sufficient.

Whichever category you fall into—this book is for you. The material is based on classes we have taught for a number of years at Columbia Business School to professionals just like you. We are going to show you how to use Python to do all kinds of useful things, like automating repetitive tasks to save yourself time and money and performing data analyses to answer important business questions on files far too large and complex to be handled in a spreadsheet.

Hopefully, you'll find that this book provides valuable insight into what's possible using technology and gives you a new skill that you can immediately use in a business context.

We have divided this book into two parts. In part 1, we will learn the basics of Python (loops, variables, lists, and whatnot), and in part 2, we'll dive into ways Python can be used to analyze datasets in a real-world business context.

Unless you are already familiar with Python, you should begin by reading part 1 in order, from start to finish—resist the temptation to jump around. You will learn the fundamental knowledge you need to do anything in Python. This part of the book also contains a number of exercises, and we encourage you to spend some time working on them. If you just read the book without trying these problems, you'll still learn something, but you may not remember it as well. The companion website for this book contains digital versions of every piece of code, but for the same reason, we recommend typing it in by hand rather than just copying and pasting the code. If some questions pop into your mind like, "What happens when I do X?" then try doing it! In the worst-case scenario, it doesn't work. Then, you can revisit what we were showing you. Either way, you'll learn something new.

Part 2 is about using Python to analyze data in a business context. You should begin by reading chapter 5, which introduces a different way to write code in Python. This chapter also introduces the story of Dig, a restaurant chain based in New York that we will return to again and again in this part of the book. We have found that many Python books, even basic ones, seem to be written for engineers—they focus on functionality rather than on how that functionality might be *used*. By rooting part 2 in a real-life case study, we show you what Python can do for *you* rather than teaching it in a vacuum. In the remaining chapters, we discuss how Dig's challenges can be addressed using data. We build on the Python fundamentals you learned in part 1 to show you how to use massive datasets to answer these questions.

Our aim is to teach you the basics of Python and to provide you with a map so that you can decide what you want to learn more about on your own. As a result, we'll sometimes use informal terminology, and skip over some more technical details. This is a deliberate choice on our part—it will prevent us from getting too bogged down with details that aren't essential and will help you get to applications as quickly as possible. In our conclusion, we will point you to resources you can use to take what you've learned to the next level, if you're interested.

One of Python's key strengths is the speed at which it evolves. Thousands of developers around the world donate their time and energy to improve the language and make it faster, richer, and more powerful. The speed at which Python develops is so rapid that some features we cover in part 2 didn't even exist when we started writing it. We have created a companion website to this book (available at https://www.pythonformbas.com) to ensure that it stays up to date as the language evolves. As we become aware of relevant changes, we will endeavor to post them there. In addition, the website will contain digital versions of every piece of code in the book and the datasets we use in part 2, as well as appendices on topics we did not have the space to cover in this book.

In writing this book, we benefited from the help of many people to whom we are infinitely grateful. First and foremost, the students who sat in our classes as we developed the material and gave us their invaluable feedback—if only we were sure not to forget anyone, we would name them all here. We are particularly thankful to (in alphabetical order) Joao Almeida, George Curtis, Nicholas Faville, Nicola Kornbluth, Royd Lim, Brett Martin, Veronica Miranda, Jason Prestinario, and Saron Yitbarek, all of whom took the time to read earlier versions of the manuscripts and give us their comments. It has been a privilege to be at Columbia Business School at a time of tremendous innovation in the area of technology and analytics. The school encouraged us to push the boundaries of what a "traditional" MBA class looks like, and this book was born of these efforts. We are particularly grateful to Dean Costis Maglaras and to members of the Decision, Risk, and Operations Division for their steadfast support. Last but not least, we are eternally grateful to Shereen Asmat, Molly Fisher, and Dig's leadership team for graciously volunteering their time to talk to us about their company. At their request and to protect proprietary information pertaining to their business, many of the details in this book are based on our conversations but otherwise are fictionalized, and the dataset we work with was synthetically generated.

We both love coding, and we love sharing our excitement with others—there is nothing like seeing a student run their first line of code, or their first data analysis. It has been a true pleasure taking our experience doing this in classrooms and converting it to a book for you to read. We look forward to going on this journey with you all!

From coronavirus-induced self-isolation in New York April 2020

PART I

WELCOME TO PART 1. I'm Mattan Griffel and I'm going to teach you a little bit about the basics of Python. I'm going to try to make it interesting and explain some boring things in (hopefully) new and interesting ways. Let me first tell you a little bit about myself.

I'm a two-time Y Combinator–backed entrepreneur. I previously started a company called One Month, an online coding school that teaches people how to code in just thirty days, and I'm currently the founder and chief operating officer of Ophelia, a telemedicine company focused on helping people overcome opioid addiction. I'm also an award-winning faculty member at Columbia Business School, where I teach coding to MBA students and executives. Throughout my career, I've taught tens of thousands of people how to code.

But I have a confession to make: I didn't start off as a coder, and I never got a degree in computer science. I began as in early-twenty-something in New York City with an idea for a startup. I was working in marketing as my first job out of college, and I'd spend my evenings dreaming about my startup idea, but I had a problem: my idea required building software, and I didn't know anyone personally who could do that for me. I tried so hard to find a technical cofounder—I went to hackathons and meetups and pitched people over drinks—but no luck.

Eventually, several of my friends grew tired of hearing me complain about how hard it was to find a developer. One of them, John, confronted me over coffee:

"Either you have to learn how to code so that you can build this by yourself," he told me, "or I need you to stop talking about it because it's getting annoying."

The thought had never even crossed my mind. Why would I learn how to code? Isn't that what software engineers and people working in IT were for?

John shared a personal story with me. Years earlier, during a summer break in high school, John was working as a parking garage attendant with a friend. When they were bored, they often shared stories of what had happened the night before. One of them had gone out with friends after drinking several Four Lokos and had a pretty crazy night (Four Loko was a caffeinated alcohol drink that eventually was banned in several states because it was downright dangerous). They joked for a while about what it would be like if people could share stories about their Four Loko–induced debauchery on a dedicated website.

John decided that while he was bored at his job that summer, he was going to teach himself how to code. John picked up a few books and found some online guides, and a few months later, fourlokostories.com was born. It became pretty popular for a while—getting hundreds of thousands of pageviews and tens of thousands of Facebook likes.

My friend John has since moved on to bigger and better projects. He's actually founded several other companies, many of which started with a random idea and John spending a weekend writing some code. Hearing his story over coffee that day, I was dumbstruck.

"You taught yourself how to code in one summer?" I asked John.

"Yeah, just don't spend a lot of time on the basics," he said. "Pick a project and start working on it as soon as possible. And learn a newer language like Python or Ruby."

That conversation changed my life forever. I ended up quitting my job in marketing and decided I'd try to learn how to code on my own. I didn't have an entire summer, though, so I gave myself one month to see how far I could get. I started with a series of videos on the website Lynda.com, which I raced through in about a week. Even though I didn't really understand most of what I learned at first, I kept going because it was exciting, and I enjoyed the feeling of building something with my own two hands (even though it was all digital and I couldn't actually touch it).

Looking back on that period of my life, I remember being pretty frustrated at times and then really excited when I finally got things to work. One day, I remember doing something that broke all the code I had been writing, and I couldn't get any of it to run for two whole days. Then, when I finally fixed it, I had no idea how I fixed it or how I had broken it in the first place. In retrospect, that's a pretty common experience, even for professional software engineers. You may even feel that way as you read this book.

After spending some time learning how to code every day for about a month, I had built the first version of my startup idea. It was embarrassing and it didn't work most of the time, but it was *mine*.

It's hard to express how good it feels when you finally get your code to run. I've always admired artists for their ability to see something inside their heads (a painting, a sculpture, a story, or whatever) and then actually conjure it into reality. For the first time in my life, through code, I felt like an artist.

Another confession: I'm still not a great coder—plenty of professional software engineers can write better or faster code than me. But one thing I discovered along the way is that I'm quite good at teaching coding to people who have never done it before, and I enjoy it as well.

Most people think that because they never did well in math or science in high school, that they're never going to be able to learn how to code. That's not true. Learning to code is more like learning French or Spanish than it is like doing math. Writing code can be a lot more fun and creative than you might expect.

People think coding is so hard because it tends to be taught really poorly. One of the things I experienced while learning how to code was that most of the online guides and books I found either went way too fast or way too slow. They started by assuming I already had a lot of experience with code, or they started with the basics and spent so much time on that material that I never got to do anything useful with it and I got bored.

Instead, I hope that this book will be an entertaining and helpful guide to learn how to code using Python. Let's try to have some fun along the way.

1

GETTING STARTED WITH PYTHON

1.1 WHAT YOU'LL LEARN IN THIS CHAPTER

By the end of this chapter, you'll have a better understanding of Python, including where it came from and what it can be used for. You'll install Python and a handful of other tools on your computer, and you'll gain a basic understanding of the command line, the place where we'll begin running Python code. Finally, you will run your first Python script and get some exposure to what coding in Python is actually like.

1.2 INTRODUCTION TO PROGRAMMING USING PYTHON

It's quite common for beginners to get overwhelmed when they first start learning a programming language like Python. To paraphrase Donald Rumsfeld, there are "*known unknowns*, and there are *unknown unknowns*." The more you learn about a topic like Python, the more you'll realize what you don't know. The scope of the Python language is *huge*, but you really only need to know a tiny bit for it to be useful.

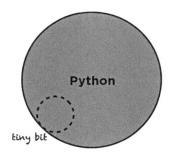

Most experienced programmers only barely scratch the surface. A 2019 survey by Stack Overflow found that almost 90 percent of programmers are self-taught,[1] meaning that even professional programmers constantly come across new topics and concepts they don't know but have to figure out how to learn.

As an analogy, let's consider a language like English. According to the Global Language Monitor, the English language currently has 1,057,379.6 words.[2] (Ever stop to think about what a 0.6 word is? We, too. We still don't know.) Yet the average fluent adult knows only twenty to thirty-five thousand words.[3] Would you say that the average language speaker isn't "fluent" just because they don't know all the words? Probably not.

Learning a programming language like Python is pretty similar to learning a language like English. Of course, it can be frustrating when you don't quite know the word you need to use to express an idea, or what code to write to solve a particular problem. That's what we're here to help you with. Along the way, we'll also point out some common mistakes that beginner coders make, which should protect you from doing anything too embarrassing.

1.2.1 Introduction to Programming

Given the vast number of programming languages—C, Java, C++, PHP, JavaScript, Python, Perl, Ruby, Visual Basic, Go—it's hard to know where to start.

When most people start their journey learning how to code, the sheer number of options to begin is overwhelming. It's definitely enough to make someone feel anxious, and many people tell us that they're afraid of spending too much time learning the wrong thing. Imagine taking six months to learn Python only to find out that you should have been learning JavaScript instead.

Let us take a moment to calm your concerns. You'll probably be all right no matter where you start. A lot of what you're learning when you first learn a programming language isn't specific to that language at all—it's the basics of how programming languages work in the first place. Most programming languages share these building blocks. If you've never coded before, however, it can be hard to understand why that is.

To help you understand what's going on behind the "black box" of coding, we start by taking you on a tour of how a programming language like Python could be used to build something that we all probably use every day—a website.

In this book, we won't be showing you how to build a website using Python—it's quite a complex topic that could take up a whole book on its own, and building websites doesn't rank high on the list of what we'd expect an MBA to do with Python. This is still a good way to introduce the topic of coding because it covers many of the major areas of coding and because we interact with websites every day.

Most of the websites we visit are actually *web applications*. Applications are like apps that you download on your phone or computer (think Microsoft Word or Excel) except that with a web application, instead of downloading it, the application sits on a server somewhere (in the "cloud"). You interact with a web application by opening your browser and going to a website like facebook.com or twitter.com.

How are web applications built? Every web application has a *front end* and a *back end*. The front end is the part that you see.

Different programming languages are used to write the front end and back end. The front end of a web application is generally built using three programming languages:

1.   HTML (Hypertext Markup Language)
2.   CSS (Cascading Style Sheets)
3.   JavaScript

These three languages work together to make nearly every page on the web. The HTML describes what's on the page, CSS makes it look the way it does, and

JavaScript adds some of the flair and behavior of a page (things like popup notifications and live page updates).

That's the front end, and there's a lot more to be said, but that's outside the scope of this book. We'll leave that to you to explore in greater depth if you're interested. For now, we'll shift our focus to the part of a web application that most people don't see: the back end.

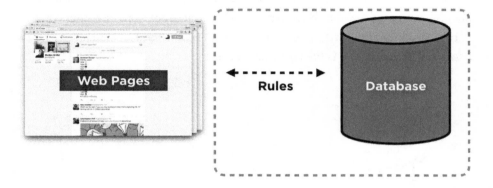

The back end is the metaphorical "black box" of coding. Think of it as the web application's "brain"; it carries out the bulk of the work, and then hands it over to the front end so that it can be displayed to you as pretty web pages. For example, if you search for a friend on facebook.com, the back end will look through Facebook's enormous database to find them, and then present it to the front end so that it can be shown to you in your browser.

The back end usually consists of two things: a database and a set of rules. The database stores all of the information that your web application needs (e.g., usernames and passwords, photos, status updates, and everything else).

The rules in between a database and the webpages are what enable the web application to figure out what information to get from the database and what to do with it every time a user does something on the website. When it comes to database languages, one is more popular than almost any other: SQL (commonly pronounced "sequel" or "S-Q-L"). We won't talk much about SQL, given that it's outside of the scope of this book.

Most programming languages you've heard of fit in between the database and the web pages. Some that you might have heard of include Python, Ruby, PHP, and Java. This is by no means an exhaustive list of languages, but it is where most of the languages we have mentioned fit in.

They're all basically the same, just a little different. We often are asked: "I'm thinking of building X idea (a dog walking app, a better way to find roommates, a way to find cool events in your area, whatever). What programming language should I learn?" Once you learn how programming languages actually work, you'll realize that this is kind of a funny question. It's like saying, "I've got this story I really want to tell, it's a story of two star-crossed lovers. What language should I use to tell it? English? French? Spanish?"

You probably can tell that story using any one of those languages, because that's what languages are for. Of course, the languages are all different. In some languages like French or Spanish, you've got masculine and feminine words. In other languages like Chinese, you indicate past and future tense by putting a word at the end of your sentence. Programming languages work the same way. You can do the same things with most programming languages, although the code itself might look a little different. Consider this example:

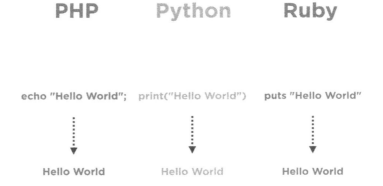

This figure shows three different snippets of code from three different languages: PHP, Python, and Ruby. You can easily spot some of the differences. The word used is different in each case: echo, print, and puts. PHP uses semicolons at the end of its sentences, but Python and Ruby don't. Python uses parentheses, whereas PHP and Ruby don't need them. But when you run the code (we'll talk about what "running code" means in a bit), you get the same output.

PHP   Python   Ruby

echo "Hello World";   print("Hello World")   puts "Hello World"

Hello World   Hello World   Hello World

All three lines of code print out Hello World. (This is, by the way, traditionally the first lesson you learn when you're learning a programming language—how to print Hello World—and it's always boring!)

What makes something a programming language? Python, and all the other programming languages, are languages for humans to talk to computers. Programming languages started off being very computer-friendly but not very human-friendly. The following is an example of how you might tell a computer to do something simple like print out "Winter is coming." in binary code:

```
00000000  7f 45 4c 46 01 01 01 00  00 00 00 00 00 00 00 00  |.ELF............|
00000010  02 00 03 00 01 00 00 00  80 80 04 08 34 00 00 00  |............4...|
00000020  c8 00 00 00 00 00 00 00  34 00 20 00 02 00 28 00  |........4. ...(.|
00000030  04 00 03 00 01 00 00 00  00 00 00 00 00 80 04 08  |................|
00000040  00 80 04 08 9d 00 00 00  9d 00 00 00 05 00 00 00  |................|
00000050  00 10 00 00 01 00 00 00  a0 00 00 00 a0 90 04 08  |................|
00000060  a0 90 04 08 0e 00 00 00  0e 00 00 00 06 00 00 00  |................|
00000070  00 10 00 00 00 00 00 00  00 00 00 00 00 00 00 00  |................|
00000080  ba 0e 00 00 b9 a0 90     04 08 bb 01 00 00 00 b8  |................|
00000090  04 00 00 00 cd 80 b8 01  00 00 00 cd 80 00 00 00  |................|
000000a0  57 69 6e 74 65 72 20 69  73 20 63 6f 6d 69 6e 67  |Winter is coming|
000000b0  73 68 73 74 72 74 61 62  00 2e 74 65 78 74 00 2e  |shstrtab..text..|
000000c0  64 61 74 61 00 00 00 00  00 00 00 00 00 00 00 00  |data............|
000000d0  00 00 00 00 00 00 00 00  00 00 00 00 00 00 00 00  |................|
*
000000f0  0b 00 00 00 01 00 00 00  06 00 00 00 80 80 04 08  |................|
00000100  80 00 00 00 1d 00 00 00  00 00 00 00 00 00 00 00  |................|
00000110  10 00 00 00 00 00 00 00  11 00 00 00 01 00 00 00  |................|
00000120  03 00 00 00 a0 90 04 08  a0 00 00 00 0e 00 00 00  |................|
00000130  00 00 00 00 00 00 00 00  04 00 00 00 00 00 00 00  |................|
00000140  01 00 00 00 03 00 00 00  00 00 00 00 00 00 00 00  |................|
00000150  ae 00 00 00 17 00 00 00  00 00 00 00 00 00 00 00  |................|
00000160  01 00 00 00 00 00 00 00                           |........|
```

Binary is the lowest level at which instructions can be written for a computer. It's the most computer-friendly (it's really fast), but it's also the least human-friendly (as you've noticed, it's basically unreadable). Next, you can move up one level, which is Assembly language:

```
section .text
    global _start

_start:

    mov edx,len
    mov ecx,msg
```

```
    mov ebx,1
    mov eax,4
    int 0x80

    mov eax,1
    int 0x80

section .data

msg db 'Winter is coming.',0xa
len equ $ - msg
```

This version is only slightly more readable than the binary version. It includes some familiar words, but it ends up being converted into binary anyway so that it can be read by the computer. The following is an example of how you would write the same thing in Java:

```
public class WinterIsComing {
    public static void main(String[] args) {
        System.out.println("Winter is coming.");
    }
}
```

Things are getting better now, and indeed, Java is a huge improvement over Assembly when it comes to human readability. But we still don't like the idea of beginners learning to code with Java because there's still so much overhead to learn before you can do something as simple as print text. (For example, you first have to learn the meaning of public, class, static, void, main.) And then there's Python:

```
print("Winter is coming.")
```

What a breath of fresh air. All of that in one simple line. Python has become a popular programming language for beginners and experts alike because it emphasizes human readability.

1.2.2 What Is Python?

Python has brought computer programming to a vast new audience.
                                                    —*The Economist*, July 19, 2018

*Forget Wall Street lingo. The language Citigroup Inc. wants its incoming
investment bank analysts to know is Python.*
                                                    —Bloomberg, June 14, 2018

The programming language Python was named after Monty Python (the British comedy group), not a snake (as many people think). It was created in 1991 by Guido Van Rossum. He's been known in the Python community as the "Benevolent Dictator for Life" (BDFL).

Guido worked at Google from 2005 to 2012, where he spent half of his time developing the Python language. Interestingly, much of the popularity of Python comes from the fact that when Google was first conceived by Sergey Brin and Larry Page at Stanford, they wrote their first web crawlers using Guido's relatively new Python.[4] As Google started to grow, they made the smart business move of hiring Guido. Google also spent a lot of resources building data science tools in Python and released them for free to the open-source community. As a result, many aspiring developers who wanted to learn Python from the best and brightest were enticed to work at Google. This gave Google a competitive business advantage in terms of hiring the most talented programmers.

We often are asked which big companies are using Python. The answer is that *most* large companies and certainly almost every tech company uses Python in some capacity. Examples include Google, Facebook, YouTube, Spotify, Netflix, Dropbox, Yahoo, NASA, IBM, Instagram, and Reddit. The list goes on and on. Python is so prevalent because it can be used for so many different things and is easy to use alongside other programming languages. For example, even if a company's main product isn't built using Python, they may use Python for machine learning, artificial intelligence (AI), or data analysis behind the scenes.

As a result, Python is currently the fastest-growing major programming language.[5] According to Stack Overflow, an online community for developers, it's also considered to be the most wanted programming language.[6]

Companies like Citigroup and Goldman Sachs have begun training their business analysts in Python. "Programming is going to be like writing was when we were in school," says Kimberly Johnson, the chief operating officer of mortgage giant Fannie Mae. Kimberly refers to Python as the language of the future, especially for MBAs.[7] At Columbia Business School, where we both teach, Python is by far the most popular language, both among MBA and engineering students.

1.3 SETTING UP YOUR DEVELOPMENT ENVIRONMENT

Before we can write and run Python code, we have to do a few things. This is what we call setting up your "development environment." It consists of three steps:

1. Install a text editor.
2. Install Python.
3. Set up the command line.

Although this process can be fast for some, others may run into problems depending on how their particular computers are set up. We recommend allocating about an hour to get everything set up properly, but you may not need this much time.

Note that the software we use in this book should work on both Windows computers and Mac computers (but unfortunately not on most cloud-based laptops like Chromebooks, as of writing this). We've gone through some effort to test it on both environments. When appropriate, we include screenshots for both to ensure that no one feels left out.

1.3.1 Install a Text Editor

You'll need to install a text editor for writing code. We'll be using a popular text editor called *Atom*. For this book, it doesn't really matter what text editor you use, so if you have a preferred text editor, feel free to use that.

Even experienced developers sometimes run into problems and get frustrated installing all the right tools on their computers. For example, when joining a new company, it's not uncommon for it to take several whole days to get all the software installed properly. Our advice is to just stick with it if you're running into problems, practice your troubleshooting skills (we'll include some troubleshooting advice in the book and on our website), and know that it should get easier from here on out.

How to install *Atom*:

1. Go to https://atom.io and click the download button.
2. Install *Atom* and ensure that it's accessible on your computer.

The first time you open *Atom*, you may see a bunch of notifications and announcements that you can close. Next, you'll see a blank tab that should look something like this:

This is where we'll write our code, but we don't need this for now, so feel free to close down *Atom* for the time being.

1.3.2 Install Python

Now it's time to install Python. Actually, if you're on a Mac, Python comes preinstalled by default (but depending on when you got your computer, it's unlikely to be the most recent version). Windows doesn't come with Python by default.

Either way, head over to https://www.pythonformbas.com/install and follow the steps to install Python so that we can ensure that we're working with the latest version. As a warning, if you install Python in some other way, you may reach a point where you're not able to follow along with the exact instructions we provide in this book.

Shortly we'll walk through a way to check whether everything was installed successfully. Unfortunately, several things can go wrong during this process. We've included a set of *Frequently Asked Questions* on our website at https://www.pythonformbas.com/install to help you out.

1.3.3 Set Up the Command Line

The command line is an application we can use to run Python code (among many other things). We're going to set up our command line so we can access it quickly and know that it works.

macOS:

The Mac version of the command line is a program called Terminal that comes with your computer. To find it:

1. Click on the magnifying glass in the top, right-hand corner of your screen (or just hold the *command* key and hit the spacebar). A search bar should pop up.
2. Type "Terminal".
3. Click on the Terminal application that looks like a black box. This should open the Terminal.
4. Go to your dock on the bottom of your screen and right-click or Ctrl and click on the Terminal icon to pull up a menu. Select *Options > Keep in Dock*.

Now that you have your Terminal open and it appears in your dock, you can easily access it.

Windows:

On Windows, we're going to use a program called *Anaconda PowerShell Prompt* that comes included with the Anaconda installer:

1. Click *Start*.
2. Type "Anaconda Powershell Prompt".
3. Click on the *Anaconda Powershell Prompt* application that looks like a black box. This should open *Anaconda Powershell Prompt*. It will look like a black window with white text. (Major warning: Windows comes with other

similar-looking but different applications; e.g., *Anaconda Prompt*, *Windows PowerShell*, *Windows PowerShell ISE*. Make sure you don't use one of these by accident. The title of the window should read *Anaconda Powershell Prompt*.)

4. Go to your taskbar at the bottom of your screen and right-click on the *Anaconda Powershell Prompt* icon to pull up a menu. Select *Pin this program to taskbar*.

Now that you have your *Anaconda PowerShell Prompt* open and it appears in your taskbar, you can easily access it.

If anything goes wrong during these steps, check out the *Frequently Asked Questions* on our website at https://www.pythonformbas.com/install and you may find a solution.

1.3.4 A Quick Sanity Check

To ensure that you installed Python properly, open a new command line window (Terminal or *Anaconda PowerShell*, depending on which you're using), then type `python --version` (that's two hyphens, also called dashes), and hit enter:

```
                            mattan — -zsh — 80×24
(base) mattan@Mattans-MacBook-Pro ~ % python --version
Python 3.8.3
(base) mattan@Mattans-MacBook-Pro ~ %
```

Don't worry if your command line doesn't look exactly like ours.

Also, don't worry if you don't have the exact same version of Python. As long as you see anything above Python 3.8, you should be able to run all of the Python code in this book.

While you're at it, type `pip --version` and hit `Enter`. As long as you see any version number (and you don't get an error message), you should be good to go.

This step ensures that the Python package installer is set up correctly on your computer.

The key is that if you've done everything correctly, you shouldn't get an error message. If you do see an error message, or if something else went wrong (which unfortunately happens all too often), check out the *Frequently Asked Questions* on our website at https://www.pythonformbas.com/install and you may be able to find a solution.

1.4 COMMAND LINE BASICS

Open up Terminal if you're on a Mac or *Anaconda PowerShell* if you're on a PC.

This is your command line. If this is your first time ever looking at a command line, it's pretty intimidating. Let us break it down for you.

On a Mac (we'll walk through the Windows version in a second), you'll see something like this (the specifics of what you see in your command line are actually not all that important; if you see something different from what we show when you open your command line, that's probably fine.):

```
Last login: Wed Sep 19 13:24:00 on ttys001
(base) mattan@Mattans-Macbook-Pro ~ %
```

The first line tells you the last time you logged in. You can basically ignore it. It's possible to turn this off, but we won't get into that now and leave it to you as a challenge in case you'd like to figure it out.

The second line is more interesting:

```
(base) mattan@Mattans-Macbook-Pro ~ %
```

This line tells you a few things. The first part (base) has to do with a feature of the Anaconda installer—it's possible to have different versions of Python installed

---

DON'T LISTEN TO OTHER DEVELOPERS' ADVICE (FOR NOW)

If you talk to friends or colleagues who already know how to code, they'll often try to give you advice about where and how to start learning how to code. Some may recommend you start with a more basic coding language like C++ or Java so you can "really understand" what's happening at a lower level before moving on to Python. Ignore advice like this for now (except for ours, of course!)

A lot of times when coders give you advice, they're really just recommending you learn the same way they did. The problem with advice about learning more basic programming languages first is that you'll spend a lot (really, we mean *a lot*) of time learning the basics before you're able to actually learn something that you can actually use—for example, apply to a business problem.

For now, you just need to get started and learn some useful stuff as quickly as possible. That's what this book is about. Don't worry, you will have plenty of time to go back and learn the basics later, when it actually may be more useful and interesting anyway.

on your computer at the same time—but we won't be using that feature here, so again, you can safely ignore it.[8]

Then there's mattan, which is our username on our computer. After that there's a @ and Mattans-Macbook-Pro which is the name of our computer. Then there's a space and a ~ (tilde), which actually tells you where you are on your computer right now. That's right, you're *somewhere* on your computer when you open the command line. We'll get into that in a bit. Finally, there's a %, another space, and then a rectangle (the *cursor*).

So far, we've been showing the Mac version of the command line, but on a Windows computer, you'll see something like this instead:

```
(base) PS C:\Users\mattan>
```

The prompt starts with (base), which means the same thing as it did on a Mac. Then you've got PS, which stands for *PowerShell*. After that you've got C:\Users\ mattan, which tells you where you are on your computer right now (we'll explain what that means in a moment), a >, a space, and then a blinking line (the *cursor*).

The area behind the blinking cursor indicates where you can type and is known as the *Prompt* (as in, it's prompting you to type stuff). At the prompt, you can enter a command that you've memorized or looked up, hit Enter, and see the output of your command.

1.4.1 The pwd command

For example, type the letters pwd and hit Enter. On a Mac, you should see something like this:

```
/Users/mattan
```

Or, on a PC, it may look something like this:

```
Path
------
C:\Users\mattan
```

What did we do with pwd, exactly? The command pwd stands for *print working directory*, and by running it, we're commanding our computer to tell us what folder we're currently in.

From now on, when we say to "run" a command, what we mean is open up the command line, type a command into your prompt, and then hit Enter. Sometimes we'll indicate this as follows:

```
% pwd
/Users/mattan
```

Here, the % is shorthand for the prompt (we're cutting out all the other information you see in your command line). This is pretty common when you're looking at code examples online. Whenever you see a % in front of some code, it means you should type or copy and paste it into the command line (but don't type the % itself). Sometimes you won't see a % and it will be up to you to figure out that you're supposed to run it in your command line—yes, this can be confusing when you're starting out, but it becomes intuitive over time.

Go ahead and run pwd three times and each time say "print working directory" out loud. This will help you remember it.

1.4.2 The open . and start . commands

We keep saying that you're *somewhere* on your computer when you open up the command line. What do we mean by that? Well, if you're on a Mac, try running the following command (remember not to actually type the % part):

```
% open .
```

(That's open, a space, and a period.)
If you're on a Windows, try the following:

```
% start .
```

(That's start, a space, and a period.)
A new window should open with some folders inside of it. This happens to be the folder you're currently inside. This is the default folder you start in when you open your command line. It's called your *home directory*.

(By the way, we know we're throwing a lot of new terms your way, but it's actually not that important for you to memorize them. We're letting you know what they are called so that you can develop a familiarity with them for when we use them again. But don't get nervous or stressed out trying to write down and memorize each new term. When there's an important term for you to remember, we'll let you know.)

1.4.3 The ls command

Now try running ls and see if you can figure out what it's doing.

Here's what we get:

```
% ls
Applications
Movies
Music
Desktop
Documents
Pictures
Downloads
Public
anaconda3
Library
```

Windows users will see a bunch more information as well, including last write time and length. You can safely ignore all of that information if it seems confusing to you. If you compare it with the window that opened when you ran open . (on a Mac) or start . (on a Windows), you'll notice that you see the same folders as you do in the output from the command line:

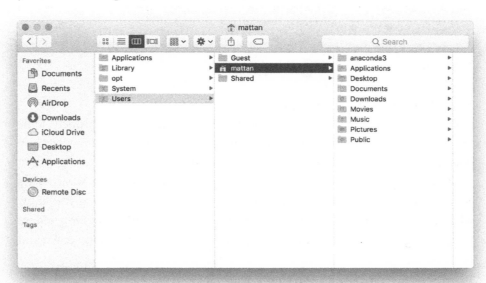

The command `ls` stands for *list* and it basically means "tell me what folders and files are in the folder that I'm currently in."

1.4.4 The cd command

The last command you need to know about is `cd`, which stands for *change directory*. `cd` lets you move from your current folder to another folder like this:

```
% cd Desktop
```

You won't get any output from running this command, but you can check that it worked by running pwd:

```
% pwd
/Users/mattan/Desktop
```

`cd` lets you move into any of the folders inside the folder you're currently in. (Technically, `cd` is the command and the thing that comes after the space, the folder name, is called an *argument*.)

If you want to move into a folder whose name has spaces in it, you'll need to put the folder name in quotes. For example:

```
% cd "Work Documents"
```

Because the command line interprets each space as a new argument, it doesn't know that you want it to be the name of one folder. In practice, developers will often just use _ (underscores) instead of spaces in folders and file names to avoid confusions like this.

If you find yourself inside of a folder that doesn't have any other folders in it, and you want to go back, you can run the following:

```
% cd ..
```

The `..` stands for the folder one level up from the folder you're currently in (sometimes called the *parent folder* or the *enclosing folder*). So basically what you're doing with `cd ..` is saying "take me back a level."

Now that you know pwd, `ls`, and `cd`, you have the three commands you need to move around your computer in the command line. There are hundreds of other commands out there, but these are the only three you need to know right now to run Python code.

Take a few minutes to practice them now. Try choosing a random folder somewhere on your computer, open up the command line, and see if you can figure out how to get to it. If you get lost at any point, you can run:

```
% cd ~
```

cd with a ~ (tilde) as an argument will always take you back to your home directory (where you start when you first open up the command line). In the worst-case scenario, you can always quit the command line and open it up again. Then, you should be back where you started.

1.4.5 The clear command

It is not particularly important, but the `clear` command lets you clear out any previous commands you've run.

```
% clear
```

This is helpful if you don't like the clutter of seeing a bunch of text every time you use the command line.

1.4.6 Create a Folder for Our Code

Now that we've learned a few basic commands, let's create a new folder on your desktop where you can save the code that we write as we move through this book. We recommend putting it on your desktop so that it's easy to see and get back to, but you can also create this new folder anywhere you want as, long as you know how to get back to it again later.

Make sure you're in your home directory by opening up a new command line window or running cd ~:

```
% cd ~
% pwd
/Users/mattan
```

Now cd into your desktop:

```
% cd Desktop
% pwd
/Users/mattan/Desktop
```

Then run the following:

```
% mkdir code
```

Check your desktop. You should see a new empty folder named code. We didn't teach you the `mkdir` command earlier because it's probably easier to just right click somewhere on your desktop and select *New Folder*, but we're showing it to you just now because it's fun.

Even though you just created a new folder in the command line, you're not *inside* of it yet. You still need to cd into it:

```
% cd code
% pwd
/Users/mattan/Desktop/code
```

You did it. Now close down your command line, open up a new one, and navigate to your new folder. To get some practice, repeat this task three more times.

1.5 IT'S TIME FOR HAPPY HOUR

Now that we've explored the command line, let's step away from it for a second to run our first bit of Python code. (It's okay if the words "run Python code" don't mean anything to you at the moment. Just go with it for now, and it will start to make more sense soon.)

We've provided a file at https://www.pythonformbas.com/code named happy_hour.py (go there now and download this file). In Python, a file with code that you can run is sometimes called a *script*. Don't worry about what's inside the file for now.

First things first, move it into your newly created code folder on your desktop. That way you can easily find it later. Then open up a new command line window. Navigate to your code folder using the cd command. (Remember how to do this from the previous section on the command line? If not, go back and review it.) At this point, check to make sure you're in the right folder by running pwd and ls.

```
% pwd
/Users/mattan/Desktop/code
% ls
happy_hour.py
```

You should see the happy_hour.py file that you've put into your code folder. Make sure you see it when you run ls; otherwise, this next step won't work. If you don't see it, you either (a) didn't move the file into the right folder, or (b) didn't navigate into that folder in the command line.

Now that you have taken care of that, run the file in the command line by typing python happy_hour.py and hitting enter:

```
% python happy_hour.py
How about you go to McSorley's Old Ale House with Mattan?
```

Hmm . . . interesting. Did you get this same result?

First, you may have gotten an error when you tried to run the command. That's okay. Even if you didn't get an error, it's worth learning about different kinds of errors that come up, because you're bound to run into them at some point.

One error you might have gotten is the following:

```
can't open file 'happy_hour.py': [Errno 2] No such file or
directory.
```

If you got that error, it means that it can't find the file you're trying to run. Either you're in the wrong folder, or the file that you thought you moved isn't actually there. Go back and make sure the file is where you think it is (in the code folder on your desktop).

Another error you might have gotten looks something like this:

```
% python
Python 3.8.3 (default, Jul 2 2019, 16:54:48)
[Clang 10.0.0 ] :: Anaconda, Inc. on darwin
Type "help", "copyright", "credits" or "license" for more information.
>>> happy_hour.py
```

```
NameError: name 'happy_hour' is not defined
>>> python happy_hour.py
SyntaxError: invalid syntax
```

The error you see here is interesting but slightly more complicated to explain. If you typed in just the word `python` and hit `Enter` without adding a space and putting `happy_hour.py` at the end, you accidentally opened up something called *Interactive Mode*. We'll return to this in a second, but for now, just exit out of it by typing either `exit()` and hitting `Enter`, or pressing `Ctrl` and `D` on a Mac or `Ctrl` and `Z` on Windows. You should be back at the command line prompt.

But let's say you did manage to get the file to run. Even so, you probably didn't see the same output that we had in our example. Try running it again a few times and see what you get (note that if you press the up arrow, the last piece of code you ran will be displayed in the terminal—no need to retype it multiple times).

```
% python happy_hour.py
How about you go to The Back Room with Mattan?
% python happy_hour.py
How about you go to Death & Company with Samule L. Jackson?
% python happy_hour.py
How about you go to The Back Room with that person you forgot to
text back?
```

Notice the output is different each time. What do you think is happening?

Before we tell you, we want you to try something. Open up `happy_hour.py` in your text editor (*Atom*) and read the code on your own. You can do this in two ways:

1. Open *Atom*, go to File > Open . . . , find the file and click Open.
2. Right click on `happy_hour.py`, select Open With, and find *Atom* in the list of applications.

Unfortunately, just double-clicking `happy_hour.py` probably won't open the file in *Atom* by default (it will open it with your computer's default text editor, whatever that is). It is fairly easy to make *Atom* the default text editor, though. See the box "Changing Your Default Text Editor" for instructions.

CHANGING YOUR DEFAULT TEXT EDITOR FOR .PY FILES

To change your default text editor for .py files on a Mac, right click on any file with a `.py` extension and select Get Info. Under Open With find *Atom* and then click the Change All . . . button to apply the change to all `.py` files.

On a Windows, go to Start Menu, search for "default apps" and click on it, scroll down the window and click on "Choose default apps by file type," scroll down to `.py` and choose *Atom* as the default.

These instructions may change with operating system updates, so you may have to do some Googling to get this to work.

Once you've opened `happy_hour.py`, you should see the following:

```python
import random

bars = ["McSorley's Old Ale House",
    "Death & Company",
    "The Back Room",
    "PDT"]

people = ["Mattan",
    "Sarah",
    "that person you forgot to text back",
    "Samule L. Jackson"]
random_bar = random.choice(bars)
random_person = random.choice(people)


print(f"How about you go to {random_bar} with {random_person}?")
```

This is Python code. Don't worry about the fact that we haven't taught you anything about Python or code yet. Just take a minute of two to read through this code, line by line, and see if you can figure out what's going on at a high level.

Even if it looks like gibberish, don't let your eyes gloss over it. Study it and start to ask what each part might be doing. Do you see patterns or repetitions? Look for clues, even if none of it makes sense to you yet.

Ready, go!

Hopefully, you've read through the code on your own. If not, please take a second to do that now. Part of the skill of coding is being able to read other people's code that you haven't seen and figure out why it's doing what it's doing. So, we need to start working out that muscle now.

Here's how we would read the file. We would break the file down into three parts:

1. Top
2. Middle
3. Bottom

The top section seems to be doing some setup:

```python
import random

bars = ["McSorley's Old Ale House",
    "Death & Company",
    "The Back Room",
    "PDT"]

people = ["Mattan",
    "Sarah",
    "that person you forgot to text back",
    "Samule L. Jackson"]
```

First, note we have some sort of `import random` line of code. We don't yet know what it does.

Then, it seems like two lists are being created: bars and people. We might not understand the exact characters yet (why are there square brackets [] and quotation marks ""?), but we get the general idea.

The middle section of code seems to be doing some of the work:

```python
random_bar = random.choice(bars)
random_person = random.choice(people)
```

Our guess (okay, we know, but let's pretend we all are seeing this for the first time) is that this code is choosing a random bar and a random person from the list of bars and people. Remember that `import random` that we saw earlier? Perhaps that has something to do with the `random.choice` we've got here.

Finally, the bottom section looks like what we see in the command line:

```
print(f"How about you go to {random_bar} with {random_person}?")
```

Except that {random_bar} and {random_person} seem to be filled in with whatever random bar and random person is chosen in the middle section.

Whether or not you mentally broke up the file into a top, middle, and bottom section of the code is irrelevant. We're sharing with you how we might read this—after having seen thousands of different files of code in our lifetimes.

In addition to learning to understand code, one of the things you'll be learning is how you break down problems, your process for reading and analyzing, and what methods work best for you personally.

Often, you'll see files with code structured in a similar way. First, you have some code that does a bit of setup (think of this as getting the ingredients together for a recipe). Next, you have code that actually does the work (the steps involved in actually following a recipe), and then, you have the result (delicious food that you can hopefully serve).

You might think at this point that we'd start to teach you something about Python, but instead we've got a challenge for you.

1.5.1 Challenge 1: Happy Hour Fixes

We'd like you to do three things:

1. Oops, we spelled Samuel L. Jackson's name wrong. Can you fix it for us?
2. Add one friend to the list. Did you get an error?
3. Have it print out two random people instead of just one.

Take a few minutes to do this, but not more than five or so.

If you get stuck, keep at it for a bit, but don't get too frustrated if you ultimately can't figure it out. The point of these challenges is to test the limits of what you currently know how to do, so that your mind expands a bit and you hopefully learn something new. The point is not to get so frustrated that you give up. Be kind to yourself.

Did you figure it out? The first part of the challenge should have been pretty easy. Just move around the l and the e in this line (line 11):

```
"Samule L. Jackson"]
```

So that it reads:

```
"Samuel L. Jackson"]
```

Congratulations! You just edited your first bit of code.

Don't forget to save your changes—this is something a lot of first-time coders forget, and then they wonder why their code still isn't working when they run it.

A file with code in it is just like a Microsoft Word file or an Excel file. If you make a change but forget to save, then your change won't actually take effect. It stays in limbo until you try to close the file (in which case, it'll ask something like "Do you want to save the changes you made?").

Imagine you made a change to a Microsoft Word file, but you forget to save it, and then you emailed the file to a friend or a coworker. Will they see the change you made, or will they see the old version? They'll see the old version unless you save it first and then send them the new version of the file. Code works the same way.

In other words, if you want to see your code changes when you run the file in the command line, make sure you save your code first.

Coincidentally, there's a little trick you can use in *Atom* to check if you have a pending change in a file that needs to be saved. The tab at the top of *Atom* has the name of the file. If you've made a change in the file but haven't saved it yet, you'll see a blue • (e.g., `happy_hour.py` •).

When you save the file, the • disappears. Now, when you run the code in the command line, it'll run exactly what you see in *Atom*.

Let's return to our happy hour file. What about adding a friend to the list of people? If you're good with small details, you may have noticed that each entry in the list of people has quotation marks around it, and a comma afterward (except for the last one). So, if we wanted to add Daniel to the list, we would make the code look something like this:

```
people = ["Mattan",
    "Sarah",
    "that person you forgot to text back",
    "Samuel L. Jackson",
    "Daniel"]
```

A common mistake is to do something like the following:

```
people = ["Mattan",
    "Sarah",
    "that person you forgot to text back",
    "Samuel L. Jackson"
    "Daniel"]
```

Do you see the difference? It's subtle. The second example is missing a comma at the end of the second-to-last line:

```
"Samuel L. Jackson"
```

This introduces a particularly tricky bug because it doesn't produce an error when you try to run the file. And the problem doesn't necessarily show up right away:

```
% python happy_hour.py
How about you go to Death & Company with that person you forgot to
text back?
% python happy_hour.py
How about you go to PDT with Samuel L. JacksonDaniel?
```

Do you see what happened when we ran the file that second time? It smushed together Samuel L. Jackson and Daniel so what we got was Samuel L. JacksonDaniel.

Why this happens is something that will make more sense once we get to strings and the print() function. For now, it's enough to know that without the comma, it just doesn't work correctly.

When it comes to programming, one thing that often trips up beginners is the fact that a little thing like a missing comma can make your code not work, or at least not work correctly.

When it comes to code, computers can't interpret text in the same way that a human can. A human can see a bit of text with a comma missing and assume that you meant to put a comma there. They'll understand what you meant to write. A computer, in contrast, makes no assumptions about what you meant. If you don't put it in the code, the computer won't do it. This is a good thing because it means your computer won't ever do things you didn't tell it to do (you know what they say about assumptions), but it's annoying because it means you have to be pedantic about everything.

Our favorite illustration of this in English is the sentence "Let's eat Grandma!" which means something quite different than the phrase "Let's eat, Grandma!" Remember: punctuation saves lives.

If that idea scares you because you're not a detail-oriented person, that's okay. It takes a bit of getting used to, but eventually your eye will start to notice the small stuff naturally without you having to think much about it.

Back to the final challenge, which was to change the code so that it prints out two random names instead of just one.

This was by far the trickiest part of the challenge, so if you didn't figure it out, that's okay.

The key is to look at this line:

```
random_person = random.choice(people)
```

Did you guess that if you include another line just like it, then you can grab another random person from your list of people? Like this:

```
random_person2 = random.choice(people)
```

You also might have created a second list of people, but that isn't necessary in this case. You can pull from the same list.

The only other change you'd need to make to actually see the output would be to change the final print line:

```
print(f"How about you go to {random_bar} with {random_person}?")
```

To add the second randomly selected person:

```
print(f"How about you go to {random_bar} with {random_person} and
{random_person2}?")
```

Note that our line of code is already starting to get long. This may be a good point to mention that in Python, line breaks matter. The previous line of code, while it's printed in this book as being two lines, needs to be all on one line of code otherwise Python won't be able to run it. We'll come back to this topic later. Where possible, we've tried to break down long lines of Python code into shorter ones so that they can be printed in this book the same way they should be typed.

In some cases though, that isn't really possible due to limitations in the number of characters that can be printed on one line in this book.

Back to our file, let's run the updated code a few times:

```
% python happy_hour.py
How about you go to McSorley's Old Ale House with Mattan and Daniel?
% python happy_hour.py
How about you go to The Back Room with Samuel L. Jackson and Sarah?
```

At this point, you might be happy, but if you kept running the code, you might eventually realize a problem:

```
% python happy_hour.py
How about you go to McSorley's Old Ale House with Daniel and Daniel?
```

Every once in a while, the two randomly selected people will be the same person. In computer programming, this type of error is sometimes called a *bug* or an *edge case*. An edge case occurs when your code works normally most of the time, but occasionally it does something wrong.

You might want us to tell you how to fix it. But this time, we'll flip the question around and ask you: How would you fix it?

Take a second and think at least conceptually about how you might get around a problem like this. We may not know enough about Python to fix this problem yet, but it's something we'll be able to come back to soon.

1.5.2 Challenge 2: Build Your Own Randomizer Script

We have a final challenge for you. Your challenge is to take 10 minutes or so and create your own randomizer script (remember, a script is just a file with Python code inside of it that you can run).

There are many ideas for randomizer scripts available on the web, and some of them are quite popular. For inspiration, the next two examples feature two of our favorites (we apologize in advance for the crude language):

It's This for That (http://itsthisforthat.com) generates a random startup idea by combining a startup buzzword with a niche market.

What the f*** is my social media strategy? (https://whatthefuckismysocialme-diastrategy.com/) generates a random social media strategy consisting mostly of marketing buzzwords mashed together—although most of them read surprisingly like real social media strategies.

Take 10 minutes to create your own randomizer script like one of these examples using `happy_hour.py` as a template. If you're feeling proud of your script, email it to us at authors@pythonformbas.com. We'd love to see what you came up with.

1.6 WRAPPING UP

In this chapter, we introduced you to the Python programming language and started scratching the surface of what you can do with it. We also set up a development environment—including installing Python and a text editor—and explored the command line.

Finally, we ran our first Python script—our happy hour generator—and looked at the code behind it. We played around with modifying some of the code and also used it as the structure to create our own Python scripts.

In the next chapter, we'll dive into the basics of Python and get a better understanding of some of the new concepts and tools that we're getting exposed to.

2

PYTHON BASICS, PART 1

WE'VE LEARNED what it means to "run" Python code, but we don't yet have a grasp of the basic building blocks of a Python script. In this chapter, we'll start learning the basics of what we can do with Python.

2.1 WHAT YOU'LL LEARN IN THIS CHAPTER

By the end of this chapter, you'll be able to create a basic Python script that takes input from a user, do some work to it, and then get back an output. You'll also learn about two different ways of running Python code, how to use the `print()` function, how to read and troubleshoot Python errors, comments and variables, some of the Python data types (e.g., floats, integers, and strings), and how to get user input.

2.2 TWO WAYS OF RUNNING PYTHON CODE

There are two ways of running Python code. The first, which we've already seen, is to run a script in the command line like this:

```
% python script.py
```

A script is any bit of valid Python code saved into a file with a `.py` file extension. Python scripts can be downloaded or created from any text editor (including
but not limited to *Atom*).

You might be wondering, "What's so special about the `.py` extension?" The
answer is nothing.

For example, if we wanted, we could rename `happy_hour.py` to `happy_hour.txt`
or `happy_hour.html`. (A lot of operating systems now hide file extensions because
they think most people would prefer not to see them, so you might have to change
your system settings if you want to see them by default and be able to change them.)

The purpose of a file extension at the end of a file name is to tell your computer
what application to use to open it when you double-click it. For example, files
with the `.txt` file extension will be opened with whatever plain text editor is
installed on your computer by default and files with the `.html` file extension will
be opened by your default browser. The `.py` file extension tells your computer that
the file is a text file that contains Python code, and that when you double-click it,
your computer should open it with the default text editor. It's possible to override
the default application that is used for a particular file type; we discussed this in
the box "Changing Your Default Text Editor" in section 1.5.

A second way to run Python code is to use something called *interactive mode*.
You can access Python's interactive mode by typing `python` in the command line
(without a filename after it) and hitting *Enter*:

```
% python
Python 3.8.3 (default, Jul 2 2019, 16:54:48)
[Clang 10.0.0 ] :: Anaconda, Inc. on darwin
Type "help", "copyright", "credits" or "license" for more
information.
>>>
```

As you can see, a bunch of this information is related to the version of Python
installed, and some additional reminders tell us we can do things like type `help`
for more information. In this book, we'll skip all that information moving forward to save space:

```
% python
>>>
```

Note that the prompt has changed to `>>>`. This is to indicate that you're no
longer in the command line—you're now inside Python. Any of the previous

command line commands we ran (like pwd, ls, or cd) will no longer work in this mode:

```
% python
>>> pwd
Traceback (most recent call last):
    File "<stdin>", line 1, in <module>
NameError: name 'pwd' is not defined
>>>
```

But what *will* work in Python interactive mode is Python code. Try this out:

```
% python
>>> 1 + 1
2
>>> print("Winter is coming.")
Winter is coming.
>>> "Mattan" * 1000
'MattanMattanMattanMattanMattanMattanMattanMattanMattan
MattanMattan ...
```

Whoa, that's a lot of Mattans. To exit Python's interactive mode and go back to the command line:

- Press Ctrl and D on a Mac
- Press Ctrl and Z on Windows
- Or type exit() and hit *Enter*

If you ever forget how to do this, just type exit and hit *Enter* to get a reminder:

```
>>> exit
Use exit() or Ctrl-D (i.e. EOF) to exit
```

The letters EOF stand for *end of file*, which basically means you're telling Python that there's no more code to run.

Why would you want to use interactive mode rather than writing your code in a file, or vice versa?

Python's interactive mode is a great way to save some time when you're experimenting with code. If you don't know exactly what you're trying to do or how you're trying to do it, you can play around in this mode. Once you've figured out what code you want to use, it makes sense to save it to a file so you can just run that file in the future rather than having to rewrite the same code every time.

Let's leave the interactive mode for now, and we'll return to this later.

2.3 PRINTING

We want you to create a new file called `print.py` and save it into your `code` folder. To do this:

1. Open *Atom*. It should open an empty file by default. If it doesn't click *File > New File*.
2. Click *File > Save* (or `Command` and `S` on a Mac and `Ctrl` and `S` on Windows).
3. Navigate to your `code` folder on your desktop.
4. Change the file name to `print.py` (don't forget to add the `.py` extension).
5. Click *Save*.

Double-check your `code` folder to make sure your new file is there. Once you've checked, type the following into your empty `print.py` file:

```
print("Winter is coming.")
```

Now save the file and run it in your command line:

```
% python print.py
Winter is coming.
```

Did this work for you? If not, make sure your file is saved to the right place and that you're in the right place in your command line (remember you can use `ls` to check if you can see the file). Basically, `print()` is a function that prints things out into the command line. We'll be introducing several more functions over the next few chapters and will be discussing functions in further depth in section 4.2, "Introduction to Functions." For now, know that functions take inputs inside of parentheses. And when we refer to the name of a function, we'll always be putting parentheses after the name—like `print()`—to distinguish them from variables (which we'll cover shortly).

Next, add another line to `print.py`:

```
print("Winter is coming.")
print("You know nothing", "Mattan Griffel")
```

(Feel free to replace the second part with your own name to make it personal.) Then run the file again:

```
% python print.py
Winter is coming.
You know nothing Mattan Griffel
```

(If you don't see this new line in your output, ensure that you save your file before running it.)

Even though we added two bits of text—"You know nothing" and "Mattan Griffel"—to that second `print()`, separated by commas, Python turned that comma into a space and printed them next to each other.

PRINT IN PYTHON 2

In Python 2 (a previous version of Python), you could write `print "hi"` (without parentheses), but this doesn't work in Python 3. It's probably the first error you'll get if you try to copy code from Python 2 and run it in Python 3. If you see the following:

```
>>> print "hi"
    File "<stdin>", line 1
        print "hi"
                 ^
SyntaxError: Missing
parentheses in call to 'print'
```

You know you're running code meant for Python 2 in Python 3. The easiest way to fix it is to just manually add parentheses around the text after the word `print`, like this:

```
>>> print("hi")
hi
```

2.3.1 Printing Challenge

Change the code in `print.py` so that it prints out the lyrics of your favorite song or poem. Take a few minutes to do this now.

Done?

Here's what we came up with (one of the lines is printed in bold, for reasons that will shortly become obvious):

```
print("since feeling is first")
print("who pays any attention")
print("to the syntax of things")
print("will never wholly kiss you;")
print("wholly to be a fool")
print("while Spring is in the world")

print("my blood approves")
print("and kisses are a better fate")
print("than wisdom")
```

```
print("lady i swear by all flowers. Don't cry")
print("—the best gesture of my brain is less than"
print("your eyelids' flutter which says")

print("we are for each other: then")
print("laugh, leaning back in my arms"
print("for life's not a paragraph")

print("and death i think is no parenthesis")
```

This poem is called "Since Feeling is First" by e e cummings and it's one of Mattan's favorites (Daniel would like you to know that his favorite is "Funeral Blues" by W. H. Auden.) And what do we get when we run it?

```
% python print.py
    File "print.py", line 13
        print("your eyelids' flutter which says")
                ^
SyntaxError: invalid syntax
```

Uh, oh! That's not right. What's going on here? (Note that this error is a result of a mistake in the code above, which you might not have made in your own version of this challenge—so you might not get this error message. Bear with us, nevertheless, as we discuss the process of debugging Python code.)

The first time you see an error message, you may want to throw your hands in the air and give up. Don't. Error messages are your friend—let us show you why. We're going to run into error messages all the time when writing Python code, so we'd better get used to them and learn how to troubleshoot them.

Let's take a deeper look at a Python error.

2.4 DEBUGGING ERRORS AND GOOGLING

Let's take another look at this error:

```
File "print.py", line 13
    print("your eyelids' flutter which says")
        ^
SyntaxError: invalid syntax
```

What is it trying to tell us? The first part—File "print.py"—is the file that Python was running when it ran into an error. This might seem fairly obvious, because that's the file we were running. But let's imagine you were writing a lot of code. Developers need a way to structure and organize lots of code, and one way of doing that is to separate it into multiple files that share code with each other (we'll see later how to do this in section 4.3, "Importing Python Packages"). When you have code in multiple files, it can be helpful to know which file had the particular error.

The next part, *line 13*, tells us the line where the error occurred.

Take a look at the next two lines of the error:

```
print("your eyelids' flutter which says")
     ^
```

This is an actual print out of the line of code Python was running when it ran into the error, with a ^ underneath where Python thinks the error appears. This is not always correct, but it is Python's best guess.

The last line of the error, SyntaxError: invalid syntax, contains both the category of the error—you will encounter a few general error types—and a specific error message.

What can we learn from this error message? Unfortunately, very little. Sometimes Python errors are more helpful than other times. In this case, even after taking a hard look at line 13 (printed in bold in our previous example), it doesn't look like anything is wrong. So now what do we do?

We Google it.[1] Believe it or not, a major part of becoming a good coder is Googling to find an answer to a problem that you don't already know how to solve. It's important that you learn how to troubleshoot and solve your own problems rather than having us give you all the answers. (Sometimes we don't have the answers!)

Almost always, the first thing we do when we run into a Python error that we don't recognize is Google the error message plus the word "python."

| SyntaxError: invalid syntax python | |

Google Search   I'm Feeling Lucky

Often, you'll see a site called Stack Overflow (https://stackoverflow.com) in your Google search results:

python - 'Syntax Error: invalid syntax' for no apparent reason ...
https://stackoverflow.com/.../syntax-error-invalid-syntax-for-no-apparent-reason ▾
2 answers
Jun 16, 2014 - For problems where it seems to be an error on a line you think is correct, you can often remove/comment the line where the error appears to be ...

Stack Overflow is a popular website where developers post questions and other developers answer them for free. How amazing is that? Free tech support. Because Python is such a popular programming language, chances are that if you're running into an error, someone else has run into it before and has already solved it.

Following is a screenshot of the first Stack Overflow page given in our Google search results.[2]

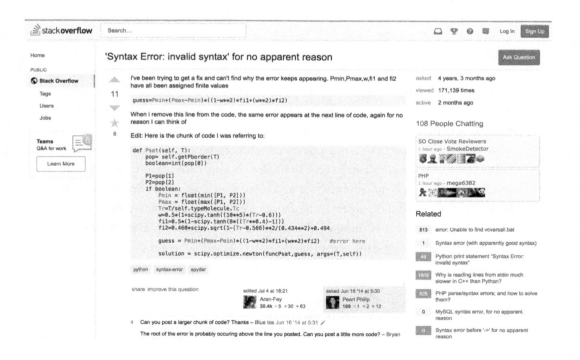

Notice that the question title, *'Syntax Error: invalid syntax' for no apparent reason*, is very similar to our problem.

Then you'll see a description of the problem, and the question asker has included the sections of the code that have produced this error. When it comes to asking a good question, the following can help make sure you get a helpful answer quickly:

1. A quick introduction of the problem. What were you trying to do? What happened? (Include the actual error message.)
2. Steps to help others reproduce the problem in case they want to see it for themselves. Ideally, this looks like a piece of code they can directly copy and paste into Python to reproduce the error.
3. Any relevant bits of your code that are related to the problem.

We highly recommend reading the Stack Overflow article "How Do I Ask a Good Question?"[3] before posting.

In the case of the *'Syntax Error: invalid syntax' for no apparent reason* question, notice how the question asker summarizes the problem and includes the line of code that the problem occurs on:

I've been trying to get a fix and can't find why the error keeps appearing. Pmin,Pmax,w,fi1 and fi2 have all been assigned finite values

```
guess=Pmin+(Pmax−Pmin)*((1−w**2)*fi1+(w**2)*fi2)
```

When i remove this line from the code, the same error appears at the next line of code, again for no reason I can think of

Don't worry. This question includes a lot of code, and it's not necessary that you understand exactly what it's doing. Below each question on Stack Overflow you'll often find comments in which people ask for more information or clarification. If anyone submits answers to the question, you'll see them below the comments. In this case, several answers are given.

The top answer as of writing this, posted by user *paxdiablo* on June 16, 2014, has a green checkmark next to it, which means it was selected as the approved answer by the person who asked the original question. Let's read their answer:

2 Answers

39

For problems where it seems to be an error on a line you think is correct, you can often remove/comment the line where the error appears to be and, if the error moves to the next line, there are two possibilities.

Either *both* lines have a problem or the *previous* line has a problem which is being carried forward. The most *likely* case is the second option (even more so if you remove another line and it moves again).

For example, the following Python program `twisty_passages.py` :

```
xyzzy = (1 +
plugh = 7
```

generates the error:

```
  File "twisty_passages.py", line 2
    plugh = 7
          ^
SyntaxError: invalid syntax
```

despite the problem clearly being on line 1.

In your particular case, that *is* the problem. The parentheses in the line *before* your error line is unmatched, as per the following snippet:

```
# open parentheses: 1  2                 3
#                       v  v               v
fi2=0.460*scipy.sqrt(1-(Tr-0.566)**2/(0.434**2)+0.494
#                                 ^              ^
# close parentheses:              1              2
```

Depending on what you're trying to achieve, the solution *may* be as simple as just adding another closing parenthesis at the end, to close off the `sqrt` function.

I can't say for *certain* since I don't recognise the expression off the top of my head. Hardly surprising if (assuming PSAT is the enzyme, and the use of the `typeMolecule` identifier) it's to do with molecular biology - I seem to recall failing Biology consistently in my youth :-)

share edit flag

edited Jul 16 '16 at 4:22

answered Jun 16 '14 at 5:34

paxdiablo
612k ● 166 ● 1218 ● 1646

This particular answer mentions that sometimes Python tells you that a particular error appears on one line, but if you remove that line, the error jumps to the next line. They give an example:

```
xyzzy = (1 +
plugh = 7
```

Sure enough, if you were to run this code, you'd get the same error message we saw before—*SyntaxError: invalid syntax.*

Why is this? When we run a file in Python, it reads the file from top to bottom, and from left to right. In the example code, the first line is incomplete: xyzzy = (1 +.

Python gets to the end of the line, doesn't find another number to add, or a closing parenthesis, and goes on to the next line to keep looking for it. Then it gets to `plugh = 7` and realizes something definitely is wrong. So, it gives us an error.

If we go back and look at *line 12* of our code in `print.py` (this was *our* solution to the challenge, so you probably won't have the same code), we had the following:

```
print("—the best gesture of my brain is less than"
```

It turns out we forgot the parenthesis at the end. We can make a quick fix:

```
print("—the best gesture of my brain is less than")
```

Now we run the code again:

```
% python print.py
    File "print.py", line 17
        print("for life's not a paragraph")
                ^


SyntaxError: invalid syntax
```

What's going on here? Didn't we just fix this problem? This happens all the time, and it's easy to get frustrated if you're not paying close attention. Look closely, and you'll see that this error is actually different from the error we were getting before. Now it's saying the error is on *line 17*.

Sometimes you make more than one mistake in your code, and one of them ends up masking the other one. The only way to see the next error is to fix them one at a time. Believe it or not, this is progress. Don't get frustrated, just keep at it.

We recommend running your code line by line as you write it. This practice can help you catch errors as you make them rather than all at once at the end (when it can be hard to figure out what you did wrong and where).

Sure enough, if we go back to the line before the error (*line 16*), we see that we're missing a closing parenthesis here as well:

```
print("laugh, leaning back in my arms"
```

Once we fix this by adding the missing parenthesis at the end, the file prints just fine:

```
% python print.py
since feeling is first
who pays any attention
to the syntax of things
will never wholly kiss you;
wholly to be a fool
while Spring is in the world
my blood approves
and kisses are a better fate
than wisdom
lady i swear by all flowers. Don't cry
—the best gesture of my brain is less than
your eyelids' flutter which says
we are for each other: then
laugh, leaning back in my arms
for life's not a paragraph
and death i think is no parenthesis
```

A final thought on this example is that empty lines in your Python code are not actually printed out to the command line. Python just skips empty lines of code entirely. Can you figure out how to print out an empty line in the command line? We'll leave this for you to experiment with on your own.

2.5 COMMENTS

Let's add some attribution to the top of our print.py file (you can replace this with the title and author of the song or poem that you choose):

```
# "Since feeling is first" by e e cummings
...
```

(The ellipsis ... represents the rest of the file of code, so we don't have to keep showing you the whole thing every time we print out a code example—we'd run out of pages.)

In Python, lines with a pound sign (#)—also known as the hashtag symbol or number sign—in front of them are called *comments*. Comments also are skipped by Python (meaning they're not actually run), so they're useful for things like attribution, writing notes to other developers who might be reading your code, and writing notes to yourself for later (like to-dos).

You can put them at the end of a line of code as well, like this:

```python
print("lady i swear by all flowers. Don't cry") # I love this line
```

Comments also are useful for troubleshooting. Because Python skips anything after a #, you can "comment out" a bunch of lines of code (rather than simply deleting them) to see how your code will run without those lines:

```python
# "Since feeling is first" by e e cummings
print("since feeling is first")
print("who pays any attention")
print("to the syntax of things")
print("will never wholly kiss you;")
print("wholly to be a fool")
print("while Spring is in the world")

# print("my blood approves")
# print("and kisses are a better fate")
# print("than wisdom")
# print("lady i swear by all flowers. Don't cry") # I love this line
# print("—the best gesture of my brain is less than")
# print("your eyelids' flutter which says")

print("we are for each other: then")
print("laugh, leaning back in my arms")
print("for life's not a paragraph")

print("and death i think is no parenthesis")
```

Now notice how those lines are skipped when we run our code:

```
% python print.py
since feeling is first
who pays any attention
to the syntax of things
will never wholly kiss you;
wholly to be a fool
while Spring is in the world
we are for each other: then
laugh, leaning back in my arms
for life's not a paragraph
and death i think is no parenthesis
```

There's a convenient keyboard shortcut for commenting out code in *Atom*, which is Command and / on a Mac or Ctrl and / on a Windows after selecting one or multiple lines of code. Try it out now. If you ever forget the keyboard shortcut, you can find it again in *Atom* in the *Edit* dropdown menu under *Toggle Comments*.

2.6 VARIABLES

Now we are going to introduce an important Python concept, the *variable*. If you've ever taken a high school algebra class, you likely already know how variables work. Here's a quick pop quiz:

```
a = 1
b = 2
c = a + b
```

What is the value of c? If you said 3, then you are correct and you know how variables work. Variables are just ways to save things in your code. Think of them as little boxes to store things like numbers and text. To get some practice with variables, let's create a new file called variables.py and add the following to it:

```
# Variables are just nicknames
# they're plain, lowercase words

name = "Mattan Griffel"
orphan_fee = 200
teddy_bear_fee = 121.80
total = orphan_fee + teddy_bear_fee

print(name, "the total will be", total)
```

Then go ahead and run the code to see what you get:

```
% python variables.py
Mattan Griffel the total will be 321.8
```

A helpful way to think of variables is the box analogy. When you're moving from one house to another, you can put a bunch of things into a box and label the box something like *books* so that you remember what's inside of it. This makes it easier to move those things around. In Python, variables are like boxes that can contain text, numbers, and (as we'll see later) other things like lists as well.

Creating a new variable and giving it a value is called *variable assignment* (we'll use that term occasionally throughout the book, so you'll become familiar with it). Once you've assigned a variable, you can use it anywhere in your code and whatever's inside the variable box will get plugged in there when the code runs. But what happens if you try to use a variable that hasn't actually been created yet? For example:

```
...
print(subtotal)
```

VARIABLES AND THE PYTHON STYLE GUIDE

The official Python Style Guide says that variables should be "lowercase with words separated by underscores as necessary to improve readability."[4] So that's the convention we'll be following in this book.

When it comes to Python (and other programming languages), there are two kinds of rules: those you *have* to follow and those you *should* follow as a matter of convention. The conventions are the ones that the community has agreed on, either implicitly or explicitly, to standardize different approaches to writing code. The goal is to make it easier to read, share, and understand other people's code. Variable naming is one of those conventions.

Years ago, long before the Python Style Guide was released in 2001, if you looked at other people's code you'd find them using all sorts of different conventions for variable naming like `camelCase` or abbreviation (e.g., `tbf`). You'll still find examples of this all over the place once you start looking, but we recommend using lowercase words separated by underscores.

What happens is that when you run your code, you'll get the following kind
of error:

```
File "variables.py", line 9, in <module>
     print(subtotal)
NameError: name 'subtotal' is not defined
```

Note the error class (`NameError`) and the error message (`name 'subtotal'
is not defined`). Note that this is also the most common error that will come
up if you accidentally misspell a variable name. If you want `variables.py`
to run again without an error, make sure to either define `subtotal`, remove
`print(subtotal)`, or comment it out like so:

```
   ...
   # print(subtotal)
```

Another thing about conventions: the spaces around the equal signs aren't
necessary but they're preferred as it makes the code easier to read (e.g.,
`orphan_fee = 200` versus `orphan_fee=200`).

If you ever have a question like, "What happens if I do X? Will it still work?"
our recommendation would be to try it for yourself and see what happens. You're
unlikely to make a mistake that can't be easily corrected, and the answers to many
of these "What happens if . . . ?" questions are somewhat arbitrary. Why do things
in Python work one way but not another? Because the people who created the
language decided it should work that way.

Learning and becoming comfortable with a programming language like Python
means trying out enough things that you can begin to anticipate what happens
under different circumstances. In other words, when you're not sure, give it a shot
and see what happens.

2.7 NUMBERS AND MATH

It should be no surprise that in Python you can do math using many symbols
you're probably already familiar with. Create a new file called `math2.py` (Python
actually has a built-in module called `math`—we'll learn more about these later in

section 4.3.1—so naming this file math.py could lead to problems that we want to avoid for now.) Inside of math2.py write the following code:

```
# In Python you can do math using these symbols:
# + addition
# - subtraction
# * multiplication
# / division
# ** exponents (not ^)

print("What is the answer to life, the universe, and everything?",
40 + 30 - 7 * 2 / 3)
print("Is it true that 5 * 2 > 3 * 4?")
print(5 * 2 > 3 * 4)
```

Running it should give you the following:

```
% python math2.py
What is the answer to life, the universe, and everything?
65.33333333333333
Is it true that 5 * 2 > 3 * 4?
False
```

One thing you may have noticed is that our first actual line of code in math2.py is a bit long:

```
print("What is the answer to life, the universe, and everything?",
40 + 30 - 7 * 2 / 3)
```

If you read the Python Style Guide, you'll learn about the convention that all lines of code should be less than eighty characters long. In this book, long lines of code need to be printed out across multiple lines for you to be able to read them. In Python, however, breaking one line of code into multiple lines doesn't always work.

One way to fix this is to wrap multiple lines of Python code in parentheses. In our previous example, it actually is possible to break the long line of code into multiple lines, because it's already inside the parentheses from the print() function:

```
print("What is the answer to life, the universe, and everything?",
40 + 30 - 7 * 2 / 3)
```

Though this only works if you don't add a new line break in the middle of the text in quotes. When Python gets to the end of the first line, it notices you never closed the parenthesis that you opened at the start of the line, so it assumes the next line is just a continuation.

A second approach is to use variables to break the code into smaller chunks when possible. Here's an example of what we mean by that:

```
...
answer = 40 + 30 - 7 * 2 / 3
print("What is the answer to life, the universe, and everything?",
answer)
...
```

(Again, don't actually type the ... part, that's just our way of skipping over some of the code we've previously written so that we only have to show the relevant code.)

This approach often has the added benefit of making your code easier to read. Good variable names can make your code clearer because you're essentially labeling different sections of your code.

After trying each of these approaches, run the file again to see that the code still works as it did before:

```
% python math2.py
What is the answer to life, the universe, and everything?
65.33333333333333
Is it true that 5 * 2 > 3 * 4?
False
```

Anyone who has read *The Hitchhiker's Guide to the Galaxy* knows that the answer to life, the universe, and everything should be 42, not 65.333. It turns out we forgot our order of operations. Edit math2.py to add in parentheses around 40 + 30 − 7:

```
...
answer = (40 + 30 - 7) * 2 / 3
...
```

Now run `math2.py` again:

```
% python math2.py
What is the answer to life, the universe, and everything? 42.0
...
```

There we go. However, do you notice something strange here? It's printing `42.0` instead of just `42`. What's going on?

2.7.1 Integers Versus Floats

To understand why our file prints out `42.0` instead of `42`, we have to peel back another layer of the onion to talk about something really technical: the difference between integers and floats.

Let's open up Python interactive mode for a second.

```
% python
>>> 1 * 1
1
```

Why are we showing you this in the interactive shell? Because if we did this in a file, we'd have to print it out, and we'd have to go back to the command line to run the file each time. This approach saves us two steps.

```
>>> 11 * 11
121
>>> 111 * 111
12321
>>> 1111 * 1111
1234321
>>> 111111111 * 111111111 # Nine 1s
12345678987654321
```

Okay, that had nothing to do with integers versus floats (we just find it interesting). Let's return to what we were talking about, integers versus floats:

```
>>> 42
42
>>> 42.0
42.0
>>> 42.000000
42.0
```

Even though, to a human, 42 and 42.0 are the same number, this is not true for a computer. To understand why, consider that to store a decimal number, Python needs to set aside some space to store the whole part of the number (42) as well as separate space to store the fractional part of the number (in this case, 0). For a whole number, Python needs to store only the whole numbers.

Going back to our "box" analogy, if you were moving houses, you might use a different size box to transport a large lamp versus smaller stuff like utensils. The same is true here: when you create a variable, Python automatically figures out what kind of box size it needs to store that variable and creates the variable accordingly. (It might be interesting to you to know that in some other languages, such as C++, the programming language won't automatically figure out the box type for you; you have to specify it.)

In a programming language, the "type of box" is called a *data type*. The whole number data type in Python is called an *integer*, and the decimal data type in Python is called a *float*. We're going to be learning about other data types later—like strings, lists, and dictionaries—but, for beginners, this concept may seem weird and abstract until we get more experience with other ways of storing data later in this book.

In general, Python does a good job of handling this complexity. For example, try the following two lines:

```
>>> 2 + 2
4
>>> 2 + 2.0
4.0
>>> 4 / 2
2.0
```

In the first line, we are adding two integers, and the result is an integer. In the second, we are adding an integer and the float, and Python gives us a float. In the third, we are dividing two integers, and even though the result is a whole number, Python is still giving us a float.

At the risk of stretching our "moving houses" analogy a little too far, if you were trying to combine a box with a lamp and a box with cutlery, you would have to use the larger of the two boxes for the combined package. In the same way, when you add an integer and a float, Python realizes the result needs to be in a float. Similarly, when you carry out a division, even if it might not necessarily result in a decimal number, Python knows it *might*, and so it makes sure to give you back a float, just in case.[5]

In some cases, you want to specifically convert a float into an integer or vice versa. You can do this as follows:

```
>>> float(42)
42.0
>>> int(42.0)
42
>>> int(10.58)
10
```

Note that `int()` isn't the same thing as rounding, which you can do with `round()`:

```
>>> round(10.58)
11
```

The `int()` function will simply remove the decimal part, whereas the `round()` function rounds up or down to the closest whole number. As a side note, a convenient feature of the `round()` function is that it also accepts an optional second argument (we'll talk more about function arguments in section 4.2) that lets you tell it how many decimal points you want to round to:

```
>>> round(10.58, 1)
10.6
```

How can we apply our new knowledge of the `int()` function to our `math2.py` file to get it to print out `42` instead of `42.0`? We can convert our answer variable into an integer before printing it:

```
...
answer = (40 + 30 - 7) * 2 / 3
print("What is the answer to life, the universe, and everything?",
int(answer))
...
```

Note that we also could have used round() here. Alternatively, we could have used int() earlier when we created the answer variable in the first place, like this:

```
...
answer = int((40 + 30 - 7) * 2 / 3)
print("What is the answer to life, the universe, and everything?",
answer)
...
```

For what we're trying to accomplish, the two approaches will produce identical outcomes. The only difference will be that the answer variable in the first case will contain a float and in the second case will contain an integer.

Let's check whether it worked by running the file again:

```
% python math2.py
What is the answer to life, the universe, and everything? 42
...
```

This is just what we wanted!

2.8 STRINGS

Create a new file called strings.py and type the following:

```
# Strings are text surrounded by quotes
# Both single (' ') and double (" ") can be used

kanye_quote = 'My greatest pain in life is that I will never be able
to see myself perform live.'
print(kanye_quote)
```

Strings are just a fancy name for text in Python.[6] So far, we've been using double quotes (" ") for most of our strings, but we can use single quotes (' ') as well as you'll notice in strings.py. The two are basically interchangeable—as long as you use the same thing on both sides.

Because the `kanye_quote` line is already quite long, it makes sense to split it across two lines. We've already noted that we can do this by splitting the line into two strings and wrapping them in parentheses:

```
...
kanye_quote = ('My greatest pain in life is that I will never '
'be able to see myself perform live.')
print(kanye_quote)
```

Why is it useful that you can create strings with either single or double quotes? At some point, you're likely to run into a problem when you want to use quotes inside of your strings, for example, when quoting dialogue or using apostrophes.

Add the following to `strings.py`:

```
...
hamilton_quote = "Well, the word got around, they said, "This kid is
insane, man""
print(hamilton_quote)
```

Can you figure out why what we've added won't work? It's because Python will read `"Well, the word got around, they said, "` as a string. If you start a string with a double quote (`"`), Python isn't smart enough to know that your use of another double quote inside the string wasn't meant to end the string.

One simple solution is to switch the kind of quotes you use to start and end your string:

```
# Switch to single quotes if your string uses double-quotes
hamilton_quote = 'Well, the word got around, they said, "This kid is
insane, man"'
print(hamilton_quote)
```

That should produce the following output:

```
% python strings.py
...
Well, the word got around, they said, "This kid is insane, man"
```

See how the quotes are printed out?

DOING "MATH" WITH STRINGS

Python handles the addition of two strings intuitively, as follows:

```
>>> "Hello" + "Mattan"
'HelloMattan'
```

Python automatically realizes that adding two strings means sticking them together. Notice, however, that there is no space between the two words. How would you introduce a space there?

What happens if we try to add a string to an integer:

```
>>> "The meaning of life is " + 42
Traceback (most recent call last):
    File "<stdin>", line 1, in <module>
TypeError: can only concatenate str (not "int") to str
```

This doesn't work.

We were asking Python to combine a string and an integer. In our moving analogy, this is equivalent to trying to combine two boxes with dumbbells and a crystal vase. The two boxes are so different that it's unclear exactly how to combine them, so Python gives up and throws an error.

The conclusion is that you need to explicitly convert the integer to a string before adding them together using the `str()` function:

```
>>> "The meaning of life is " + str(42)
'The meaning of life is 42'
```

A final point worth knowing (because it will come up very soon) is that Python also allows you to multiply a string by an integer, as follows:

```
>>> "candy" * 4
'candycandycandycandy'
```

That's a lot of candy! The string is simply repeated four times.

2.8.1 String Functions

Although we'll cover functions in much further depth later, it's worth noting that Python has several functions that are specifically useful when it comes to strings. Unlike the other functions we've seen so far, we have to run these functions *directly on* a string itself by putting a . after it like so:

```
# A few string functions
print(kanye_quote.upper())
print(kanye_quote.lower())
print("ok fine".replace("fine", "great").upper())
```

If you add this code to your strings.py file, when you run it you should see the following:

```
% python strings.py
...
MY GREATEST PAIN IN LIFE IS THAT I WILL NEVER BE ABLE TO SEE MYSELF
PERFORM LIVE.
my greatest pain in life is that i will never be able to see myself
perform live.
OK GREAT
```

What's going on here?

On the first line, we're printing the entire contents of kanye_quote in all uppercase by adding .upper() to the end. On the next line, we're printing it all lowercase by adding .lower() to the end. Finally, we're taking the string "ok fine" and doing two things: replacing the text "fine" with "deal" and *then* uppercasing the entire thing.

The main reason these functions look different from the rest is that we can run them directly on a string by adding a . and the function name (plus parentheses) after either a string or a variable that contains a string. In Python, these kinds of functions are technically called methods. They're usually specific to the kind of data types you're working with (we'll see some others later when we introduce lists and dictionaries), and as we saw earlier, they can be connected one after another (this is sometimes called "chaining").

String functions can be used to do many handy things, which we'll come back to later in this book. In section 3.5.2, we'll introduce other string functions such as .split() and .join() that will allow us to separate a string into something called a list, and also convert a list back into a string.

There are many more string functions (and other functions, generally) that we will not have time to cover in this book, but we encourage you to explore them further if you're interested by reading the Python documentation online. You can find more string functions by going to https://docs.python.org/3/library/stdtypes .html and reading the section on *String Methods*.

2.8.2 F-Strings

Remember back in happy_hour.py when we saw a string that looked like this?

```
print(f"How about you go to {random_bar} with {random_person}?")
```

What's going on with that f before the string and the curly braces ({ }) inside of it?

It turns out that Python strings have the ability to let you write Python code directly inside of them. Try adding the following to the bottom of `strings.py`:

```
...
# F-strings let you write Python code directly inside of a string
# inside of curly brackets ({ })
print(f"1 + 1 equals {1 + 1}")
```

These kinds of strings are known as *f-strings*. Running the code should give you the following output:

```
% python strings.py
...
1 + 1 equals 2
```

If you are wondering why the f character is necessary, we encourage you to run an experiment to see what happens if you remove it.

```
print("1 + 1 equals {1 + 1}")
```

When we remove the f from the front of the string, we get the following:

```
% python strings.py
...
1 + 1 equals {1 + 1}
```

The f character in front of the string is important because it tells Python to actually go in and run what's inside the curly braces instead of just printing out the whole thing as is (brackets and all).

It's common for Python developers to use f-strings to insert variables directly into a string and format them a certain way. To get a deeper understanding of what's possible with f-strings, try adding the following to `strings.py`:

THE F IN F-STRINGS

You may be curious at this point: What does the f stand for? Some quick Googling will turn up the fact that it stands for *format*, but that answer may not be satisfying.

A little more sleuthing on this relatively new feature of Python uncovers the following note from the developers:

"Other prefixes were suggested, such as 'i'. No option seemed better than the other, so 'f' was chosen."

In order words, after thinking about it for a bit, the developers of Python couldn't come up with a better option—so they went with f.

```
...
name = "mattan griffel"
print(f"{name.title()}, the total will be ${200 + 121.80 :,.2f}")
```

When you run this, you should get the following result:

```
% python strings.py
...
Mattan Griffel, the total will be $321.80
```

As you can imagine, {name.title()} will take whatever is inside the name variable, convert it to title case (i.e., capitalize each word), and then insert it directly into the string. Inside the next set of curly brackets—{200 + 121.8 :,.2f}—we're adding 200 and 121.80 and inserting the result directly into the string as well.

What's the deal with :,.2f?

That's actually a feature of f-strings, and it's how we can tell Python to format the number as a float with two decimal points, and commas for the thousands separator. In other words, what we'll see printed out is 321.80 instead of 321.8. That's handy when we want to display something like a currency value, which typically is displayed to two decimal places, even if the second one is 0.

The full power of what you can do with f-strings and when you should use them is probably not yet clear, and we'll have to use them in a few other examples before you understand why they're useful. We're introducing them at this point so that we can use them later.

A quick rule of thumb is that whenever you've got some text and you'd like to put some variables into that text directly, it's probably best to use an f-string (and don't forget the curly brackets around the variable inside the string). However, now that we've introduced f-strings, don't go overboard using them when there's no reason to do so. For example, the following isn't necessary:

```
print(f"Winter is coming.")
```

STRINGS VERSUS VARIABLES

Let's quickly recap: What's the difference between:

```
'a string'
```

And this?

```
a_string
```

They look pretty similar, but they're different. The first is a string. The second is a variable that includes an instruction for Python to go to the "box" labeled a_string and look at whatever's inside it.

This string doesn't actually have any variables or Python code inside it to run. It will still work, but it's just unnecessary. You need to use an f-string only if you have {}s inside that string with some Python code inside it. Similarly, you could write:

```
print(f"{name}")
```

But the following is much simpler:

```
print(name)
```

2.9 GETTING USER INPUT

Thus far, we've been dealing only with information that we've manually put in ourselves. But what if we want to take user input and do something with that? That's where the input() function comes in handy.

Create a new file called input.py and enter the following:

```
name = input("What's your name? ")
print(f"Hi {name}!")
```

Now run the file:

```
% python input.py
What's your name?
```

You'll notice that we're not taken back to the command line prompt. The Python code asks us a question, pauses, and waits for us to respond. Type in your name and see what happens:

```
% python input.py
What's your name? Mattan
Hi Mattan!
```

Cool. So what we have here is a way to get some input from a user, save it into a variable, and then do whatever we want with it. (By the way, we like to put a space after the question mark in the input() question, just so that it doesn't all seem so smushed together when you're asking the user for some information. Try it without the space to see what we mean.)

Let's try to collect some other info. Edit `input.py`:

```
...
age = input("How old are you? ")
print(f "Hi {name}! You're {age} years old.")
```

And then run it:

```
% python input.py
What's your name? Mattan
How old are you? 32
Hi Mattan! You're 32 years old.
```

It's interesting, but not very useful yet. Let's make our `input.py` do some work for us. We want it to tell us our age in *dog years* instead of human years:

```
name = input("What's your name? ")
age = input("How old are you? ")
age_in_dog_years = age * 7

print(f"Hi {name}! You're {age_in_dog_years} in dog years. Woof!")
```

And now we run the code to see if it works:

```
% python input.py
What's your name? Mattan
How old are you? 30
Hi Mattan! You're 32323232323232 in dog years. Woof!
```

Oops! What do you think is going on here? Take a look at your code again and see if you can figure it out. If you're feeling brave, you can try to fix it on your own before moving on.

What's happening here is that all user input that we get from `input()` comes in as a string. As noted in the previous box "Doing 'Math' with Strings," `'30'` is a string, which is different from the integer 30. But as we saw in section 2.8, when we multiply a string by an integer, Python assumes we just want to repeat the string multiple times (which is what's happening here). To actually multiply the numbers, we first have to convert the string into a number:

```
% python
>>> "32" * 7
'32323232323232'
>>> int("32") * 7
224
>>> float("32") * 7
224.0
```

We can use either `int()` or `float()` to do the conversion, depending on what input we're expecting the user to give us. Given what we just showed you, do you think you can get `input.py` to work properly? Give it a shot now.

We can think of at least two (okay, there are more) obvious ways to fix this. The first is to convert the user's input into an integer right when we get it:

```
age = int(input("How old are you? "))
```

The second is to convert the age variable into an integer right before you're about to perform math:

```
age_in_dog_years = int(age) * 7
```

We prefer the first option. In the second example, the age variable will still contain a string. This could be confusing later if we need to use the age variable again—we would have to keep converting it into an integer every time. We'd probably expect a variable named age to have a number in it based on the fact that age is usually a number. It's unlikely that someone would give us their age in intervals of less than a year (e.g., `32.4`) but if that's something we were expecting, then we might use `float()` to convert the user's input into a float instead.

The final code in `input.py` should look like this:

```
name = input("What's your name? ")
age = int(input("How old are you? "))
age_in_dog_years = age * 7

print(f"Hi {name}! You're {age_in_dog_years} in dog years. Woof!")
```

And, when we run it, it should give us the following output:

```
% python input.py
What's your name? Mattan
How old are you? 32
Hi Mattan! You're 224 in dog years. Woof!
```

It worked! Give yourself a treat.

2.9.1 Tip Calculator Challenge

Before moving on, here's one more challenge so you can review what we've covered so far:

Write a script called `tip_calculator.py` that asks you how much your bill totaled and that recommends three standard tip amounts (18 percent, 20 percent, and 25 percent). Include comments in your code. Take 10 minutes or so.

2.9.2 Tip Calculator Challenge Solution

Here's what we came up with:

```
# Tip Calculator

# Convert the user's input into a float
amount = float(input("How much was your bill? "))

# Calculate the tip amounts
print(f"15%: ${amount * .18 :,.2f}")
print(f"18%: ${amount * .20 :,.2f}")
print(f"20%: ${amount * .25 :,.2f}")
```

Take a look and compare your answer to ours. Ours is not necessarily the best or most ideal solution; it's just one possible solution.

One thing to note about our solution is that we converted the user's input using `float()` instead of `int()` because we're expecting the user to give us a bill amount that probably will include cents.

We also used `:,.2f` to display the tip amounts as a currency with two decimal points. We could have used `round()` as well to round to two decimal points, but the downside with `round()` is that tip amounts like `$1.90` would still end up being displayed with only one decimal point (e.g., `$1.9`) because Python hides unnecessary digits by default.

If you solved this challenge a different way and you're satisfied with your solution, that's fine too.

2.10 WRAPPING UP

What have we covered so far? Take a moment to look at the following list and try to remember some of the Python terms we've gone over together so far. The actual practice of trying to recall something, even if it feels like you're struggling, will make it easier to remember it in the future. So far we've learned about the following:

- Command line basics (`pwd`, `ls`, and `cd`)
- Two ways of running Python code (running a script or in Python interactive mode)
- `print()`
- `# Comments`
- Variables
- Numbers and Math
- Strings
- Getting user input with `input()`

Hopefully, you're enjoying yourself so far. If you're feeling overwhelmed, know that we've already covered the hardest part for most people, which is actually just getting started.

In chapter 3, we'll introduce a few new data types, and some more advanced concepts in Python, such as if statements and loops. These new concepts, plus what we've learned so far, will allow us to do a lot more with Python, and move us closer toward the goal of using Python to solve some real business problems.

3

PYTHON BASICS, PART 2

WE NOW KNOW ENOUGH to be able to write some basic scripts in Python, but a few important pieces are still missing. What happens when numbers and strings are not enough? How can we really unlock the power of Python to do things for us quickly? In this chapter, we'll continue to build on the concepts we learned in the last chapter, and we'll start seeing how Python can be used to solve even more complex problems.

3.1 WHAT YOU'LL LEARN IN THIS CHAPTER

By the end of this chapter, you'll have learned most of Python's basic functionality. You'll learn how to run checks in Python, work with logic, create lists, run code loops, and create dictionaries. Along the way, you'll get a chance to apply your newfound knowledge to FizzBuzz, a common developer challenge problem.

3.2 CONDITIONAL STATEMENTS

Thus far, all the code we've written runs no matter what happens. But often you will want to write code that takes into account different possibilities for what could happen—different paths, if you will. Let us demonstrate.

3.2.1 if Statements

We'll start by creating a new file called `if.py`:

```
answer = input("Do you want to hear a joke? ")

if answer == "Yes":
    print("What's loud and sounds like an apple?")
    print("AN APPLE")
```

You'll need to indent the last last two lines using your Tab key. This is our first time using indentation in Python, and it's something we'll come back to shortly. If you've copied everything properly, when you run the file you should see the following:

```
% python if.py
Do you want to hear a joke?
```

Do you see what happens? The code pauses, asks us a question, and waits for us to respond. Type "No" and then hit Enter.

```
% python if.py
Do you want to hear a joke? No
```

Okay, so nothing happened. Now try running it again and typing *Yes* (you may notice this is case sensitive, which we'll talk about in a bit).

```
% python if.py
Do you want to hear a joke? Yes
What's loud and sounds like an apple?
AN APPLE
```

So now we're seeing something printed that we didn't see before. And it all seems to be controlled by that magical `if answer == "Yes"`. The general structure of an `if` statement is as follows:

```
if x:
    # Do something
```

PYTHON BASICS, PART 2 **73**

Where x is anything that can be true. How does == (two equal signs) in answer == "Yes" work? It checks to see whether two things are the same. It returns True if they are or False if they aren't. Let's open Python interactive mode and play around with some examples:

```
% python
>>> "Yes" == "Yes"
True
>>> "No" == "Yes"
False
```

It is important to realize that even though they look similar, = and == are very different. Can you follow what's happening in this example?

```
>>> answer == "Yes"
Traceback (most recent call last):
    File "<stdin>", line 1, in <module>
NameError: name 'answer' is not defined
>>> answer = "Yes"
>>> answer == "Yes"
True
>>> answer = "No"
>>> answer == "Yes"
False
```

First, we're checking if the answer variable contains the string "Yes", but we get an error because we haven't actually defined the answer variable yet. Once we do, we can check to see that it is equal to "Yes". And if we later overwrite the answer variable and set it equal to the string "No", then we can see that answer == "Yes" returns False.

To summarize, = is used to assign a value to a variable, whereas == is used to check equality. Some programming languages do not distinguish between these two (e.g., VBA, Excel's scripting language), but Python does.

A question we often are asked is, "Is == case sensitive?" What if we didn't know? How could we figure it out?

```
>>> "Yes" == "yes"
False
```

Aha! So == *is* case sensitive. We'll learn how to deal with this later. By the way, we can use != (that's an exclamation point and an equal sign) to check if two things are different:

```
>>> "yes" != "Yes"
True
>>> answer != "Blue"
True
```

There are a lot of other symbols you can use to compare two things in Python (e.g., we already saw > earlier), but we'll come back to those later.

Now a more general question: How does the if statement work? It checks to see if something is true or false, and if it's true, then it runs any code after the : (colon) that is *indented*.

The indentation part is really important. For an if statement to work in Python, it needs to have a colon at the end of the line, and you need to have some code (one or more lines) indented afterward. Why? Because otherwise Python doesn't know where the thing that comes after if ends.

What happens if you forget to do either of these things (e.g., you forget to put a colon or tab in your code afterward)? What kind of error do you get? It's worth trying to replicate this so that you'll be able to recognize the error later if you make that mistake (*when* you make that mistake; trust us, we've forgotten our fair share of colons).

3.2.2 else and elif Statements

Let's make another change to if.py:

WHITESPACE IN PYTHON

Indentation is really important in Python. This is the first time we've seen tabbed code in Python, but it won't be the last (we'll need it again for loops and functions).

When indenting your code in Python, you can use either a tab (by hitting the Tab key) or four spaces (by hitting the spacebar four times). Which one you choose to use can be a contentious issue, and most developers prefer one over the other. In an episode of the HBO show *Silicon Valley*, the main character Richard Hendricks actually threatens to break up with his girlfriend because she uses spaces instead of tabs.

One slightly annoying thing about Python is that it forces you to choose either tabs or spaces within a file. If you try to run a Python script that uses both tabs and spaces for indentation, you get the following error:

```
TabError: inconsistent
use of tabs and spaces in
indentation
```

It's a pretty straightforward problem, but it's annoying, nonetheless. You're most likely to encounter this problem when copying and pasting code that someone else has written, and they happen to use a different convention from you.

Practically speaking, most developers end up using a setting in their text editor that automatically converts tabs into four spaces. Fortunately, *Atom* should do this automatically for you by default.

```
answer = input("Do you want to hear a joke? ")

if answer == "Yes ":
    print("What's loud and sounds like an apple?")
    print("AN APPLE")
else:
    print("Fine.")
```

The `else` lets you say what code you want to run if the `if` part doesn't turn out to be true. Now when we run the file we can get the following:

```
% python if.py
Do you want to hear a joke? No
Fine.
```

What if we want to check for a third option? Let's add something else to `if.py`:

```
answer = input("Do you want to hear a joke? ")

if answer == "Yes":
    print("What's loud and sounds like an apple?")
    print("AN APPLE")
elif answer == "No":
    print("Fine.")
else:
    print("I don't understand.")
```

Adding an `elif` lets us add other conditions. It's like another `if` (in fact, it's a shortening of *else* and *if*). So now we can run our code and get the following:

```
% python if.py
Do you want to hear a joke? Yes
What's loud and sounds like an apple?
AN APPLE
% python if.py
Do you want to hear a joke? No
Fine.
% python if.py
Do you want to hear a joke? Blue
I don't understand.
```

We can put in as many `elif`s as we want, but we can only have one `if` and one `else`. Think of it as a series of paths that our code can step through:

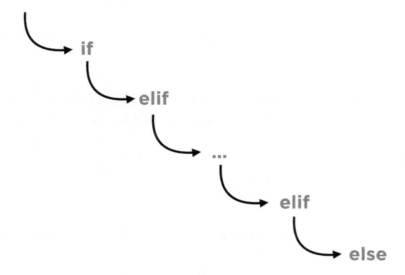

It works like a waterfall, in the sense that Python always starts with the `if` and then moves down to the next one only if the one before it wasn't true. Once it finds an `if` or an `elif` that's true, Python won't check any of the ones after it. As a result, the code under `else` will only run as a last-case scenario. You can think of it as a catchall or as a safety net.

This may seem pretty clear so far, but now we're going to throw a curveball your way. Let's test your problem-solving skills. What would happen if you used two `if`s instead of an `if` and an `elif`?

```python
answer = input("Do you want to hear a joke? ")

if answer == "Yes":
    print("What's loud and sounds like an apple?")
    print("AN APPLE")
if answer == "No":
    print("Fine.")
else:
    print("I don't understand.")
```

In case it's not clear, the difference here is on the line:

```
if answer == "No":
```

This code would produce the following bug:

```
% python if.py
Do you want to hear a joke? Yes
What's loud and sounds like an apple?
AN APPLE
I don't understand.
```

Both the code under the first `if` and also under the `else` runs! Why is that? Because first it checks the first `if`:

```
if answer == "Yes":
    print("What's loud and sounds like an apple?")
    print("AN APPLE")
```

Which runs because `answer` is `"Yes"`. But then it still checks the second `if`:

```
if answer == "No":
    print("Fine.")
else:
    print("I don't understand.")
```

The first part, `answer == "No":`, is `False`. Therefore, Python then runs what's underneath the `else` part. In other words, putting two `if`s instead of one `if` and one `elif` splits the chain of checks that Python performs, so each one runs independently.

We'll note that you can put an `if` directly inside another `if` (and even more `if`s inside of those `if`s, if you want). In other words, you can come up with all sorts of complex conditions like *if A and B but not C then do D*. Keep in mind that an `if` inside of another `if` would require you to indent twice (tabs are important!) like so:

```
if x:
    if y:
        # Do something
```

As we continue to learn more about Python concepts like loops and functions, we'll start to see `if` statements used inside loops inside functions and so on. This is called *nesting* and it's relatively common, but it can be really confusing to try to understand what exactly is happening if you're not used to seeing it.

3.3 LOGIC IN PYTHON

We've already seen one example of logic in Python, when we introduced the `==` operator, which returns `True` if the things on either side of the operator are the same and `False` otherwise. You might wonder whether Python has any other ways of comparing two items (doing logic), and indeed it does. These ways include, but are not limited to, the following:

```
==,!=, >, >=, <, <=, not, and, or
```

The best way to understand how these symbols work is to actually play around with them in Python interactive mode. We'll start with just `True` and `False`.

```
% python
>>> True
True
>>> False
False
```

Note that `True` and `False` (with capital T and F) are actually things in Python. You might ask, "Are they variables?" And the answer is no, they're just `True` and `False`. They're an entirely different data type from what we've learned thus far. Technically, they're called *Booleans* (named after George Boole, who first defined an algebraic system of logic in the mid-nineteenth century).

3.3.1 Equal to

The operator `==` checks to see if the things on both sides are the same or not and returns `True` if they are or `False` if they're not.

```
>>> answer = "yes"
>>> answer == "yes"
True
>>> answer == "no"
False
```

Remember, even though they look similar, = and == do different things in Python: = assigns a value to a variable, and == checks to see if two things are equal.

3.3.2 Not Equal to

The operator != is the opposite of ==. It tells us if two things *aren't* the same.

```
>>> answer = "no"
>>> answer != "yes"
True
>>> answer != "no"
False
```

3.3.3 Greater Than, Less Than

We've actually already seen > (greater than) and < (less than) in our lesson on math in Python. They work as you might expect:

```
>>> 10 > 12
False
>>> 10 < 12
True
```

It's also possible to check if something is greater than or equal to, or less than or equal to something else with >= and <=:

```
>>> 1 + 1 + 1 >= 3
True
>>> 1 + 1 + 1 <= 3
True
```

3.3.4 not

The operator not is probably the easiest to explain because it just takes whatever value we have (True or False) and then flips it.

```
>>> not True
False
>>> not False
True
>>> not 1 + 1 + 1 >= 3
False
```

You might notice that unlike the other operators we've looked at, not takes only one "thing" and inverts it, unlike == which took two "things" and checked if they were equal, or < which took two "things" and checked if one was greater than the other.

Notice the last example. As you can imagine, once you start combining symbols together, it can get kind of complicated to understand which one runs first. In this case, everything to the right of not runs first, and then not is applied to the result. It's bad practice to rely on this because it can lead to mistakes if you forget the correct order, so we recommend using brackets to specify the order in which you want to run things—in this instance, the clearest way would be to write not (1 + 1 + 1 >= 3).

3.3.5 and

We can use and to combine some of the logic checks we learned previously:

```
>>> username = "admin"
>>> password = "123456"
>>> username == "admin" and password == "123456"
True
```

The operator and only returns True if both sides are True. In this case, username == "admin" is True and password == "123456" is True so when we combine them the result is still True. But if we change password:

```
>>> password = "wrong password"
>>> username == "admin" and password == "123456"
False
```

The second part is no longer True, so and makes the whole thing return False. Again, notice how the == is evaluated before the and, as expected. To ensure this happens, you might want to use (username == "admin") and (password == "123456") instead.

3.3.6 or

The operator or returns True as long as either side is True. And it returns False only if both sides are False.

```
>>> answer = "yes"
>>> answer == "Yes" or answer == "yes"
True
>>> answer == "No" or answer == "no"
False
```

3.3.7 in

A final operator worth mentioning is in, which checks if one variable is in another variable. You can use it to check whether one string contains another. For example,

```
>>> "d" in "hello"
False
>>> "d" in "goodbye"
True
>>> "d" in "GOODBYE"
False
```

Notice that in is case sensitive, like our other string-based operators. Another, far more useful way, in can be used involves lists, which we haven't covered yet. Nevertheless, let's show you a quick example now. You can probably figure out how it works:

```
>>> people = ["Mattan", "Daniel", "Sarah"]
>>> "Mattan" in people
True
```

If you want to learn more about Python's truth terms, look up "Python comparison operators" or "Python logical operators."

3.3.8 Logic Practice

Logic in Python (and in general) can get quite a bit more complicated once you start combining these truth terms. We've created a practice file `logic_practice.py` that you can download at https://www.pythonformbas.com/code, and we'd recommend that you spend the next ten minutes working through this file line by line:

```
True and True
False and True
(1 == 1) and (2 == 1)
"love" == "love"
(1 == 1) or (2 != 1)
True and (1 == 1)
False and (0 != 0)
True or (1 == 1)
"time" == "money"
(1 != 0) and (2 == 1)
"I Can't Believe It's Not Butter!" != "butter"
"one" == 1
not (True and False)
not ((1 == 1) and (0 != 1))
not ((10 == 1) or (1000 == 1000))
not ((1 != 10) or (3 == 4))
not (("love" == "love") and ("time" == "money"))
(1 == 1) and (not (("one" == 1) or (1 == 0)))
("chunky" == "bacon") and (not ((3 == 4) or (3 == 3)))
(3 == 3) and (not (("love" == "love") or ("Python" == "Fun")))
```

The idea in this example is that each line is either `True` or `False`, and it's up to you to figure out which. It starts off easy and gets harder as it goes down. When it comes to parentheses, ensure that you solve what's inside the parentheses first before doing the rest.

One idea is to write what you think the answer is as a comment at the end of the line like this:

```
True and True # True
```

If you want to double-check your answer, you can either copy and paste that entire line into Python interactive mode:

```
% python
>>> True and True
True
```

Or you can just put that line inside of a `print()`:

```
print(True and True)
```

And then run the file to see the output:

```
% python logic_practice.py
True
```

3.4 MAKING IF.PY CASE INSENSITIVE

Let's apply something we just learned to our `if.py` script. You may have noticed that the following line is case sensitive:

```
...
if answer == "Yes":
    print("What's loud and sounds like an apple?")
    print("AN APPLE")
...
```

Meaning, if you type "yes" (lowercase "y") you'll get the following:

```
% python if.py
Do you want to hear a joke? yes
I don't understand.
```

We can fix this by adding an or:

```
...
if answer == "Yes" or answer == "yes":
    print("What's loud and sounds like an apple?")
    print("AN APPLE")
...
```

And you could also put the same thing in the elif so that your final if.py looks like this:

```
answer = input("Do you want to hear a joke? ")
if answer == "Yes" or answer == "yes":
    print("What's loud and sounds like an apple?")
    print("AN APPLE")
elif answer == "No" or answer == "no":
    print("Fine.")
else:
    print("I don't understand.")
```

This way, it'll accept both "Yes" and "yes" (or "No" and "no") as options:

```
% python if.py
Do you want to hear a joke? Yes
What's loud and sounds like an apple?
AN APPLE
% python if.py
Do you want to hear a joke? yes
What's loud and sounds like an apple?
AN APPLE
```

What happens if we had written this instead?

```
...
if answer == "Yes" or "yes":
    print("What's loud and sounds like an apple?")
    print("AN APPLE")
...
```

Even though this looks similar to the code we wrote previously (answer == "Yes" or answer == "yes":), it actually would be wrong and introduce a particularly tricky bug. We would get the following:

```
% python if.py
Do you want to hear a joke? yes
What's loud and sounds like an apple? AN APPLE
% python if.py
Do you want to hear a joke? no
What's loud and sounds like an apple? AN APPLE
% python if.py
Do you want to hear a joke? blue
What's loud and sounds like an apple? AN APPLE
```

It looks fine at first, but you realize pretty quickly that something is wrong: you'll always get back the same answer no matter what you type. Why is that?

It has to do with two things:

1. **The order in which Python checks if things are True or False.** Remember that an or will be true if either side is true. So, first it'll check if answer == "Yes" is true, and then it'll check if "yes" is true.
2. **The fact that all nonempty strings in Python are interpreted as True.** This is weird, but it's true. The value of any string on its own is considered True by Python when it needs to be interpreted as a True/False value.

In other words, even though our brains may read this as:

```
if answer == ("Yes" or "yes"):
```

Python actually reads it as:

```
if (answer == "Yes") or ("yes"):
```

Weird huh? This highlights the importance of using parentheses liberally.

What if we wanted to expand our code even further to check the user's answer against a set of values? Let's say we want to accept "Yes", "yes", "Y", and "y" as possible answers. Could you do this?

```
if answer == "Yes" or answer == "yes" or answer == "Y"
or answer == "y":
    ...
```

This is fine, and it would work, but an easier solution might be to use the in we told you about earlier.

```
if answer in ["Yes", "yes", "Y", "y"]:
    ...
```

This is somewhat shorter, and probably easier to read.

Another potential improvement might be to use a string function. As covered in section 2.8.1, string functions operate on strings and do something to them. Remember that lower() takes a string and converts it to lowercase. For example "Hello".lower() returns 'hello'.

We can use this in our if statement:

```
if answer.lower() in ["yes", "y"]:
    ...
```

This basically allows us to make the user's input case insensitive: "Yes", "YES", "yeS", and "yEs" will all produce the same thing when lowercase.

Interestingly, most websites like facebook.com and twitter.com use this feature when you sign up with an email address. Because email addresses are case insensitive, they lowercase whatever text you give them before saving it into the database, and when you log in, they lowercase whatever email address you type in before comparing it against what's saved in the database. Otherwise, two people could sign up using the same email address but different capitalization, or you might not being able to log in because you didn't type your email address exactly the same way as when you signed up.

Why lowercase instead of uppercase? It doesn't really matter, as long as they do the same thing consistently. Our final code should look like this:

```
answer = input("Do you want to hear a joke? ")

if answer.lower() in ["yes", "y"]:
    print("What's loud and sounds like an apple?")
    print("AN APPLE")
elif answer.lower() in ["no", "n"]:
    print("Fine.")
else:
    print("I don't understand.")
```

If we wanted, we could separate the options into their own variables:

```
...
affirmative_responses = ["yes", "y"]
negative_responses = ["no", "n"]
if answer.lower() in affirmative_responses:
    ...
elif answer.lower() in negative_responses:
    ...
```

Some developers might argue that this is better, because the variable names themselves act as a sort of comment explaining what ["yes", "y"] and ["no", "n"] actually are. Other developers might argue it was already clear before and you're just making the code longer (and possibly harder to read) for no good reason.

We'll leave it to you to think about which option you prefer and why. These kinds of questions, even though they might seem trivial at first, are at the root of some of the most interesting questions around coding and software development. Specifically, how do you write code that is clear and easy to change later?

Entire businesses have been brought down because their developers didn't consider questions like this—their code got buggier and software improvements got harder to make. For example, some people have argued that in the late 1990s, Netscape (a publicly traded company) made the single biggest strategic mistake that any software company can make by deciding to rewrite all their code from scratch because they felt it was slow and inefficient.[1] The rewrite ended up taking three years.

3.5 LISTS

The next aspect of Python we want to introduce you to is the *list*. We first encountered lists in `happy_hour.py`, and most recently in `if.py`, but it's time to really understand how to work with them. Lists are ways of grouping things in Python.

Create a new Python file called `lists.py` and type in the following:

```
# Python, lists are a way of grouping
# (usually) similar things together
the_count = [1, 2, 3, 4, 5]
stocks = ["FB", "AAPL", "NFLX", "GOOG"]
random_things = [55, 1/2, "Puppies", stocks]
```

Here we have three lists that we've created and saved into three different variables—`the_count`, `stocks`, and `random_things`. You'll notice that when you're saving a list into a variable, it usually makes sense to name it something plural so that you remember that it contains a list.

Creating a list in Python is pretty straightforward, you start with [and end with] (a pair of square brackets—which "open" and "close" the list), and then you put any items you want inside the square brackets separated by commas. The items or things in Python lists are often called *elements*.

In the last example (`random_things`) you might have noticed two things:

1. Inside of a list, each element doesn't necessarily have to be the same kind of thing.
2. A list can have a list inside of it.

Actually, this second point may not have been so obvious. Even though it looks like the last element of `random_things` is a variable (`stocks`), variables are just boxes you put other things into. When you run Python code, variables will always get replaced with whatever's inside of them. In other words, the contents of the `random_things` list is actually:

LIST FUNCTIONS

There are a number of useful functions that we can use on lists in Python:

- `len()` gives us the number of elements inside a list
- `sum()` adds up the numbers inside of a list
- `min()` gives us the minimum value in a list
- `max()` gives us the minimum value in a list

To run each of these functions, put the list (or a variable containing the list) directly into the parentheses. For example, `len([1, 2, 3, 4, 5])` would be 5 and `sum([1, 2, 3, 4, 5])` would be 15.

Note that `sum()` only works if the list contains numbers. Conversely, `min()` and `max()` work on lists of numbers *or* strings (in which case, we'll get back the first or last value when arranged in alphabetical order). In addition to these four list functions, we'll mention a handful of others later.

```
[55, 0.5, 'Puppies', ['FB', 'AAPL', 'NFLX', 'GOOG']]
```

Try printing out `random_things` in your file and what you see in the command line should match. (Note also that technically 1/2 is a math expression that is replaced with the float `0.5`.)

For people who aren't used to reading code, this might be confusing. You can put lists inside of lists and lists inside of those lists (and so on). It can get confusing because it can be hard to keep track of where the commas are and where one list ends and another begins. This is a skill that comes with practice.

3.5.1 Building Lists from the Ground Up

When creating a list, you can either create it with all the elements already inside of it (like we just did), or you can start with an empty list and add things into it one at a time. To see what we mean, add the following code to your `lists.py`:

```
...
# You can start with an empty list
# and append or remove
people = []

people.append("Mattan")
people.append("Sarah")
people.append("Daniel")
people.remove("Sarah")
print(people)
```

`[]` is an empty list in Python. We're saving that to the variable `people`, which we can then append (add) stuff into and remove from.

TUPLES

In Python, you may occasionally see something called a *tuple* which is basically a list but with parentheses instead of square brackets:

```
% python
>>> numbers = (1, 2, 3, 4, 5)
```

Tuples and lists can do a lot of the same things, with the one major difference being that once you've created a tuple, you can't change it (in programmer-speak, this is called being "immutable"). Watch what happens if we try to `append()` another number to the tuple we just created:

```
>>> numbers.append(6)
Traceback (most recent call
last):
    File "<stdin>", line 1,
in <module>
AttributeError: 'tuple'
object has no attribute
'append'
```

So, if tuples are basically lists with less functionality, why do they exist? The answer is that they're faster, with the added benefit that sometimes developers want to be able to create lists that can't be changed later.

Our recommendation is to not worry about using tuples for the time being. We mention them only because you may occasionally see a tuple being used in someone's code (something that looks like a list but with ( ) instead of [] around the outside). Now you know it's basically just a list.

Let's reopen our old `happy_hour.py` script from section 1.5. Remember we had that problem of potentially picking the same random person twice?

```
...
random_person = random.choice(people)
random_person2 = random.choice(people)
...
```

How could you avoid this problem by removing the first person from the list before picking the second random person? One way would be to remove the first randomly chosen person from the list before randomly selecting a second person:

```
...
random_person = random.choice(people)
people.remove(random_person)
random_person2 = random.choice(people)
...
```

3.5.2 Creating a List from a String

Consider the following bit of code:

```
"New York, San Francisco, London"
```

Is it a list? No. In Python, this is a string, even though it looks like what we might call a list. Because it doesn't have square brackets around it, it's not a list.

```
["New York, San Francisco, London"]
```

Technically this is a list, but it's not really what we want. This list only has one element (note that the commas are inside a string, which doesn't count). In Python, lists let you do a lot of useful things, such as picking randomly from a list, shuffling a list around, and checking to see if something's in a list, among other things.

How could we turn a string into a list? We could use Python's `split()` function:

```
% python
>>> "New York, San Francisco, London".split()
['New', 'York,', 'San', 'Francisco,', 'London']
```

By default, the `split()` function splits a string wherever the spaces are. If we want to change that, we can pass in what we want to split on:

```
>>> "New York, San Francisco, London".split(", ")
['New York', 'San Francisco', 'London']
```

There's the list we want! Add the following to `lists.py` to help you remember:

```
# Use split() to turn a string into a list
cities = "New York, San Francisco, London".split(", ")
print(cities)
```

Similarly, you may have wondered if it's possible to print out a list in a way that looks more natural (e.g., without the square brackets). Try adding the following to `lists.py`:

```
# Use join() to turn a list into a string
groceries = ["Milk", "Eggs", "Cheese"]
print(" and ".join(groceries))
```

Here's what you should see when you run the code:

```
% python lists.py
...
Milk and Eggs and Cheese
```

The `join()` function turns a list into a string. You add it with a dot directly after a string (for example, a comma with a space after it, like this: `', '`) and you pass it a list as an argument. It then puts a comma and a space in between each element of the list and gives you the result as a string.

The function itself is a little counterintuitive initially. It can be used with any list-like object (such as tuples, and even strings), so it makes more sense to make it a string function. If you want to see something trippy, try this: `"-".join("hello")`. In this book, lists are the only list-like objects we'll be considering, so you can safely ignore these complications.

3.5.3 Accessing Elements of Lists

You can get individual things out of a list by using another set of [] (square brackets) after the list with a number inside. Add the following to your lists.py:

```
# Access elements of a list using []
first_city = cities[0]
second_city = cities[1]
last_city = cities[-1]
first_two_cities = cities[0:2]
print(first_two_cities)
```

Notably, here, lists are zero-indexed, meaning the first thing in a list is at position zero, the second thing is at one, and so on. This is confusing to a lot of non-programmers, but it's something you get used to after a while.

In our example, first_city will contain the string "New York", last_city will contain the string "London", and first_two_cities will contain the list ['New York ','San Francisco'].

We've just shown you another thing you can do using square brackets in Python besides just creating a list. This can also trip up a lot of beginners, because you're basically doing something like this:

```
first_city = ['New York', 'San Francisco', 'London'][0]
```

The first set of square brackets defines or creates a new list, but the second set of square brackets (the [0] at the end) tells Python to get the first element out of the list. One clever thing in Python is that you can always use [-1] to get the last element of a list (or [-2] to get the second to last element and so on), so you don't have to know exactly what position it's in.

Notice that we were able to use cities[0:2] to grab just the first two cities. This is called *slice notation* in Python and it allows you to get a subset of elements in a list using the following format:

```
list[start:stop]
```

A key point is that slice notation will grab from the element at the first number up until but not including the second number. In other words, [0:2] gives us the first and second element in a list, but *not* the third (which would be the element at [2]). We can also leave either side empty in slice notation, which will either give us every item in a list up until some element number:

```
list[:stop]
```

Or it will give us every item in a list from some element number through the rest of the list:

```
list[start:]
```

In case this is confusing, it's worth taking some time with slice notation in Python interactive mode to get a better understanding:

```
% python
>>> cities = ['New York', 'San Francisco', 'London']
>>> cities[:1]
['New York']
>>> cities[1:]
['San Francisco', 'London']
```

USING SLICE NOTATION ON STRINGS

An interesting quirk in Python is that strings can be treated like lists in some ways. For example, take string **"New York, NY"**. We can grab the first character of the string with [0] or the first three characters with [0:3] as if it were a list:

```
% python
>>> "New York, NY"[0]
'N'
>>> "New York, NY"[0:3]
'New'
```

But we can also get the last two characters of this string as if it were a list by doing the following:

```
>>> "New York, NY"[-2:]
'NY'
```

Here, we're relying on both slice notation *and* the fact that we can use −2 as the position of the second to last character to basically say "give us everything from the second to last character to the end of the string" (in other words, give us the last two characters). Quite handy, huh?

What if you want to figure out the position of a specific item in a list? Python has a function called index() that allows you to do just that:

```
>>> a = ["Mattan", "Daniel", "Priya"]
>>> a.index("Daniel")
1
```

This tells me that "Daniel" is the second element in the list (remember that Python numbers lists starting at zero).

The downside of using lists to store things is that you have to remember the position they were in if you want to get those things out (it would be like having to memorize the page number of a word in the dictionary every time you want to look up the definition). Later, in section 3.8, we'll learn about another data type in Python called a dictionary that solves this problem by letting us use strings instead of numbers to look things up, but first, we want to show one of the most useful things that you can do with lists: looping.

3.6 LOOPING OVER LISTS

Because the topic of looping over a list is so important, let's create a whole new file called loops.py:

```
# Use for to loop over a list
numbers = [1, 2, 3]
for number in numbers:
    print(number)
```

This will produce the following output when run:

```
% python loops.py
1
2
3
```

At a high level, the way a for loop works is that it goes through every element of a list one at a time, and it runs the same code for each one. It's a shortcut for writing less code. In this case, we just went through a list with the numbers one, two, and three and printed each one, one at a time.

We say it's a shortcut, because a longer way of doing the same thing in Python would be the following:

```python
numbers = [1, 2, 3]

number = numbers[0]
print(number)
number = numbers[1]
print(number)
number = numbers[2]
print(number)
```

Do you see how this would produce the same output as when we used a loop? (If not, try it yourself.)

The general structure of a for loop in Python is as follows:

```python
y = [...]
for x in y:
    # Do something to x
```

What are x and y in this example? The y is a list that the for loop needs to run properly. It has to already exist (like a list of numbers, a list of stocks, or a list of people).

The x is something we define in the for loop. It's like you're creating a new variable for the purpose of the for loop, and as it runs. the value of x will change until it has gone through every element of the list (in order). The x does not need to exist before you run the for loop, and if it does exist, it will be overwritten.

Note the tabbing again. This is how Python knows what to repeat as part of the for loop. When it gets to the end of what's tabbed, it goes back to the beginning of the loop for the next element in the list.

We like to think of for loops as an "apply all" shortcut.

For example, let's say we have a list of stock tickers, but they're all lowercase:

```python
stocks = ["fb", "aapl", "nflx", "goog"]
```

How could we use a `for` loop to print out each one in all caps? See if you can give it a shot on your own before looking at our answer.

Here's how we'd probably do it:

```
stocks = ["fb", "aapl", "nflx", "goog"]
for stock in stocks:
    print(stock.upper())
```

Note that we have two variables here: `stock` and `stocks`.

Usually when you're creating a variable to hold a list, it makes sense for it to be plural (e.g., `stocks`, `numbers`, `random_things`, or `people`). If you are looping over that list and want to create a variable to refer generically to an individual element in the list, it makes sense to go with the singular version (e.g., `stock`, `number`, `random_thing`, or `person`). These variables are just indexes for Python to use when going over the list.

Often, you will find that developers use a shorter name for the looping variable like `i` or `j`. On the positive side, it makes the code far more concise. On the negative side, it makes it a little less readable, because it's hard to know what the variable contains just by seeing its name. As you become more proficient with Python, you'll develop your own preferences in this respect.

3.6.1 Looping Challenge

Use a `for` loop to print out the squares of the numbers one to ten. Take five minutes to do this now.

3.6.2 Looping Challenge Solution

The simplest way to solve this problem is to start with a list of the numbers from one to ten, and then loop over each one to print out the square:

```
numbers = [1, 2, 3, 4, 5, 6, 7, 8, 9, 10]
for number in numbers:
    print(number * number) # same as number ** 2
```

This would produce the following output:

```
1
4
9
16
25
36
49
64
81
100
```

If you want to get fancy, you could add some ornamentation:

```
numbers = [1, 2, 3, 4, 5, 6, 7, 8, 9, 10]
for number in numbers:
    print(number, "squared is", number * number)
```

Which would produce the following:

```
1 squared is 1
2 squared is 4
3 squared is 9
4 squared is 16
5 squared is 25
6 squared is 36
7 squared is 49
8 squared is 64
9 squared is 81
10 squared is 100
```

As a bonus challenge, can you figure out a better way to loop over the numbers from one to ten?

Why would you need a better way? What if you had to loop over the numbers from one to one hundred? Would you create a list with each number in it? What about one to one million?

A quick Google search for "Python 1 to 10" should unearth the range() function, which works like this:

```
for x in range(10):
    print(x)
```

And produces:

```
0
1
2
3
4
5
6
7
8
9
```

The range() function is kind of weird because it produces a list[2] of numbers starting with zero up to (but not including) the number you give it. It also gives you the option of specifying what number you want to start with, so that you could get the numbers from one to ten with range(1, 11):

```
for number in range(1, 11):
    print(number, "squared is", number * number)
```

This is a bit shorter than the version in which we created our own list, but it also makes it much easier to change the range of numbers you're looping over.

For fun, try printing out the squares of the numbers from one to one million. If you accidentally type an extra zero like we did the first time, and your Python script keeps running for a while, you can just press Ctrl and C to interrupt it and stop it early.

3.6.3 How to Do Something X Times

Incidentally, you can use a for loop to run the same code a certain number of times.

```
for _ in range(10):
    print("Hey ya!")
```

The range(10) function will produce a list of ten things (the numbers from zero to nine), and so the loop will run once for each of those numbers. What's up with the _ character in the for loop? Python developers like to use _ as the variable name in this specific case to indicate that it won't actually be used inside the loop (because you still need to put something in that spot). You could instead just put i (or some other variable name in that spot) and not use it within the loop, but _ is tidier.

3.6.4 Creating a New List of Squares

So far we've only been using print() inside of our for loops, but we can do much more. For example:

```
squares = []
for number in range(1, 11):
    squares.append(number * number)
print(squares)
```

This does the following:

1. Creates an empty list called squares
2. Loops through the numbers from one to ten
3. Squares each number
4. Appends each square into the squares list
5. Prints out the squares list when it's all done

Of course, Python has many ways of doing something like this (arguably faster), but this is one way to do it.

In case you're still confused about what exactly is supposed to go inside versus outside the loop, let us show you two wrong ways to do it and what happens in each case:

Mistake 1

```
for number in range(1, 11):
    squares = []
    squares.append(number * number)
print(squares)
```

Here we've put `squares = []` inside the `for` loop. What do you think will happen? Run the code and you'll see the following output:

```
[100]
```

This is because you've overwritten the value of the `squares` variable and reset it to an empty list on every loop. At the end you're left with only the final value, which doesn't get overwritten because the loop ends.

Mistake 2

```
squares = []
for number in range(1, 11):
    squares.append(number * number)
    print(squares)
```

Here we've put `print(squares)` inside the `for` loop. What do you think will happen? This time you get the following output:

```
[1]
[1, 4]
[1, 4, 9]
[1, 4, 9, 16]
[1, 4, 9, 16, 25]
[1, 4, 9, 16, 25, 36]
[1, 4, 9, 16, 25, 36, 49]
[1, 4, 9, 16, 25, 36, 49, 64]
[1, 4, 9, 16, 25, 36, 49, 64, 81]
[1, 4, 9, 16, 25, 36, 49, 64, 81, 100]
```

In this case, because you print out the value of the `squares` variable at the end of every loop, you get this pretty pyramid pattern, which isn't necessarily what you want (although using `print()` inside of a `for` loop can be an effective way to debug a problem and figure out exactly what's happening in your code).

LIST COMPREHENSIONS

Python has a built-in, faster way of generating one list from another. It's called a list comprehension and it takes the following form:

```
[number * number for number in range(1, 10)]
```

This is basically the same as what we've been doing, but all in one line. This list comprehension structure can be a little confusing for beginners, but it's worth being aware of. The advantage to a list comprehension is that not only is it shorter but also you don't have to first create an empty list to append values into.

3.7 FIZZBUZZ

Have you ever heard of *FizzBuzz*? It's a common developer interview question. Some developers hate this interview question because it forces them to think on the spot, under the pressure of time, and doesn't allow them to refer to resources they may be used to checking when they don't know how to do something (like Stack Overflow). Nevertheless, here's the challenge:

3.7.1 FizzBuzz Challenge

Write a program that prints the numbers from one to one hundred. But for multiples of three print "Fizz" instead of the number and for the multiples of five print "Buzz". For numbers that are multiples of both three and five print "FizzBuzz".

We need one additional thing to solve this, which is how to check if a number is divisible by three or five. We can do this using the % (modulo) symbol in Python, which tells us what's left over (the remainder) if we divide one number by another. For example, 3 % 3 is 0, 4 % 3 is 1, 5 % 3 is 2, 6 % 3 is 0, and so on.

In other words, we can check if number is divisible by three by doing number % 3 == 0. That will return True or False.

Take ten minutes now to give this challenge a shot!

Feeling stuck? Read on for some tips.

First, we highly recommend spending at least a few minutes trying this challenge before giving up and reading our solution. We promise you will learn quicker banging your head against the wall (figuratively) for ten minutes than just skipping ahead to the solution. In a sense, this problem is representative of many problems you'll encounter in coding, and you can't always assume that someone else has already figured it out for you.

Second, we recommend breaking down the larger problem into smaller steps. In fact, this is a good idea with coding problems in general. It gives you a more reasonable starting point and allows you to test things out along the way so you know what's working and what isn't.

For example, we would break this challenge into the following subchallenges:

1. Print out the numbers from one to one hundred.
2. Check if the number is divisible by three, in which case print "Fizz".
3. Check if the number is divisible by five, in which case print "Buzz".
4. Check if the number is divisible by three and five, in which case print "FizzBuzz".

Even if it's not clear to you how to accomplish steps two through four, step one should be fairly easy. A few pages ago we saw how to print out the numbers from one to ten, so one to one hundred should be similar.

Start out by just solving the first problem, then move on to the next one. Something about the word "if" in there might help you realize you'll probably need to use an `if` statement somewhere (inside the `for` loop, perhaps?)

Again, set a time cap of ten minutes or so, but don't take too much longer than that. When you're ready, continue reading to see our solution.

3.7.2 FizzBuzz Challenge Solution

Let's tackle this problem in a few steps.

1. Print out the numbers from one to one hundred.

Look back at the looping challenge solution in section 3.6.2 to see how to do this:

```
for number in range(1, 101):
    print(number)
```

This produces the following output:

```
1
2
3
...
99
100
```

If you forgot how to specify the beginning and end of range(1, 101), that's fine. You could either look it up online or figure it out through trial and error. Note that what you actually call the variable in the for loop (whether it's number or x) doesn't matter as long as you call it that consistently.

2. Check if the number is divisible by three, in which case print "Fizz".

The key here is to figure out how to put an if inside of a for loop. We know (because we told you) that you can check if number is divisible by three by doing (number % 3) == 0. Just put that inside of an if statement:

```
for number in range(1, 101):
    if (number % 3) == 0:
        print("Fizz")
```

The problem here is that this will only produce the following output:

```
Fizz
Fizz
Fizz
...
```

With this code, we're only seeing "Fizz" for each number that is divisible by three, and we're not seeing any of the other numbers printed out. This is because our if doesn't have an else. We need to remember to use an else to print out the number itself in case it's not divisible by three.

```
for number in range(1, 101):
    if (number % 3) == 0:
        print("Fizz")
    else:
        print(number)
```

This will give us output we're looking for:

```
1
2
Fizz
...
98
Fizz
100
```

In general, we recommend running your code early and often to make sure it's actually doing what you think it's doing and so that you can catch errors as they come up rather than at the end when they can be harder to troubleshoot.

3. Check if the number is divisible by five, in which case print "Buzz".

If you figured out the last step, this addition is relatively simple. Just add an extra elif to check if number is divisible by five:

```
for number in range(1, 101):
    if (number % 3) == 0:
        print("Fizz")
    elif (number % 5) == 0:
        print("Buzz")
    else:
        print(number)
```

This will give you the following:

```
1
2
Fizz
4
Buzz
...
98
Fizz
Buzz
```

4. **Check if the number is divisible by three and five, in which case print "FizzBuzz".**

This last step is somewhat tricky, because it's not as simple as just adding another `elif` like we did in step three:

```python
for number in range(1, 101):
    if (number % 3) == 0:
        print("Fizz")
    elif (number % 5) == 0:
        print("Buzz")
    elif ((number % 3) == 0) and ((number % 5) == 0):
        print("FizzBuzz")
    else:
        print(number)
```

If you actually ran this code and checked the output, it would produce the same output we got after making the change in step three. In particular, for numbers that are divisible by three and five (e.g., fifteen, thirty), we still only see "Fizz":

```
...
13
14
Fizz
16
17
...
```

We get this result because `if`, `elif`, and `else` are checked successively and in order. Consider fifteen, for example, which is divisible by three *and* five. What will happen when the loop gets to that number? The first line will check whether this number is divisible by three, it will find that it is, and it will execute the line `print("Fizz")`, bypassing everything else.

This problem has a number of possible solutions, but one of the simplest solutions flips around the order of your `if` and `elif`s so that it checks for the most specific case first:

```
for number in range(1, 101):
    if ((number % 3) == 0) and ((number % 5) == 0):
        print("FizzBuzz")
    elif (number % 3) == 0:
        print("Fizz")
    elif (number % 5) == 0:
        print("Buzz")
    else:
        print(number)
```

This will give us the output we're looking for:

```
1
2
Fizz
...
14
FizzBuzz
16
...
98
Fizz
Buzz
```

Nice!

Now, there are still a number of possible optimizations at this point. For example, you may have figured out that ((number % 3) == 0 and (number % 5) == 0) is the same as (number % 15) == 0, which would make your code shorter—although it's debatable whether shorter is always better. Some might argue that the first approach is more explicit and makes it easier to find and change the conditions later if you needed to.

Coders even compete over who can come up with the shortest possible solution to FizzBuzz and other challenges, such as on the coding practice site HackerRank.com (which we'd recommend checking out if you want to try out some additional practice problems).

The shortest possible solution to FizzBuzz we've been able to identify so far (by searching online) is the following one-liner:

```
for x in range(100):print(x%3//2*'Fizz'+x%5//4*'Buzz'or x+1)
```

Again, just because something is short doesn't mean it's good. We would argue that the one-line solution to FizzBuzz is unnecessarily complicated and almost impossible to read.[3]

3.8 DICTIONARIES

Lists in Python are useful because they let you group different things together. You can also use `for` loops to avoid rewriting the same code over and over. But you'll see shortly why lists are not always the best way to store certain kinds of data in Python. To deal with one limitation of lists, we'll be introducing a new data type called the dictionary.

Let's say for example that we want to store a whole bunch of information related to a publicly traded stock in Python, so we decide to create a list:

```python
stock = ["Microsoft", "MSFT", "NASDAQ"]
```

We also want to keep track of that stock's most recent open and close trading price. We can add that into the list as well:

```python
stock.append(108.25) # Open Price
stock.append(106.03) # Close Price
```

Now if we want to access some particular piece of information, we have to remember exactly what position all the pieces of information are in (or print out the entire list and count). For example, the ticker is the second element in the list and the close trading price is the fifth. (Or was it the fourth? It's easy to forget.) Something like this could work:

```python
print(f"{stock[1]} is trading at {stock[4]}")
```

But this clearly isn't ideal. The problem is that even though these pieces of information should be grouped together, we lose track of something important if we just throw them into a list. They're all properties or qualities of one thing—like how people have hair color, eye color, height, weight, and many other properties—and, when working with lists, Python doesn't give us a way to label what each element actually is.

But Python has another data structure called a *dictionary* that works like a list and lets us label things using strings[4] instead of just a number for each position. That way, the order doesn't matter, and we can use the string to access any part of the data.

To see how dictionaries work, let's go ahead and create a file called `dictionaries.py` and write the following code:

```
# Dictionaries let you label values using strings
stock = {"name": "Microsoft", "ticker": "MSFT", "index": "NASDAQ"}
```

Note that to create a dictionary we use {} (curly brackets) on the outside instead of the square brackets we used for lists. In Python, when creating a dictionary that has a lot of things in it, it can be easier to split it across multiple lines:

```
# Dictionaries let you label values using strings
stock = {"name": "Microsoft",
         "ticker": "MSFT",
         "index": "NASDAQ"}
```

Usually, the labels are all lined up to make it easier to read. The exact number of tabs or spaces don't matter, because Python interprets the entire thing as one line. Also, as long as they're inside the curly brackets, the line breaks don't matter either (the same is true for lists, as we saw in `happy_hour.py`).

Inside the dictionary, the thing to the left of each colon is called a *key* and the thing on the right of the colon is called a *value*. We call these key/value pairs:

```
'key': value
```

With dictionaries, a key *always* has a value, and vice versa. The key is a string, but the value can be basically anything—a string, a number, a list, or even another dictionary. Within each dictionary, each key is unique (meaning we can't use the same key more than once). There's always a colon in between each key and value, and don't forget to put a comma between each key/value pair.

To get something out of a dictionary, we can use [] (square brackets) just like we did with lists. Except that with dictionaries, we put a key inside the square brackets instead of a number. Add the following to `dictionaries.py`:

```
print(f"{stock['name']}'s stock ticker is {stock['ticker']}")
```

The values we get back with `stock['name']` and `stock['ticker']` should be `'Microsoft'` and `'MSFT'` because that's what we initially set as the values of those keys when we created our `stock` dictionary.

The f-string allows us to use a key to look up a value from the `stock` dictionary and insert that value directly into a string. One thing to be careful about is whether to use single versus double quotes for keys inside of an f-string. If your f-string uses double quotes on the outside, your keys need to be single quotes (e.g., `f"{stock['name']}'s`) because otherwise Python will think the string should end where the key starts.

Keep in mind that the following two snippets of code both look similar:

```
stock[1]
```

and

```
stock['ticker']
```

But the first would work only on a list whereas the second would work only on a dictionary. The thing inside the `[]` gives us a hint as to which one we're working with.

One way to understand the difference between a list and a dictionary is to think of how an actual dictionary works. When you pick up a dictionary to look up the definition of a word, you flip through the pages until you find that word (the key) and then read the definition (the value). If actual dictionaries were structured like lists, we'd have to memorize the page number on which the definition of each word appeared, which would make dictionaries practically impossible to use.

GET A LIST OF KEYS IN A DICTIONARY

It's possible to get a list of keys in a dictionary using the `.keys()` function:

```
>>> stock = {"name": "Microsoft",
...          "ticker": "MSFT",
...          "index": "NASDAQ"}
>>> stock.keys()
dict_keys(['name', 'ticker', 'index'])
```

This can be helpful when using a dictionary that is storing a lot of things and we've lost track of what keys we can use on it.

3.8.1 Dictionary Challenge, Part 1

Dictionaries are often used to store information about things like users. Create a dictionary called user in dictionaries.py. Give it the following keys: 'name', 'height', 'shoe size', 'hair', and 'eyes'. Fill in the values of those keys with your own information. Once you've done that, individually print out each of the values saved in your dictionary.

3.8.2 Dictionary Challenge Solution, Part 1

Your user dictionary should look something like this:

```python
user = {'name': 'Mattan',
        'height': 70,
        'shoe size': 10.5,
        'hair': 'Brown',
        'eyes': 'Brown'}
```

Remember that the tabs and new lines don't matter in this case, they're just meant to make it easier to read (you could put the whole dictionary on one line if you wanted to). How you print out the values is up to you. We used f-strings:

```python
print(f"Name: {user['name']}")
print(f"Height: {user['height']}")
print(f"Shoe Size: {user['shoe size']}")
print(f"Hair Color: {user['hair']}")
print(f"Eye Color: {user['eyes']}")
```

When our code is run, the result should be:

```
Name: Mattan
Height: 70
Shoe Size: 10.5
Hair Color: Brown
Eye Color: Brown
```

Of course, if we wanted, we could print it all out in one line with something like this:

```
print(f"{user['name']}'s height is {user['height']}, shoe size is
{user['shoe size']}, hair color is {user['hair']}, and eye color is
{user['eyes']}")
```

But this is starting to get quite long for one line of code.

3.8.3 Adding Key/Value Pairs

Given that we've already created a stock variable that contains a dictionary, adding a new key/value pair is quite easy. Add the following to dictionaries.py:

```
...
stock["open price"] = 108.25
stock["close price"] = 106.03
print(stock)
```

You should see the following printed out as the value of stock:

```
{'name': 'Microsoft', 'ticker': 'MSFT', 'index': 'NASDAQ', 'open
price': 108.25, 'close price': 106.03}
```

Adding a new key/value pair uses basically the same code as looking up a value using a key (e.g., stock["open price"]) except that we set it equal to something. Because keys are just strings, we can use spaces in key names.

Another thing to be aware of is that keys are case sensitive. For example, trying to print stock["Open Price"] will produce the following error:

```
Traceback (most recent call last):
    File "dictionaries.py", line 26, in <module>
        print(stock["Open Price"])
KeyError: 'Open Price'
```

The same `KeyError` would come up if we tried to use a key that didn't exist in our dictionary at all, like `stock["volume"]`.

THE SAFER WAY TO GET SOMETHING OUT OF A DICTIONARY

A safer way to get a value out of a dictionary when we don't know that it contains a particular key is to use the dictionary `get()` function:

```
stock.get('volume')
```

This will return the value of the key if it exists. But if the key doesn't exist, `get()` won't give us an error, it just won't give us any output. This can be helpful because it won't lead to an error message that would prevent the rest of our code from running. The `get()` function has another cool feature, which is that we can set a default value to get back in case it can't find that key in our dictionary:

```
stock.get('volume', 'Value not found')
```

It's probably safer to use `get()` when you don't know what's inside your dictionary, though it's a double-edge sword because it could also mask errors in your code that might be useful to see if something has gone wrong in your code.

3.8.4 Dictionary Challenge, Part 2

Add a `favorite movies` key to the `user` dictionary that you created as part of the Dictionary Challenge in section 3.8.1, and then print it out.

3.8.5 Dictionary Challenge Solution, Part 2

We solved this challenge in the following way:

```
...
user['favorite movies'] = ['Pulp Fiction', 'Magnolia', 'The Royal
Tenenbaums']
print(f"Favorite Movies: {user['favorite movies']}")
```

We ran this code and got the following:

```
Favorite Movies: ['Pulp Fiction', 'Magnolia', 'The Royal Tenenbaums']
```

Note that we set the value of user['favorite movies'] to a list. If we had done the following:

```
user['favorite movies'] = 'Pulp Fiction, Magnolia, The Royal Tenenbaums'
```

Then the value would have been a string and not a list; if the difference isn't clear, go back and reread section 3.5.2.

Now if you're like us, and you're bothered by the way lists look in Python when you print them out, you can instead print out the list as a string, so that it looks like this:

```
Favorite Movies: Pulp Fiction, Magnolia, The Royal Tenenbaums
```

Recall from section 3.5.2 that we can convert any list into a string using join(). We can do the same thing in dictionaries.py:

```
print(f"Favorite Movies: {', '.join(user['favorite movies'])}")
```

That should get us an output that's slightly more readable.

3.8.6 What Are Dictionaries Used For?

Dictionaries could be used to represent rows retrieved from a table (or a database), because we can use column names as keys, which allows us to label our information. Consider the following table:

Name	Height	Shoe size	Hair	Eyes	Favorite movies
Mattan	70	10.5	Brown	Brown	['Pulp Fiction', 'Magnolia', 'The Royal Tenenbaums']
...	...	...	...	...	...

If we wanted to grab the first row and do something with it in Python, we could represent it as a list:

```
user = ['Mattan', 70, 10.5, 'Brown', 'Brown', ['Pulp Fiction',
'Magnolia', 'The Royal Tenenbaums']]
```

But we'd soon get confused about what each element in the list actually represents. What do 70 and 10.5 refer to? Which 'Brown' refers to hair color and which refers to eye color? Using a dictionary essentially lets us keep track of the column names as well:

```
user = {'name': 'Mattan',
        'height': 70,
        'shoe size': 10.5,
        'hair': 'Brown',
        'eyes': 'Brown',
        'favorite movies': ['Pulp Fiction',
                'Magnolia',
                'The Royal Tenenbaums']}
```

It might be a little more confusing to read, but it contains essential information that we otherwise wouldn't have.

As a quick exercise, imagine you have a blog with multiple blog posts. You've used Python to connect to the database and grab the most recent blog post, which is being stored in a dictionary named blog_post. What are some keys and values you'd expect to find in this dictionary? Here are some keys we might expect to see:

- title
- body
- author
- created_at
- published_at

How did we know that blog_post would probably have created_at and published_at keys? Blogs tend to want to keep track of that stuff, and we've seen enough databases to know that it's a common thing to save.

At this point, you might also (quite rightly) be thinking that this could get pretty complicated fast. Many real datasets contain hundreds of columns and thousands of rows, and if we had to create a dictionary like the previous one for every dataset, we'd end up with unwieldy code. In addition, that's not really how people *think* about data—we tend to think of datasets as tables and columns and rows, and we tend to store them in Excel files rather than files of code. In part 2 of this book, we'll return to these questions and see how Python makes a powerful set of tools available for dealing with large datasets in a more intuitive way.

3.9 WRAPPING UP

In this chapter, we extended our understanding of Python by learning about `if` statements, logic in Python, lists, `for` loops, and dictionaries. We also tackled the particularly tricky FizzBuzz question often asked during programming interviews. Although we're almost ready to apply what we've learned to do some real data analysis, we first need to learn about two important topics in Python: functions and importing. These are the topics of the final chapter in part 1 of this book.

4

PYTHON BASICS, PART 3

WE'VE LEFT functions as one of the last topics to cover in part 1, so you might expect them to be difficult. On one hand, functions in Python are actually quite simple conceptually; they're just a way to save code so that you can run it over and over again later. On the other hand, a lot of nuances to functions can be difficult to wrap your head around. We'll cover the simple stuff first and then get to the more complicated aspects toward the end of this chapter. We think you'll find that the hard work is worth the effort—especially when you get to part 2.

If you've ever used Excel, you're probably already familiar with functions and what they can do. Excel has many useful built-in functions, like `sum()`, `average()`, `count()`, `concatenate()`, and even `if()`.[1]

You've already been exposed to several Python functions in this book—for example, `print()`, `len()`, and `lower()`. In this chapter, you're going to learn a lot more about unlocking the power of functions.

4.1 WHAT YOU'LL LEARN IN THIS CHAPTER

By the end of this chapter, you'll be able to create your own functions from scratch. You'll learn about function arguments, outputs, refactoring, and several things that can go wrong when working with functions—like providing the wrong number or type of arguments. Finally, You'll learn about Python packages, and see how it's possible to import functions that other people have written to dramatically increase the power of what Python can do.

4.2 INTRODUCTION TO FUNCTIONS

Let's start by creating a new file called `functions.py` and add the following code:

```
grades = [90, 85, 74]
prices = [12.99, 9.99, 5.49, 7.50]
print(sum(grades) / len(grades))
print(sum(prices) / len(prices))
```

Recall from our section on lists (section 3.5) that Python has a built-in function `sum()` that calculates the sum of a list of numbers and a function `len()` that calculates how many elements are in a list. What we're doing here is creating two lists of numbers, and then calculating and printing out the *average* of each list—where average is defined as the sum of items in a list divided by the number of items in a list (this kind of average is called the *mean*). The result should end up being:

```
% python functions.py
83.0
8.9925
```

Let's say we were planning on doing this a lot—that is, calculating the averages of numbers. In that case, it might make sense for us to turn this calculation into a function. We could do that by replacing the code in `functions.py` with the following:

```
# Functions are little snippets of code
# that we can reuse over and over
def average(numbers):
    return sum(numbers) / len(numbers)

grades = [90, 85, 74]
prices = [12.99, 9.99, 5.49, 7.50]

print(average(grades))
print(average(prices))
```

To create a new function in Python, we use the following steps:

1. Start with `def` (this stands for define) and a space.
2. Then put the function name (the recommendations we encountered when naming variables apply here as well—lowercase words with underscores instead of spaces). We'll use this later to run (or "call") the function.
3. Then we need parentheses, which is where we can put any inputs (or *arguments*) that get passed in when the function is actually run later. These will end up being used like variables inside the function.
4. We finish the function definition line with a : (colon). Don't forget this.
5. After we've named the function and set its arguments, we then have to indent all the code we want to put inside the function. Just like with `if` and `for` loops, Python looks at indentation to figure out what code is part of a function and what isn't.

The general structure of a function looks like this:

```
def function(input1, input2, ...):
    # Do something with inputs
    return ...
```

Once a function has been created, it can be run (or "called") by just referring to the name of the function with parentheses and passing in any arguments that the function needs.

In our case, the `average()` function has only one argument—numbers. Even though it's a list, a list is still considered one input in Python. We'll go into more detail about function arguments later in this chapter, but it's worth noting that we defined the `average()` function *before* we knew what numbers would actually be. We had to pick a placeholder word to use inside the function to refer to whatever we pass in later when we run or call the function.

These placeholder words, or arguments, are basically variables that exist only inside a function. We picked the word numbers because it makes sense to say that the input for a function that calculates an average of something would take a bunch of numbers as an input. But when you're creating a function, you can name your input anything you want (it's like creating a new variable) as long as you use that same variable inside of your function.

Then, when we run the function and pass in a list like grades or prices, that list *becomes* numbers inside of the function. We don't have to pass in a variable—we also can pass in a list directly:

```
print(average([0, 1, -1])
```

And that list—[0, 1, -1]—becomes what numbers gets set to inside the function. Then, the function ends up returning this:

```
sum([0, 1, -1]) / len([0, 1, -1])
```

Speaking of returning things, you also may have noticed that the one line of code in our function has the word return in front of it:

```
def average(numbers):
    return sum(numbers) / len(numbers)
```

What does return do? It defines what the output of the function will be, and you'll almost always see it on the last line of every function (more on this later). Let's take a look at another example. Add the following to functions.py:

```
address = "3022 Broadway, New York, NY 10027, USA"
city = address.split(', ')[1]
print(city)
```

When we run this code, we should see:

```
% python functions.py
...
New York
```

What's going on here? The idea is that we have a variable with an address as a string that takes a particular form: *Street Address, City, State Zip, Country.* The second line of code—address.split(', ')—splits this address into a list on a comma and a space, which returns the following:

```
['3022 Broadway', 'New York', 'NY 10027', 'USA']
```

Then we're grabbing the second element from that list with [1] (remember that lists start with their first element at [0]) and saving that to the city variable.

Let's say we think, "Hmm, I'm probably going to have to do this again. Let's turn it into a function." That function might look like this:

```
def get_city(address):
    return address.split(', ')[1]


address = "3022 Broadway, New York, NY 10027, USA"
city = get_city(address)
print(city)
```

This produces the same output we had before, but we've wrapped our address. split(', ')[1] from before inside of a function, added a return, and ensured that the function argument matched up with the code.

Note that the address variable that we pass into the function when we run it is totally different from what we named the function argument when we defined the get_city() function. This is okay, and it works because of something called *scoping*—variables created inside of functions (including the names of the inputs) are available only inside that function.

Scoping gets complicated and confusing quickly, but suffice it to say that the address inside of our function (which is whatever gets passed in when we run the function) can be different from the address we defined outside of the function. We can prove this by showing you that the following also would work:

```
...


columbia = "3022 Broadway, New York, NY 10027, USA"
city = get_city(columbia)
print(city)
```

This will still work. Think you got it? Okay, let's test your skills.

4.2.1 Function Challenge

Create a function named get_state() that takes as its input a string of the form "3022 Broadway, New York, NY 10027, USA" and returns just the state (i.e., "NY").

4.2.2 Function Challenge Solution

The `get_state()` function will need to be slightly more complicated than `get_city()` because it takes some additional steps. The idea is that if you have address of the form:

```
address = "3022 Broadway, New York, NY 10027, USA"
```

Which you can split on the commas:

```
address.split(', ')
```

To get:

```
['3022 Broadway', 'New York', 'NY 10027', 'USA']
```

Now we can grab the third element using [2]:

```
address.split(', ')[2]
```

Which gives us:

```
'NY 10027'
```

This string contains both the state and the zip code, but we only need the state. So how can we grab just that? One way is to split it just on spaces this time:

```
address.split(', ')[2].split()
```

We don't need to pass an argument into the second `split()` because it splits on spaces by default.[2] This gives us back another list:

```
['NY', '10027']
```

Now we can finally get the state by grabbing the first element of this second list with [0].

```
address.split(', ')[2].split()[0]
```

Now throw this into a function called get_state() and you get the following:

```
def get_state(address):
    return address.split(', ')[2].split()[0]

state = get_state(columbia)
print(state)
```

This produces the following output:

```
% python functions.py
...
NY
```

Of course, Python has several other ways to solve this problem. Another way would be to just grab the first two characters from 'NY 10027' with [0:2] (see the box "Using Slice Notation on Strings" in section 3.5.3) instead of using split() a second time. Try this alternative technique if you'd like.

Note that both the get_state() function we defined in this challenge and the get_city() function we created before depend on the input string to take a particular form. If we change the input, the functions may no longer work. For example, let's say that the address we gave it also included a room number:

```
"3022 Broadway, Room 142, New York, NY 10027, USA"
```

Suddenly neither get_city() nor get_state() would produce the output we'd expect. Specifically, get_city("3022 Broadway, Room 142, New York, NY 10027, USA") would return 'Room 142' and get_state("3022 Broadway, Room 142, New York, NY 10027, USA") would return 'New'.

This highlights the fact that functions are often highly dependent on the kinds of inputs that they get. We have to be careful when creating functions to think of the different forms that our input can take, and either write our code in such a way that it accounts for different kinds of inputs, or at least make sure we're always passing it the right kind of inputs. We'll return to this topic in section 4.2.10.

4.2.3 What Functions Do

Let's step back for a second to consider why functions exist. One way to think about functions is that they take one or several inputs and give you an output.

The inputs can be almost anything and so can the output. Inside the function, a series of steps are repeated over and over again, like a factory line that takes different raw materials—like steel, aluminum, glass, rubber, and paint—and produces some sort of output—like a car, for example.

In the same way, when you find yourself writing code that will probably be used over and over again in different places, it can make sense to turn it into a function. `login()` is a common function most websites have that takes a `user-name` and a `password` as inputs, checks to see if they're correct, and then logs a user into a website.

So far, both of the functions we've defined—`get_city()` and `get_state()`—have taken a string as an input and returned a string as an output, but a function could do many other things. For example, you could define a function that does any of the following:

- Takes a word (a string) and gives you the plural version of that word (a string); this probably would be a difficult function to code, depending on the language.
- Takes a lot of text (a string) and gives you the most commonly used words in that text (a list of strings).
- Takes two numbers (two integers or floats) and tells you if one is divisible by the other (`True` or `False`).

Remember in the FizzBuzz Challenge (section 3.7.1) how we kept checking whether a number was divisible by three or five? We had to repeat the same kind of code multiple times:

```
(number % 3) == 0
```

and

```
(number % 5) == 0
```

The fact that these two pieces of code look similar is a great clue that it probably makes sense to turn it into a function. Let's do that by adding the following to our `functions.py` file:

```
def divisible_by(number, divisor):
    if (number % divisor) == 0:
        return True
    else:
        return False
print(divisible_by(15, 3))
print(divisible_by(20, 3))
```

Because fifteen is divisible by three but twenty isn't, when we run the file we should see the following:

```
% python functions.py
...
True
False
```

LABELING FUNCTION ARGUMENTS

By the way, one feature of functions is that we can optionally label function arguments when we call the function:

```
print(divisible_by(number=15, divisor=3))
print(divisible_by(number=20, divisor=3))
```

> These two lines will return the same result as `divisible_by(15, 3)` and
> `divisible_by(20, 3)`, respectively. This can help us or someone else reading
> our code later remember which argument is which because the argument name
> also serves as a sort of label. The other nice thing about labeling our function argu-
> ments is that it allows us to switch around the order of our arguments:
>
> ```python
> print(divisible_by(divisor=3, number=15))
> ```
>
> This will return the same result as `divisible_by(15, 3)`. With labels, Python
> automatically figures out which input corresponds to which function argument
> based on the order in which they're passed in.

4.2.4 Refactoring and Technical Debt

The term "code smell" is sometimes used to refer to a sign that something is bad
about your code. Maybe your code is less flexible, harder to read, or more error
prone than it needs to be.

One example of a code smell is code duplication—the same or similar code
repeated more than once in one file or across multiple files.[3] Code duplication
is bad because if you want to update the way you do something, you'll have
to go back to each place your code is duplicated and remember to update it
(like "Find All and Replace"). As your code grows, this isn't always as easy as it
sounds, and it's possible that you'll miss one, which could lead to code that is
buggy or broken.

One solution to this problem is to extract all your duplicated code into one
place—like a function—and then just reuse that function. The advantage is that if
you ever decide to redesign the way your function works, or improve the code in
some way, you only have to make the change in one place.

The term "refactoring" refers to the practice of rewriting code so that it's better
in some way, even though it still functions exactly the same. How could code that
functions exactly the same be better or worse? It could be easier to read, shorter,
faster, or more flexible to change later.

When we first wrote our `divisible_by()` function it looked totally fine to us:

```python
def divisible_by(number, divisor):
    if (number % divisor) == 0:
        return True
    else:
        return False
```

We looked at it the next day and realized that we accidentally used way more code than we needed to. Can you figure out a way to do this in fewer lines? How about this?

```python
def divisible_by(number, divisor):
    return (number % divisor) == 0
```

This works because whenever we use ==, we get back True or False anyway.

Is the second, shorter way much better than the first? Generally speaking, it's better to use less code rather than more code, as long as it's still clear what the code is doing. Remember the one-line solution to the FizzBuzz Challenge that is almost impossible to understand (section 3.8.2)? Here's an example of where shorter code probably isn't better:

```python
for x in range(100):print(x%3//2*'Fizz'+x%5//4*'Buzz'or x+1)
```

Why isn't it better? Well for one thing, shorter code doesn't necessarily run faster in Python. But more important, it's harder to read, which makes it harder for other coders to understand (even if that coder is future you).

There's an important concept known as "technical debt" in coding. Technical debt is the accumulation of small (or sometimes big) imperfections in code—places where code was not written as clearly or efficiently, or with an eye for future flexibility, as it could have been. Often, the first time someone writes code, they're not going to come up with the best and clearest way to write the code. That's fine. Your initial goal when writing code should be to write code that works, rather than trying to write perfect code. When you're starting out, it can be especially hard to know what makes code better or worse, and the fear of writing bad code can be so paralyzing that it prevents you from writing anything.

As you continue to write and work on the same code over time, minor imperfections in code can add up to major technical debt that may have to be "paid off" later, so to speak. It's a good idea to look back at the code you've already written and see if you can improve (or "refactor") it.

As a nontechnical person, it can be hard to understand why refactoring is valuable, especially when it doesn't change the functionality of the code—it just makes it better in some intangible way. Companies are often so focused on the business value they want to create for customers by releasing new features and functionality to their products, that they neglect the things that don't seem to create immediate value, like refactoring.

The problem is that if you don't go back and improve your code, you start to build up technical debt. Technical debt can slow down your product development team to a crawl. Consider the scenario in which one tiny change takes much longer than it should because of things like code duplication. Over time, as your code becomes larger and larger (some large companies can have millions of lines of code in their products; e.g., the Microsoft Windows operating system supposedly has roughly fifty million lines of code[4]) the whole thing can start to resemble a giant knot, where a change in one place can have unintended effects on code in other places. Eventually technical debt can bring an organization to a crawl. Just a cautionary tale.

4.2.5 Function Challenge, Part 2

Create a function called `uppercase_and_reverse()` that takes a piece of text and gives it back to you uppercased and reversed. In practice, it should work like this:

```
>>> uppercase_and_reverse('banana')
'ANANAB'
```

Take five minutes to try to solve this challenge now.

4.2.6 Function Challenge Solution, Part 2

Did you figure it out? Let's go through it together. When defining a function, it always helps to start by figuring out what your inputs and output are going to be. In this case, it's quite simple: your input will be a string, and your output will be a string.

Next let's decide what to call the function and what we should call its argument—that is, what to name the input. Because we already know the function should be called `uppercase_and_reverse()`, all we need to decide is the input. We'll go with text (although almost anything would work, like `string` or word):

```
def uppercase_and_reverse(text):
```

This is our starting point. What should we do next? Should we tackle the uppercasing or the reversing first? In this case, it doesn't matter. We could do it in either order, although for some other functions the order will matter. Let's start with uppercasing:

```
def uppercase_and_reverse(text):
    text.upper()
```

We briefly mentioned the upper() function in section 2.8.1, "String Functions," but a quick Google search for "Python how to uppercase a string" would get you the answer pretty quickly as well.

We're not done yet, so let's store our uppercased text in a new variable (variables created inside of functions don't stick around afterward; they exist only inside of the function):

```
def uppercase_and_reverse(text):
    uppercased_text = text.upper()
```

Now we want to reverse it. We haven't covered how to do this yet, but without knowing anything, your first guess might be to try uppercased_text. reverse(). This won't work, however, because Python does not have a reverse() function. To find out what to do next, try Googling it. (Seriously, get used to Googling for answers to Python questions. It's an important skill to practice when you're learning to code.) Try Googling "Python reverse a string". We found a page on Stack Overflow that showed us the following example code:

```
>>> 'hello world'[::-1]
'dlrow olleh'
```

What is [::-1] and how does it work? The answer is we don't know, and we might want to investigate before we use this for any important application, but for the sake of this exercise it seems to do the job.[5] Let's add it to our uppercase_and_reverse() function:

```
def uppercase_and_reverse(text):
    uppercased_text = text.upper()
    uppercased_reversed_text = uppercased_text[::-1]
```

Our function still doesn't return anything though. If we tried to run it right now, it would always return the word None (more on this in section 4.2.9).

To ensure that our function outputs something, we have to add another line of code with a `return` in front of it and tell it what we want the output to be:

```
def uppercase_and_reverse(text):
    uppercased_text = text.upper()
    uppercased_reversed_text = uppercased_text[::-1]
    return uppercased_reversed_text
```

Now we can test it out with something like this:

```
print(uppercase_and_reverse('Banana'))
```

Which should give us this:

```
ANANAB
```

This works, but let's take a look at our function and see what kind of refactoring we can do. What are we doing with the `uppercased_reversed_text` variable? We are just returning it, so maybe this variable is not all that necessary. How could we get rid of it entirely? We could do the following:

```
def uppercase_and_reverse(text):
    uppercased_text = text.upper()
    return uppercased_text[::-1]
```

At this point, you might have realized that we actually can combine `upper()` and `[::-1]` into one line, and get rid of the `uppercased_text` variable entirely as well:

```
def uppercase_and_reverse(text):
    return text.upper()[::-1]
```

It's a good idea to run your code at every step along the way as you're making changes to ensure that it still works. This can help you catch any mistakes earlier rather than later.

4.2.7 Function Challenge, Part 3

Inside a new file called `finance_functions.py`, create a function to calculate future value of money based on the following formula:

$$\textit{future value} = \textit{present value} \times (1 + \textit{rate})^{\textit{periods}}$$

Then, use this formula to calculate the future value of \$1,000 at a 10 percent interest rate in five years. Take ten minutes to do this now.

4.2.8 Function Challenge Solution, Part 3

Create a new file called `finance_functions.py` and start by defining a new function:

```
def future_value():
```

At this point, we have to decide what the inputs to our function should be and what we should call them. To calculate some future value, we need three bits of information:

1. A *present value*, which will be either an integer or a float in Python (e.g., `1000` or `10.58`)
2. A *rate of return*, which will have to be a float (e.g., `0.1`) because Python doesn't have percentages built in as a data type
3. A number of *periods*, which will be an integer (e.g., `5`)

Let's call these inputs present_value, rate, and periods:

```
def future_value(present_value, rate, periods):
```

The output of our function will be the future value, which can be calculated in Python, like this:

```
present_value * (1 + rate) ** periods
```

Remember from section 2.7 that Python uses ** for exponents. Put all this together and we get the following:

```
def future_value(present_value, rate, periods):
    return present_value * (1 + rate) ** periods
```

Now we can test it by adding the following to our file:

```
print(future_value(1000, .1, 5))
```

And then we can run the file:

```
% python finance_functions.py
1610.5100000000004
```

If you're curious ot know what's going on with the .5100000000004, read the box "Floating Point Arithmetic".

FLOATING POINT ARITHMETIC

Sometimes when you're doing math with Python, you will get some weird results:

```
>>> .1 * .1
0.010000000000000002
>>> (.1 + .1 + .1) == .3
False
```

What's going on here? Computers store floats in a way that can lead to some strange errors. Take the number 0.125, for example. As a human, we actually do most of our math in something called base-10. In other words, we read 0.125 as 1/10 + 2/100 + 5/1000 + 0/10000 + . . . and so on. (Remember in math class when we had to learn about the tens, hundreds, and thousands?)

Computers use binary, either zeros or ones, which requires a base-2 system. In other words, a computer sees 0.125 as 0/2 + 0/4 + 1/8 + 0/16 + . . . and so on. The problem is that most fractions can't actually be represented in base-2. They're just approximations.

This might seem really strange, but it's actually a problem in base-10 also. For example, the decimal 1/3 can't be represented in base-10. We can write 0.3 or 0.33 or 0.3333 and get closer, but there's no way of exactly representing 1/3 in base-10.

Python deals with the issue of representing most floats in base-2 by getting close enough and then cutting off everything after a certain number of digits (in Python 3, it's seventeen digits). But every once in a while, one of these little bits gets left over in the approximation and shows up when you don't expect it to, so you get something like 0.010000000000000002.

Surprisingly, this is a problem with all computers (not just with the Python language) because they all have to do math in base-2 (at the end of the day, all computer signals reduce down to just zeros and ones). One way to deal with this is by just rounding even further:

```
>>> round(.1 + .1 + .1, 15) == round(.3, 15)
```

You might decide that you care only about accuracy to the nearest ten digits. Ultimately, even banks have to decide how many decimals out they want to calculate interest. Did you know that when NASA sends rockets to space, they only use around fifteen digits of pi? If it's good enough for NASA, it's good enough for us. For more information about this problem check out the Python documentation on *Floating Point Arithmetic: Issues and Limitations.*

The simple solution here is to use the round() function to round our answer to the nearest two decimal points before returning it:

```
def future_value(present_value, rate, periods):
    return round(present_value * (1 + rate) ** periods, 2)
...
```

Now we should get a more reasonable looking result:

```
% python finance_functions.py
1610.51
```

This highlights another nice feature of functions. Imagine if we were calculating a lot of future values in our code, but we didn't turn it into a function. Once we discovered the floating point arithmetic problem and decided we wanted to fix it, we'd have to update our code a bunch of times. It's possible that we'd miss one, which could lead to a bug in our code. If we turn it into a function, then we would only have to make that update once.

4.2.9 Function Gotchas: Not Using return

Something we see first-time coders do a lot is printing out results directly inside of functions. For example, in `finance_functions.py`, we could have written the following:

```python
def future_value(present_value, rate, periods):
    print(round(present_value * (1 + rate) ** periods, 2))


future_value(1000, .1, 5)
```

This would lead to the correct answer being displayed in the command line when we ran the code:

```
% python finance_functions.py
1610.51
```

We might think, "Oh! I saved a step!" But it turns out this is a bad idea. The problem comes when we want to save the output to a variable, which is something we often want to do:

```python
def future_value(present_value, rate, periods):
    print(round(present_value * (1 + rate) ** periods, 2))


balance = future_value(1000, .1, 5)
print(f"Your account balance is: {balance}")
```

What will the value of balance be? Check for yourself:

```
% python finance_functions.py
1610.51
Your account balance is: None
```

What's happening here is that when a function has no return, it has no output. Even though it's calculating and printing out the future value to the command line, when we try to create a `balance` variable based on the function's output, Python will set its value to None, which means literally *nothing* or *empty*.

This becomes a bigger issue when we try to do something with a variable whose value is None, for example:

```
...
balance = future_value(1000, .1, 5)
print(balance * 100)
```

This would end up producing the following error:

```
% python finance_functions.py
1610.51
Traceback (most recent call last):
    File "finance_functions.py", line 6, in <module>
        print(balance * 100)
TypeError: unsupported operand type(s) for *: 'NoneType' and 'int'
```

What Python is telling us here—`TypeError: unsupported operand type(s) for *: 'NoneType' and 'int'`—is that we're trying to multiply None and an integer together, and it doesn't know how to do that. Almost always, if you get an error that includes the term `NoneType` in it, it means you have a function that isn't returning something, so you have a variable whose value is None.

Almost all functions should return something. Interestingly enough, one function we've been using doesn't return anything. Can you guess what it is? The `print()` function doesn't have to return anything because it does something really specific (prints something to the command line), so it wouldn't make sense to save its output to a variable.

4.2.10 Function Gotchas: Not Taking inputs

Another bad idea would be to use `input()` to get inputs directly from inside the function:

```
def future_value():
    present_value = float(input("What's the present value? "))
    rate = float(input("What's the rate of return? "))
    periods = int(input("Over how many periods? "))
    return round(present_value * (1 + rate) ** periods, 2)


print(future_value())
```

Notice that this function no longer takes any explicit arguments. Running this would produce the following:

```
% python finance_functions.py
What's the present value? 1000
What's the rate of return? .1
Over how many periods? 5
1610.51
```

The problem is that we're stuck getting our inputs manually through the command line. What if we want to calculate the future value of data that we weren't getting directly through the command line—for example, stored in our database? We'd have to create another function, or we'd have to change this one, which would have to lead to other changes in our code.

If we *did* want to get our inputs directly from a user through the command line, we'd be much better off getting the inputs outside of the function and then passing those variables into the function as inputs:

```
def future_value(present_value, rate, periods):
    return round(present_value * (1 + rate) ** periods, 2)

present_value = float(input("What's the present value? "))
rate = float(input("What's the rate of return? "))
periods = int(input("How many periods? "))
print(future_value(present_value, rate, periods))
```

As a rule of thumb, functions shouldn't be too rigid about where the inputs are coming from or what is happening with the output.

4.2.11 Function Arguments

As we mentioned earlier, we have the option to explicitly label our function arguments when we pass them into a function:

```
def future_value(present_value, rate, periods):
    return round(present_value * (1 + rate) ** periods, 2)
print(future_value(present_value=1000, rate=.1, periods=5))
```

This can help clarify what each function input actually is. It also allows us to reorder the function arguments if we wanted to:

```
...
print(future_value(rate=.1, present_value=1000, periods=5))
```

More important, labeling a function argument is sometimes necessary in cases in which a function argument has a *default value*. When we define a function, we can give one of its arguments a default value like this:

```
def future_value(present_value, rate, periods=1):
    return round(present_value * (1 + rate) ** periods, 2)
```

Notice the addition of `periods=1` here. This means that we now have the option of omitting this argument when we run the function:

```
...
print(future_value(1000, .1))
```

In this case, `present_value` would be set to `1000` and `rate` would be set to .1 (because we're passing those in explicitly), but `periods` would be 1 (because that's its default value).

Many of the functions we've been using so far actually have *optional arguments* (arguments set with default values) that can be discovered by reading their documentation. For example, the `print()` function documentation (available online) mentions several optional arguments—including `sep=' '` (sep is short for separator). In other words, the default separator for inputs to the `print()` function is a space. But it's possible to override the value of sep. That means, if we wanted to, we could do weird stuff like this:

```
% python
>>> print("Dollar", "dollar", "bills", "y'all", sep='$')
Dollar$dollar$bills$y'all
```

Because the `print()` function has multiple arguments with default values, if we want to override one of them, we have to pass in the argument name explicitly (e.g., `sep='$'`). Many of the functions we'll be using have optional arguments, especially when it comes to functions we'll be introducing later that help with data analysis. The best way to learn about these functions is to go online and read the documentation.

As of writing this, the documentation for the Python `print()` function looks like this:

print(*objects, sep=' ', end='\n', file=sys.stdout, flush=False)
Print objects to the text stream file, separated by sep and followed by end. sep, end, file
    and flush, if present, must be given as keyword arguments.
All non-keyword arguments are converted to strings like str() does and written to the
    stream, separated by sep and followed by end. Both sep and end must be strings;
    they can also be None, which means to use the default values. If no objects are
    given, print() will just write end.

. . .

It's not always easy to read and understand documentation, but it's worth getting some exposure early on. In this case, the `*objects` function argument is what allows `print()` to take any number of inputs that we want to give it. It looks like we could modify four optional arguments: `sep,  end,  file,` and `flush`.

Moving forward, when we introduce a new function, try to look up the documentation and read about what the different possible function arguments are. If you do this, your Python knowledge will start growing exponentially.

4.3 IMPORTING PYTHON PACKAGES

The last major topic to cover in Python Basics is importing Python packages. A *package* (sometimes also referred to in Python as a *library* or *module*[6]) is a generic term used to describe a bunch of code that was designed to be used by many different scripts or applications. One of the nice things about Python is that it comes with many built-in packages that can be loaded easily into any Python file. And when the built-in packages aren't enough, we can turn to the more than one hundred thousand online Python packages available on the Python Package Index (pypi.org).

One of Python's greatest strengths is the wide variety of packages that are available in the language. We can import these packages to do almost anything we'd like with our code. There's a famous online webcomic series called *xkcd* by Randall Munroe whose comic "Python" makes this point nicely:

It's okay if you don't get it, it's not *that* funny. But it illustrates the seemingly magical nature of the fact that, compared with other programming languages, Python lets you easily add some pretty magical functionality.[7]

We've already imported a Python package. In happy_hour.py, we saw the following code:

```
import random

...


random_bar = random.choice(bars)
random_person = random.choice(people)

...
```

Here, we loaded the random package with import random and then used the choice() function. The general formula for importing a package and then using one of the functions from that package follows:

```
import package
package.function()
```

Running this exact code, however, will produce a ModuleNotFoundError: No module named 'package' error because a package named package doesn't actually exist.

When we load a package, we make every function in that package available in our code. To explore how this works, let's create a new file called importing.py and add the following code:

```
import statistics

print(statistics.mean([90, 85, 74]))
print(statistics.mean([12.99, 9.99, 5.49, 7.50]))
```

Running this file should give us the following:

```
% python importing.py
83
8.9925
```

Remember when we created our average() function? Would it surprise you to hear that Python comes with an average function called mean() as part of its statistics package? The statistics package contains a whole bunch of useful functions related to statistics, including median(), mode(), stdev(), variance(), and others. When we import a package at the top of a file, we can access all the functions contained in that package by prefixing the function name with the package name and a dot—for example, statistics.mean().

If we get tired of having to type out the entire package name each time we want to use one of its functions, it's possible to import a package and give it a shorter alias using as, like so:

```
import statistics as st
print(st.mean([1, 2, 3]))
print(st.mean([12, 87, 10.5]))
```

We'll see this technique occasionally when reading documentation about how to use certain data analysis packages, like `pandas`, which we'll cover later. Finally, if we know that there's only one specific function we want to use inside of a package, we can import *only* that function using `from` and `import` like this:

```
from statistics import mean

print(mean([1, 2, 3]))
print(mean([12, 87, 10.5]))
```

Note that we don't have to put the parentheses after mean in `from statistics import mean`. This technique allows us to call that function in `importing.py` without having to prefix it with the entire package name every time. There are other reasons this is preferable to importing the whole package that we won't touch on here. But it does require us to know in advance which of the functions we're going to be using.

4.3.1 The Python Standard Library

The set of built-in packages that comes with Python is collectively known as the *Python Standard Library*. Later we'll show you how we can also easily download other packages from the web and import those as well. If you followed our instructions for installing Python using Anaconda, you'll find it comes bundled with a lot of the most popular packages, which means you don't have to download them all separately.

If you Google "Python Standard Library" you'll find a page listing a whole bunch of packages like `random`, `math`, and `statistics`. You don't have to learn all the different Python packages available—many of them you'll never use, and the important ones you'll learn about in due time.

We'll dive a bit further into the random package because we already used it in our `happy_hour.py` file. After searching Google for "Python Standard Library," one of the pages we should be able to navigate to has documentation for how to use the `random` package (or just Google "Python Random" and make sure you click on the documentation for Python 3).

In the documentation for the `random` package, you'll be able to read more about the `choice()` function that we used, but you'll also find a bunch of other interesting functions all related to randomness, such as the following:

- `shuffle()`—shuffles around a list randomly
- `sample()`—takes a random sampling of numbers from a list
- `random()`—generates a random number between zero and one; just like the `RAND()` function you might be familiar with from Excel
- `uniform(a, b)`—generates a random number between any two numbers

Many more functions are available in `random`, but we just wanted to show you that they all have something in common, which is that they all have to do with randomness.

Why aren't all these standard packages and functions available in every Python file by default? Why do we have to import each one manually? For one, there are a lot of them. If we actually tried to import all of the packages included in the Python Standard Library, it would take a few seconds every time, which is pretty unnecessary.

Just for fun, open up Python interactive mode and run the following:

```
% python
>>> import this
```

You'll see a nice little poem called "The Zen of Python" by Tim Peters printed out to your command line, which starts with the following two lines:

```
Beautiful is better than ugly.
Explicit is better than implicit.
...
```

While we're at it, try running the following:

```
>>> import antigravity
```

(No, we're not kidding.) If you run `import antigravity`, your web browser should open up and go to the very same *xkcd* comic we showed you earlier. Isn't that cool? (And also, super nerdy!) The webcomic became so famous that they actually built it into Python itself.

4.3.2 Importing Python Packages Challenge

Explore the Python Standard Library documentation and pick one function each from the `statistics`, `math`, and `datetime` packages to import and learn how to use. Write a comment above each explaining how it works. Take ten minutes or so to do this now on your own (note that we don't provide our solution to this challenge).

4.3.3 Downloading and Importing Third-Party Packages

On top of the built-in packages that come included with Python, hundreds of thousands of *third-party* packages are written and made available by other coders online. Python has an official website where other developers can upload their own packages for you to download at pypi.org. Python comes with the command line command `pip`, which makes it super easy to get new Python packages from the web.[8]

One of these third-party packages is called `pandas`, which lets us use Python to read Excel and CSV files. It's so popular that even though it's not technically part of Python, it comes included automatically as part of the Anaconda installer that we use to install Python. If we didn't have `pandas` installed, we could run the following code in our command line to get it:

```
% pip install pandas
```

This code would go to pypi.org and download the `pandas` package to our computer in a specifically designated folder that can be accessed from any other file (that way, we only have to download it once). Then we can use it inside of a file. Note that this `pip install` line should be run directly in our command line, *not* in Python.

In part 2, we're going to go into much more detail on `pandas`, as well as other data analysis tools available to use with Python. Many of these third-party packages can be found online by Googling for Python packages and most can be installed using `pip`.

GITHUB

When we search Google for a Python package, we often end up on Github.com, a popular website where developers upload code and instructions on how to use it. Github also has features that make it useful for teams of coders working together on the same code together (think of it as a Dropbox for your code).

When exploring a third-party Python package, it's often a good idea to look for it on Github and see if clear documentation exists on how to install and use it. Sometimes when a package is new, or isn't popular, you might not find any documentation, which can make it difficult to figure out how to use the package. As a package develops over time, becomes more popular, or gets more developers working on it, the documentation usually gets better as well. (For example, try searching for the pandas package on Github.)

The takeaway is that when deciding among third-party packages to use for a particular task in Python, check out the documentation and see how clear it is. Another indicator we often look at when evaluating a third-party package is the number of *Stars* it has on Github (the equivalent of a *Like* on Facebook). This can help us assess the relative popularity of a particular package against others.

4.4 WRAPPING UP

This chapter took a deep dive into functions and how they can be used. We covered how functions can be used to refactor our code, and we reviewed some of the things that can go wrong with functions, such as using too many or too few function arguments or using the wrong kind of function argument.

Finally, we saw how we can use Python's `import` to get functions from other packages, which will allow us to access a whole world of third-party tools in the second half of this book when we cover the topic of data analysis in Python.

4.5 END OF PART 1

This concludes the first half of the book. Congratulations on making it this far!

We have been preoccupied for the most part with learning the basics of Python so that we could move on to what we're covering in the second half of the book, which is the actual application of Python to solving business problems. Hopefully, you've found this information to be somewhat interesting. Moving forward, the things you learn will get even more useful and practical.

Everything we're about to cover builds on the concepts we introduced in the first half of the book. Know that you can—and probably will have to—flip back to a previous section if you need a quick refresher on a concept or two.

PART II

WELCOME TO PART 2. I'm Daniel Guetta, and I'm going to teach you about data analytics in Python. Given that you've gotten this far, I probably don't need to convince you how important it is for MBAs to be data literate in the twenty-first century. But let me tell you a little bit about my background and how my experiences working at Palantir and Amazon led me to realize that the material in part 2 should be central to any MBA curriculum.

I studied physics and mathematics at the University of Cambridge and MIT, and then moved to New York to pursue a doctorate in operations research (a problem-solving and decision-making methodology that brings the power of data and analytics to management and business). My thesis research led me to the supply chain group at Amazon.com, where I saw data driving thousands of decisions every day. I became obsessed with the ability of data to make everything better, and this led me to join Palantir Technologies, a company that works with private companies and governments around the world to help them drive value using their data. I was on the private side, and worked with organizations in a broad range of industries around the world, using data analytics to help them make crucial decisions, first as a data scientist, and later as a team leader on the company's more analytical projects.

I spent many hours talking to managers—talented individuals with deep subject matter expertise and often with MBAs. They helped me understand how their businesses worked, and I helped them write and run code to translate their data into insight. I noticed that even when the Palantir team was doing most of the technical work, it was immeasurably helpful to work with clients who were willing to truly engage with and understand what we were doing. Regardless of the industry—from pharmaceuticals, to consumer-packaged goods, to law, to consumer finance—I found that an engaged counterpart was one of the strongest predictors of whether a project would succeed.

In today's increasingly data-driven world, the need to be data literate is becoming the norm, not the exception. I see this day after day, in my work with students at Columbia who are increasingly eager to develop these skills, and at almost every company I consult for. Even if you have an analyst to crunch your data, knowing what they're doing can help you ask sharper questions and better understand the answers they give you. And there's nothing like being able to run some of those analyses yourselves. In the past, a mastery of Excel was enough. As datasets (the questions we ask) have become bigger and more complicated, this is no longer true.

In part 2, we will see how Python can help. We will use a case study about Dig, a restaurant chain headquartered in New York City, to illustrate the power and importance of data analytics. We will see how Dig's challenges can be addressed using data and build on the Python fundamentals you learned in part 1 to show you how to use massive datasets to answer these questions.

You will notice that part 2 does not include standalone sections with exercises. Instead, we weave the exercises into each chapter, and use a diamond ♦ symbol throughout the text to indicate opportunities to pause and think of the challenge at hand before reading our solution. Some of these challenges will involve getting your hands dirty and writing code yourselves; others will be more conceptual. We wrote this book for a broad audience—if you are reading it out of casual interest, you should feel free to read straight through to the solutions. You will get a good idea of what's possible without potentially torturing yourself with details. If, however, you work in a position in which you are directly working with datasets and want to develop the skills required to carry out analyses yourselves, you will be well served by spending some time on these challenges.

I'm passionate about the ways data can be leveraged to make things better. Few things are more satisfying than slowly but surely extracting actionable insight from the massive datasets that run your business. I look forward to showing you the tools Python makes available to make this happen.

5

INTRODUCTION TO DATA
IN PYTHON

YOU NOW HAVE A SOLID FOUNDATION in the fundamentals of Python. In part 2 of the book, we will cover one of the most important ways Python is used in a business setting—for data analysis.

It is worth first asking why we even need to work with Python—why not just stick with Excel? There are a number of reasons for working with Python:

1. **Scale:** The latest version of Excel is limited to datasets with at most 1,048,576 rows and 16,384 columns and it becomes sluggish even with much smaller datasets. Many datasets (e.g., the Dig dataset we shall look at later) far exceed this capacity.

2. **Robustness:** If an Excel spreadsheet gets complex enough (and especially if it involves combining different datasets using `vlookup` formulas or similar functions), it can be exceptionally difficult to get a "big picture" idea of what the workbook is doing. Calculations are spread out across cells in multiple sheets, and it can take a considerable amount of work to understand exactly how any given result is obtained. This can have disastrous consequences; some have suggested that the famous "London Whale" debacle in which JP Morgan Chase lost billions of dollars (you read that right—with a "B") was actually caused by a simple error in an Excel spreadsheet.[1]

3. **Automation:** Many business applications require automation, and Excel is a poor solution in those situations. For example, suppose a company has hundreds of files, each of which list sales at one of their stores. Running the same analysis on each of these hundreds of files, or somehow combining them to perform an overall analysis, can be prohibitively difficult in Excel.

4. **Integration**: In some cases, data analysis is done in a vacuum—you need to answer a single question, and you use data to answer it. In other cases, however, the question is part of larger workflows that interact with other parts of the company. Excel is often not robust enough to be part of an operational framework, and this type of analysis is unlikely to be able to "slot in" to other parts of a company's operation. Python, by contrast, is full-featured enough to handle such diverse tasks as running a website, carrying out data analysis, and running a company's staffing system (among others).

Python can solve each of these four issues and more. It can carry out repeatable, automatable analyses on large datasets quickly and efficiently. In this part of the book, we will cover the mechanics of these operations. Perhaps more important, we will teach you how to *think* in a data-driven way—that is, how to go from identifying a business problem to figuring out how to answer it using data.

5.1 WHAT YOU'LL LEARN IN THIS CHAPTER

In this chapter, you will learn the basic tools that are required in order to work with data in Python. We will first introduce *Jupyter Notebook*, a far richer way to interact with Python than the console you have been working with so far. We will then introduce pandas, Python's most popular package for data analytics, and see how to read and write files with a variety of formats into Python using pandas, and how to export them back to disk for saving and sharing. This will take a little getting used to if your main experience with data thus far has been in Excel, but it will pay dividends when we look at specific business questions we want to answer using our data. Finally, we will introduce Dig—a restaurant chain based on the east coast of the USA and poised for expansion—which will underpin many of the examples in this part of the book.

You will then be ready to start carrying out some substantial, actionable analysis on the Dig dataset, which we will begin in chapter 6.

5.2 WHAT YOU'LL NEED FOR THIS CHAPTER

Before you work through this chapter, begin by creating a folder called "Part 2" in which you can store all the files for part 2 of this book. Inside this folder, create two more folders:

- A folder called "Chapter 5" in which we will save our works-in-progress from exercises later in this chapter. You should leave this folder empty for now.
- A folder called "raw data" in which you should download the data we'll be loading and analyzing in this part of the book. You will find this data on the book's website. Download the following files into this folder:
  - ○ `Students.xlsx`
  - ○ `Restaurants.csv`
  - ○ `Items.csv`
  - ○ `Simplified orders.zip`
  - ○ `Summarized orders.csv`
  - ○ `University.xlsx`

To summarize, you should have a folder called "Part 2," and this folder should contain two other folders—"raw data," containing the files in the bulleted list, and "Chapter 5," an empty folder.

5.3 AN INTRODUCTION TO *JUPYTER NOTEBOOK*

In part 1, you learned the basics of Python coding using a terminal. In this part, we will instead use a different tool called *Jupyter Notebook*. As we'll see shortly, this tool provides a different way to run Python code and has a few advantages. Among them, it makes it much easier to visualize the output of your code, including tables and graphs. This makes it well-suited to working with data. In fact, *Jupyter Notebook* is by far the most popular way of writing code in Python in the context of data analytics.

The Python code you'll be running using *Jupyter Notebook* is the same as the code you were running in a terminal, but you will instead be typing it in a website-like interface that looks something like this:

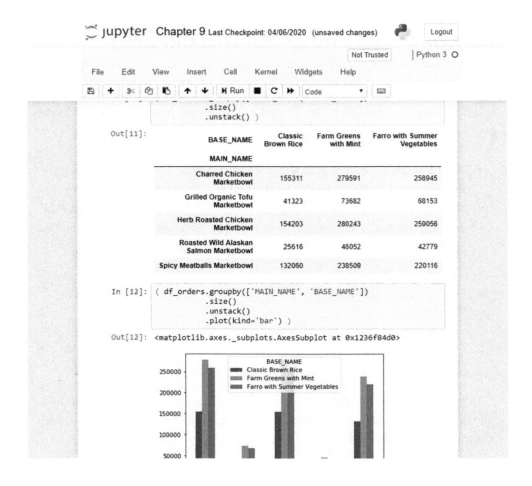

As you will quickly realize, this provides a user-friendly way to carry out even the most complex analyses and produce rich content such as tables and graphics.

5.3.1 Launching *Jupyter Notebook*

Let's first begin by launching *Jupyter Notebook*. First, open a command line prompt as discussed in section 1.4 (*Terminal* on Mac, or *Anaconda Powershell Prompt* on Windows) and type `jupyter notebook` in the terminal.[2]

A web browser window that will look something like this will appear:

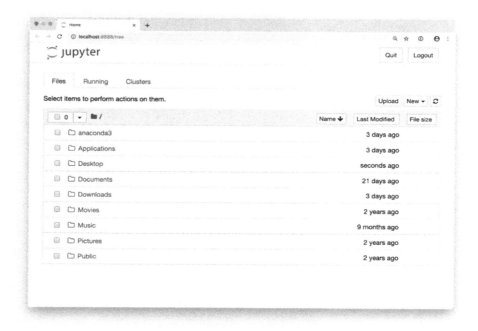

The actual folders might be somewhat different, depending on what's on your computer. In fact, the files and folders you will see on this screen are the ones in the folder you were in when you ran the `jupyter notebook` command.

One quick point—none of this is actually on the web anywhere, and you're not making your files accessible publicly. *Jupyter Notebook* just uses your web browser as an interface to navigate your computer and interact with specific files. We'll have more to say about this a little later.

Next, navigate to the folder called "Part 2," which you created in section 5.2. Click on "New" on the top-right-hand corner, and select "Python 3":

This will create a new *Jupyter Notebook* file in a new tab that looks something like this:

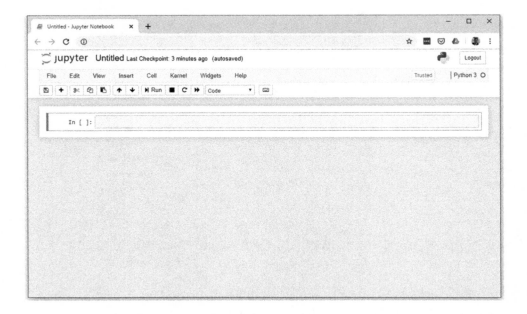

Notice that the top of this file says "Untitled." If you go back to the previous tab, you'll find that a new file called `Untitled.ipynb` has been created at that location. What you're seeing above is the file opened in *Jupyter Notebook*.

Now, rename this file—click on the text that says "Untitled" and replace it with "My first notebook." Return to the first tab, and you'll see the file has been correspondingly renamed.

5.3.2 Code Cells

A *Jupyter Notebook* is made up of multiple cells. Our notebook currently has only one cell (the rectangle you see above with the `In []` to the left of it), but we'll add more later. Each cell can be manipulated in one of two modes—*edit mode* and *command mode*. We will discuss the difference shortly.

The first purpose of these cells is to contain code. Click inside the cell (you'll notice the bar to the left of the `In []` turns green when you do this; this indicates we are entering *edit mode* for that cell), and type the code `1 + 1` into the cell:

```
In [ ]: 1 + 1|
```

Once you've typed the code, press `Ctrl` and `Enter`. This tells Python to run the code in the cell. You can also press the "Play" button (the small triangle) in the toolbar. Notice three things happen:

```
In [1]: 1 + 1
Out[1]: 2
```

- The output of this piece of code (in this case, 2) is printed right under the cell.
- The text that said `In []` changes for the briefest of seconds to `In [*]` (it's so fast you might not even seen it) and then to `In [1]`. The former means that the cell is currently running, and the latter means that this was the first cell that was run in that notebook.
- The bar to the left of the cell turns blue—this means we are no longer in *edit mode*. We have entered *command mode* for that cell. We'll have more to say about that shortly.

Now press `Ctrl` and `Enter` again, to run the cell again. Notice that the output doesn't change (because the code has not changed), but the text to the left of the cell will now read `In [2]`, because it is the second cell that has been run in the notebook (this number will never go back to 1, which is perhaps *Jupyter*'s subtle way to remind us to make every moment count since it'll never come back).

So far, so good. But what happens if we want more cells in this notebook? The first thing we need to do is enter command mode for the cell by ensuring that the bar to the left of the cell is blue. This should already be the case if you followed the previous instructions. If the bar is green (perhaps you clicked on the cell and entered edit mode), press `Esc` to enter command mode—the bar to the left will turn blue.

In command mode, we can now use a variety of commands: For example, typing the letter A will add a blank cell *above* the current selected cell. Typing the letter B will add a blank cell *below* the current selected cell. Try both.

Now that you've created multiple cells, you can edit any given cell by going into edit mode for that cell. To do that, simply click on the cell, or press Enter while the cell is selected (notice the bar to the left of the cell turns green). Similarly, you can navigate between cells using your arrow keys—press Esc to go back into command mode (the bar to the left of the cell will turn blue) and use your arrow keys to navigate.

To delete a cell, simply click on the cell, go into command mode by pressing Esc, and then press d twice in quick succession. Be careful—this will delete the cell. If you want to "undelete" the last cell you deleted, ensure that you're in command mode, and then press Z.

The key thing to understand about *Jupyter Notebook* is that all the cells in a notebook run in the *same* Python workspace—known as a *Python kernel*. To see this, type the following code in two cells:

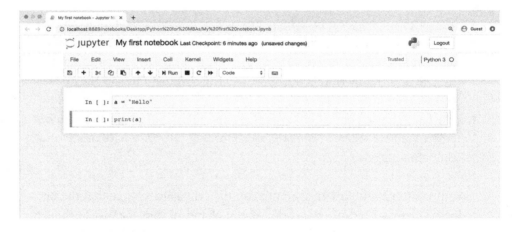

Then, run the first cell followed by the second cell. Notice that even though the variable a is only defined in the first cell, it still exists in the second cell. This makes *Jupyter Notebook* particularly convenient to carry out long, multistep analyses. If you created a whole separate notebook, however, it would run in its own separate kernel, so you could run different analyses side by side.

Recall that we have been using Ctrl and Enter to run cells. You will have noticed that this runs a cell, and *keeps that cell selected*. There are two other ways to run a cell—Shift and Enter will run the cell and select the cell below, and Alt and Enter will run the cell and create an *empty* cell below the cell that just ran. This is a lot of information to remember upon first reading, so just use and remember one of these shortcuts for now. As you get more comfortable with *Jupyter Notebook*, the other two shortcuts also will come in handy.

It can be helpful to think about the difference between running code as you did in part 1—directly in the terminal—and here in a *Jupyter Notebook*. When you used a terminal to run your code, everything happened in one place—you entered Python commands into the terminal, and the Python "engine" that ran the code (the *Python kernel*) also existed in that same terminal.

With *Jupyter Notebook*, things are slightly different. When you ran `jupyter notebook` in section 5.3.1, you did so in a command line window. This window, which remains open while you're working in the browser, runs the Python kernel, just as it did in part 1. But now, instead of typing code directly into the terminal, you type in the *Jupyter Notebook* interface in the browser. Every time you run a cell, the code is sent to the Python kernel, which will run the code and send the result back to the browser interface for you to see.

This explains behavior that sometimes causes some confusion for beginners. Suppose you go the command line window and close it while *Jupyter* is running in your browser—what happens? You should see the following popup in your browser:

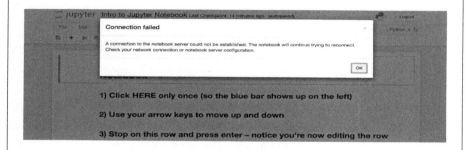

Jupyter is telling you it's unable to connect to the Python kernel—because you just closed it. You won't be able to run any code in the notebook anymore, because no kernel exists for it to connect to and actually run the code. If this happens to you, close everything and relaunch *Jupyter*.

You might be wondering why *Jupyter* goes to the trouble of separating the Python kernel and the interface in which you type code and view its results. One of the benefits of doing this is relevant in many industrial applications, when the datasets and algorithms involved are far too large and complex to run on a simple desktop or laptop computer. Instead, they need to run on high-capacity machines, often in the cloud. Unfortunately, these machines are generally in data centers that are hard to access. When you use *Jupyter Notebook*, the Python kernel (which runs all the computations) can be located on one of these cloud machines, whereas the interface in which you actually type code, which doesn't require much power, can be on your own computer. For the purposes of this book, we won't use this feature—both the Python kernel (in the command line window) and the interface (in your browser) will be on your own computer. If you work with a data science group at your company, however, you likely will encounter this more complex setup sooner rather than later.

5.3.3 Markdown Cells

Code isn't the only thing you can put in a *Jupyter Notebook.* Create a new cell, enter command mode by pressing Esc, and then press M. This will convert the cell into what's called a *markdown cell.* If you prefer, you can also select the cell and use the menu in the toolbar to select "Markdown":

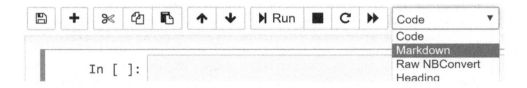

Markdown cells do not contain code—instead, they contain annotations— much like comments but formatted.

Try to type some text in that cell, and then "run" it by pressing Ctrl and Enter. Notice how the resulting text appears in a different font. This can be useful to annotate a notebook.

You won't be surprised to learn that markdown cells don't only contain plain text, they also can contain more richly formatted text using a language called Markdown. Go back to editing your markdown cell, enter the text # Section 1 into the cell, and run it. The # at the start of the cell formats it as a first-level heading. Using ## formats the text as a second-level heading, and ###, as a third-level heading. Like this:

Chapter 5

Section 5.5

Section 5.5.1

There are many more ways to format text using Markdown, but they lie outside the scope of this book. A simple Google search for "Markdown cheatsheet" should yield resources on the subject.

5.3.4 The ipynb File

The content of a notebook is saved in the `ipynb` file, so if you close your notebook and send it to someone, they'll be able to open it and immediately see the results of all the code you got the last time you ran the file.

This is a pretty convenient feature, but it often leads to confusion for people the first few times they work with notebooks.

To understand why, get your notebook back in a state where it has two cells—one containing `a = "Hello"` and one containing `print(a)`. Run the two cells one after the other—everything should work okay.

Now save the notebook by clicking on `File > Save and Checkpoint`, or press `Command` and `S` or `Ctrl` and `S` on a Mac. Then, close the tab and return to the list of folders. You should notice that the file corresponding to this notebook will have a green book icon next to it in the list of files. This means that the Python kernel corresponding to this notebook is still running in the background. If you click on the notebook and go back into it, everything will be as it would have been if the notebook had never been closed.

Where it gets interesting is what happens when you restart the underlying Python kernel. To do this, go back to the list of files, click on the little checkbox to the left of the file in the tab with the list of folders and then click the `Shutdown` button near the top. This will tell *Jupyter* that you want to completely close down the Python kernel underlying this particular notebook. This would be equivalent to completely shutting down the console in the terminology of part 1. It wipes every variable Python had stored in memory.

Now, reopen the notebook. You might expect it to be completely blank, but this is where it gets interesting—you will find that the previous output of the `print` statement is still there. *Jupyter* has saved that output in the `ipynb` file. The reason it does this is simple—sometimes you'll want to close a notebook and send it to a colleague to share your analysis, and even if the colleague doesn't have the underlying Python kernel, they'll need to be able to see the output. *Jupyter* allows them to do that.

The downside is that it will give you the impression that the kernel is still running when it isn't. To see this, *do not* run the first line, and try and run the second line—`print(a)`—directly. You should see this error:

```
--------------------------------------------------
NameError
Traceback (most recent call last)
<ipython-input-1-f04e0af0ace6> in <module>
----> 1 print(a)

NameError: name 'a' is not defined
```

Because the first line hasn't been run, the variable a has not yet been created in this particular Python kernel. Thus, Python cannot find the variable when it tries to print it, and hence the error.

If you ever encounter this error, the easy solution is to simply run the entire notebook from top to bottom, to recreate every variable as needed. The easiest way to do this is to click `Kernel > Restart & Run All`, and confirm you'd like to restart the kernel.

Inevitably, it's likely you will forget this at some point and get a `NameError` telling you some variable hasn't been defined. Do yourself a favor and save yourself a lot of frustration by remembering to just click `Restart & Run All` at that point.

One last feature of *Jupyter Notebook* is very useful, but we will delay discussing it until section 5.5.5, after we have introduced pandas DataFrames.

DIG CASE STUDY: FROM INTUITION TO DATA-DRIVEN ANALYTICS

Now that we have discussed the fundamentals of *Jupyter Notebook*, we are ready to begin working with data in Python. Many introductions to the subject use simple toy datasets, and focus on Python operations rather than on their purposes in a broader business context. In this book, we wanted to take a different approach. Indeed, as we mentioned in the introduction, our goal in part 2 is to teach you how to think in a data-driven way; this would be hard to do without a true business case and a more complex dataset to accompany that case.

For these reasons, we will anchor most of our work using a case study based on Dig, a restaurant chain with stores in New York City that is poised for expansion. The remainder of this section chronicles the story of Dig and introduces many aspects of Dig's business that will motivate many of our analyses, especially those in chapter 9. If you can't wait to dig in to the rest of the book (no pun intended), feel free to skip straight to section 5.4 in which we discuss the data we'll be using, and return to the rest of the story later.

INTRODUCTION

This case study is based on conversations with Shereen Asmat, Molly Fisher, and members of Dig's leadership team. Details about Dig, its operations, and its data have been fictionalized for the purposes of this case study to protect Dig's proprietary information.

This case was originally published in 2019 by Columbia CaseWorks of Columbia University (www8.gsb.columbia.edu/caseworks) as case number 200202, "From Intuition to Data-Driven Analytics: The Case of Dig" by C. Daniel Guetta, used with permission. Case available for purchase through The Case Center (www.thecasecenter.org).

Dig (formerly Dig Inn[1]) has built a winning concept: deliver a delicious vegetable-first menu sourced directly from farms, price each meal affordably, and have a team of skilled chefs prepare everything on site, from charred chicken to roasted sweet potatoes. On a typical day, it's not unusual to see substantial queues form outside Dig's restaurants, thankfully kept moving rapidly by the well-trained staff behind the counter. With almost thirty restaurants in New York City, Rye Brook, and Boston as of the time this case was written, and healthy venture capital backing, Dig is poised for expansion.

Founded in 2011, Dig has been shepherded by its management team from a single restaurant to a brand with a multicity reach. This evolution has involved significant changes not only in Dig's menu but also in its operations—for example, making its goods available on delivery apps, launching a catering service, and in some cases, developing a delivery-specific menu.[2] As it grew, the company had collected data on every aspect of its operations and management, but the focus was on perfecting the product and defining Dig's identity. Analyses using data were often one-off and involved painstakingly piecing together disparate datasets to answer specific questions, rather than relying on more robust systems and reporting tools, such as dashboards.

In June 2019, as Dig was ready for its next phase of expansion, the management team realized it would need to lean on its data more heavily than it had in the past. With new restaurants opening, each as different as the last, it became less and less sustainable to rely on management intuition to make decisions. The overarching challenge faced by Shereen Asmat, senior manager, data and operational products, and her team was how to support expansion beyond the three cities in which Dig operated. She was aware that as Dig's restaurant footprint and customer base grew, careful attention needed to be paid to every part of its supply chain.

"We want to build our network in the best way possible," said Asmat. "As we grow, we will face increasing complexity: differences in demand, how much local

1. Adam Eskin, "Dig Inn Is Now Dig," Medium, July 15, 2019, https://medium.com/@diginn/dig-inn-is-now-dig-bf6d8d5ecdaa.
2. Natalie Kais, "Interview: How Dig Inn Is Bringing Quality and Sustainability to Food Delivery," PSFK.com, April 2019, https://www.psfk.com/2019/04/dig-inn-interview-adam-eskin.html.

produce and meat we can order, the supply of labor and shifting landscape of labor laws in the United States, and other factors which will have an impact on our business. My team's job will be to unlock the insights in our data to help us with these growing challenges."

FROM THE PUMP ENERGY FOOD TO DIG INN

After graduating from Brown University, Dig founder Adam Eskin worked for Wexford Capital, a Greenwich, Connecticut–based private-equity firm. Tasked with searching for business concepts, Eskin came across the Pump Energy Food (the Pump), a chain of five Manhattan restaurants founded in 1997 by Steve and Elena Kapelonis.[3] The Pump was known for its menu of high-protein food targeted at fitness enthusiasts, with a menu that featured items such as egg white omelets, healthy oils, and salads. Eskin, an associate at Wexford, convinced his firm to purchase a majority stake in the Pump and was subsequently put in charge of the investment in December 2006. He made improvements immediately, setting up an office and bringing on board a branding expert to refresh the Pump's logo, website, and the look and feel of its restaurants.

With a view to reducing complexity, Eskin pared the Pump's menu from 150 items to a focused selection of healthy foods.[4] As he continued to make changes to the Pump over the next four years, he saw an opportunity to make a major pivot for the chain.

He recalled: "I quickly realized, there was an untapped market for the way I personally like to eat: fresh, vegetable-driven food you can eat every day. So, in 2011, I rebranded the business as Dig Inn with a completely new menu focused on local, seasonal produce at an accessible price point."[5]

Eskin noted that while the Pump's high-protein, low-fat foods were appealing to the bodybuilder crowd, there was a general perception that these healthy foods were "low-taste" for a broader audience. His key insight was that healthy food could be tasty. Dishes such as braised beef with fresh oregano and red wine vinegar, shaved red cabbage with mustard seed and Italian parsley, and apple-braised Swiss chard with walnuts could deliver nutrition deliciously. "People want more flavor—eating is an experience for all to enjoy," Eskin said.

Customer response to the rebranding of the Pump to Dig was great: "So far, the response has been fantastic," said Eskin. "People have become a lot more knowledgeable about food and health over the last decade, particularly when it comes to where their food comes from and how it is prepared—they seem to really appreciate the work that goes into our . . . philosophy."[6]

3. "Top Rated Diets of 2019: The Pump Energy Food," Diets in Review, 2019, https://www.dietsinreview.com/diets/the-pump-energy-food/#6E5k0UBm8tRvUbFY.99.

4. Adrianne Pasquarelli, "Restaurant Exec Is Pumping It Up," *Crain's New York Business*, May 14, 2008, https://www.crainsnewyork.com/article/20080514/FREE/864604780/restaurant-exec-is-pumping-it-up.

5. "Meet Adam Eskin of Dig Inn in Back Bay, Downtown Crossing and Prudential Center," *Boston Voyager*, March 27, 2018, http://bostonvoyager.com/interview/meet-adam-eskin-dig-inn-back-bay-downtown-crossing-prudential-center/.

6. Yvo Sin, "Pump Energy Changes Name, Not Mission, in Bringing Locally Grown Food to New Yorkers," WLNY-TV, October 19, 2011, https://newyork.cbslocal.com/2011/10/19/pump-energy-changes-name-not-mission-in-bringing-locally-grown-food-to-new-yorkers/.

DIG'S BUSINESS MODEL: DELICIOUS LOCAL FOOD AT AN AFFORDABLE PRICE POINT

At the intersection between traditional full-service restaurants and fast-food joints, the fast-casual sector is small but rapidly growing. It comprises restaurants that typically feature over-the-counter service but are more upscale than fast-food chains like McDonald's or Burger King, in terms of decor, service, and menu. Indeed, a fair share of the segment focuses on healthier ingredients than traditional fast food has, and the average fast-casual consumer is looking for healthier options.[7] As a result, the typical fast-casual meal costs $12, more than twice the average fast-food check size of $5.[8] The sector is still small, accounting for only 7.7 percent of the $780 billion in restaurant sales in 2016,[9] but it is growing meteorically. In 2018, within the top five hundred chain restaurant groups in the United States, fast-casual chains generated $42.2 billion in revenue, up 8 percent from the year before.[10]

At first glance, Dig is similar to many restaurants in the fast-casual sector, but there are some key differences. "We don't think of ourselves as a fast-casual chain," remarked Asmat. Indeed, Dig's concept differs from that of other fast-casual restaurants in key ways. The company focuses on intentional sourcing—a process that focuses on real relationships with small and minority-owned farms, creating fair contracts and helping those farmers become more sustainable.

Eskin described an early challenge: "One of our initial struggles was figuring out what types of dishes to serve on our menu—what our customers wanted, and what felt like 'us.' We tried juices, shakes, soups, sandwiches. After a lot of trial and error, we arrived at a menu that's perfect for Dig: choose-your-own bowls made from wholesome mains and sides that are way more sustaining than salad. We want to serve the kind of food you'd expect in a home-cooked meal—just made by our chefs!"[11]

To ensure the company could stay true to this mission while producing appealing menus, Dig hired a chief culinary officer, Matt Weingarten, who designed menus, including gourmet mains and sides,[12] and decided to price its meals in the $10 range. Exhibit 1 includes a menu for Dig in September 2019. Staying profitable at this price point is a challenge, and it requires a finely tuned value chain, from local farms where food is harvested and processed, to restaurants where it is cooked and served to customers.

7. "Fast Casual Industry Analysis 2019—Cost & Trends," Franchise Help, 2019, https://www.franchisehelp.com/industry-reports/fast-casual-industry-analysis-2018-cost-trends/.
8. "Fast Casual Industry Analysis 2019."
9. "Fast Casual Industry Analysis 2019."
10. Jonathan Maze, "Fast-Casual Chains Are Still Growing," *Restaurant Business*, May 2, 2019, https://www.restaurantbusinessonline.com/financing/fast-casual-chains-are-still-growing.
11. "Meet Adam Eskin of Dig Inn." Original quote referred to "Dig Inn," which was replaced with "Dig" to reflect the new branding.
12. Meagan McGinnes, "A New York City-Based Farm-to-Counter Chain Will Open in Boston Next Week," Boston.com, July 5, 2016, https://www.boston.com/culture/restaurants/2016/07/05/nyc-farm-table-restaurant-chain-open-boston-month.

EXHIBIT 1 Dig Inn—menu

Source: https://www.diginn.com /menu/

THE VALUE CHAIN: FROM FARMERS TO CHEFS TO CONSUMERS

At the very top of the value chain lie the local farmers from whom Dig sources its produce. Dig usually takes a collaborative approach to working with these farmers and sits down with them regularly to map out annual demand and place orders for fulfillment over the seasons. This allows the company to nurture its partners and be as efficient as possible in the way it procures its products. Each day, farmers and partners deliver produce to Dig's Supply Center and then send it out to the restaurants. Dig estimates that it can take as few as three days for produce to be picked, refrigerated, driven to Dig restaurants, and prepared by a team of chefs in a restaurant. In 2019, Dig is projected to purchase nine million pounds of vegetables from more than 130 farmers and partners and ranchers, including 100,000 from Dig Acres, Dig's Farm.

A key part of Dig's value chain is its ability to work with and nurture these partners, and to balance customer needs and tastes with the changing availability of produce in every season. Considerable skill is required to take the pulse of customer's likes and translate these tastes into seasonal menus. In the words of Adam Eskin:

> Our chefs face a challenge when cooking with produce that varies with the seasons. It's not one-size-fits-all cooking in our restaurants—our chefs have to respond to the raw ingredients and adjust recipes based on what they receive fresh from the farm. This type of cooking takes more time to teach, especially for our chefs-in-training, many of whom have never cooked professionally before. We recognize this challenge and are committed to mentoring our trainees—from knife skills classes to trips to the Dig Farm.[13] We do this not only to maintain the quality of our food but to help our team members grow their culinary careers.[14]

When it comes to food preparation, Dig also does things differently. "Everything is cooked in the restaurant, and every Dig employee is given training in food preparation, with a special focus on knife skills," Asmat noted. This means every employee can, and does, step in to help with food preparation when required. "It's important for us that every employee have that experience with the food we serve, but it also means we need to hire more carefully than our competitors. The skill set required to work at Dig is broader than at an average fast-casual restaurant."

Preparing every item fresh in every restaurant considerably complicates the staffing challenge. Indeed, Dig has to make sure that every restaurant is adequately staffed not only to serve its customers but also to prepare the food. This task is made tougher by the fact that demand at Dig is very variable and can depend on the time of day, the time of year, the weather, local events, and many other factors.

Staffing is not the only aspect of a Dig restaurant that is structured with a food-first mentality. Each Dig restaurant is uniquely designed, and a significant part of the restaurant's space is fashioned to ensure fresh food can be prepared, stored, and served. Finished items are portioned into large steel bowls and stocked on shelves behind a long counter, designed to show off the items and serve customers efficiently.

The majority of orders at Dig include a bowl, comprising one base (chosen from three options), two market sides (chosen from around eight options), and a main (chosen from around six options), but customers can also order any of those items alone. Dig also sells a variety of drinks and snacks.

Food ordering and provision are the last crucial links in Dig's value chain. The bulk of Dig's orders happen in-store, as described earlier, but Dig quickly realized there was a lot of value to be captured from off-site orders too. In particular, customers can order food through Dig in three ways besides in-store. They can use the app to place an order for pickup in-store; they can place an order for delivery; and, finally, Dig has a catering menu for larger orders.

Initially, these modalities relied heavily on Dig's existing infrastructure for in-store orders. Dig contracted with third-party services to deliver items, and customers

---

13. Dig's farm is called Dig Acres.
14. "Meet Adam Eskin of Dig Inn." Original quote referred to "Dig Inn," which was replaced with "Dig" to reflect the new branding.

could use those services to order from Dig. These options were immediately successful; seven years after its opening, no less than 30 percent of sales at the East 52nd Street restaurant came from deliveries.[15] There were, however, some issues: Considering every possible option in constructing a Dig bowl, there are approximately 1,500 possible Dig bowls customers might order, leaving ample room for errors, which are impossible to fix once the bowl has left the restaurant. Temperature is also an issue; in-store orders are consumed directly. Others might spend fifteen to sixty minutes sitting and being transported before they are consumed.

As Dig's fast-casual business took off, the team was eager to continue to innovate and push the boundaries on how customers experienced Dig. As they pored over customer feedback and industry trends, it became evident that delivery was a major area of opportunity. Online food delivery was an $84.6 billion industry in 2018,[16] but Dig's investigations revealed that customers were tolerating a substandard experience, from soggy food to delayed deliveries with minimal communication. To tackle this challenge, Dig beta launched Room Service in 2019—a brand-new, reimagined delivery service, with an entirely new menu and platform, built and optimized specifically for delivery.

In April 2019, Eskin and his team were looking to expand Dig beyond its current three-city footprint. Another twenty-four units were envisioned, supported by an investment of $20 million—$15 million of which came from Danny Meyer's Enlightened Hospitality Investments equity fund. Dig had previously raised $30 million in a Series D fund led by Avalt, with Monogram Capital Partners and Bill Allen, the former CEO of OSI Restaurant Partners.[17]

As part of the strategy to expand, the Dig team wanted to ensure that it had visibility over every aspect of its value chain. Entering new markets such as Philadelphia, for example, would require piecing together a new supply chain that included local farmers, finding locations, hiring staff, and designing menus and work schedules.

THE MOVE TO DATA-DRIVEN

Exciting as those expansion plans were, they would come with their own set of challenges. Intuition, skill, and experience are powerful tools. Unfortunately, they come with a downside: they cannot scale.

"We've historically had a measured approach to growth," said Asmat. "Being in New York and having restaurants in one place allowed us to have consistency in food and culture. Launching in Boston was our first take at seeing if we can maintain our standards outside the city. We needed to find local leadership that could represent the brand. We also needed to get used to reducing our reliance on geographic proximity without sacrificing our commitment to consistency."

15. Elizabeth G. Dunn, "Dig Inn Wants to Optimize Your Sad Desk Lunch," *Bloomberg Businessweek*, January 29, 2019, https://www.bloomberg.com/news/features/2019-01-29/dig-inn-wants-to-optimize-your-sad-desk-lunch.

16. "Online Food Delivery Market Report, Global Industry Overview, Growth, Trends, Opportunities and Forecast, 2019–2024," Marketwatch.com, September 2019, https://www.marketwatch.com/press-release/online-food-delivery-market-report-global-industry-overview-growth-trends-opportunities-and-forecast-2019-2024-2019-09-09-2197408.

17. Danny Klein, "Danny Meyer's Fund Invests $15M in Dig Inn," *QSR*, April 2019, https://www.qsrmagazine.com/fast-casual/danny-meyer-s-fund-invests-15m-dig-inn.

In a new world with many more restaurants, Dig found it more difficult to concurrently use intuition on every restaurant for every decision. Dig would have to start leaning more heavily on its data to assist in decision-making, and Asmat's team would have to figure out how to use data to inform decisions at every stage in the value chain.

In some sense, though, using data to make decisions would only be the last stage of this journey for Dig. Many accounts of data-driven decision-making focus on the last mile: using insightful dashboards and complex predictive analytic models, for example. But these efforts need a foundation to rest on—a solid, unified, trustworthy data asset that can act as a source of truth for the entire company.

Dig is no exception, and Asmat was only too aware of this:

> It's so easy to fool yourself into thinking collecting data is the same as collecting *useful* data, but as soon as you start analyzing it, you quickly realize how painful it can be. Take one example—our HR data. Out of necessity, we've gotten to a point where we use multiple systems to track our employees and their hours. So asking simple questions like "on average, how many workers work at each restaurant?" can take one of my most talented analysts half a day. They first need to query each dataset, combine the results, and then spend a significant amount of time to ensure their results are correct.

This is often a frustrating place to be for companies trying to make better use of their data, and it is tempting to think these growing pains can be avoided by being more rigorous with data from the start. But it's rarely so simple. "Looking back, I don't think I'd have done much differently." Asmat said. "It would have been foolish to spend valuable time and resources on this when we were trying to grow and find our identity. Frankly, I feel that the fact we even collected any data at all in our early days puts us ahead of the curve!" In fact, if Dig had wanted to focus on this earlier, it is unclear whether the company would have been able to. It is difficult to build a solid data foundation in a vacuum, without people to use it day to day and suggest incremental improvements. It's easy to think these issues only affect large legacy companies with huge amounts of data and lumbering infrastructures, but no one is immune.

This is only one example of the issues that can arise. Comparing simple metrics across datasets can be a challenge. For example, consider "net sales"—does that include online orders? What about returns, refunds, and credits? And, of course, things get more complicated when you start to compare completely different datasets, for example, in assessing the impact of staffing on sales.

Before they could systematically use their data to assist decision-making, Asmat's team had to create processes that would take these disparate data assets and combine them into a database that could be used to quickly and efficiently answer questions—a "source of truth." "Much of our work so far has been around getting our infrastructure ready to support these decisions," said Asmat, "and we've invested considerable resources into making this happen—including a team of data engineers that works closely with my team."

A key part of creating such a database is deciding what tools to use to host it. The scale of data at most companies today makes simple desktop tools such as

Microsoft Excel or *Microsoft Access* inadequate. Thankfully, there is a veritable cottage industry of companies that provide cloud-based solutions for precisely this purpose. Among others, Dig uses *Google BigQuery* and *Looker*. Exhibits 2 and 3 provide screenshots of these tools as used by Asmat's team at Dig.

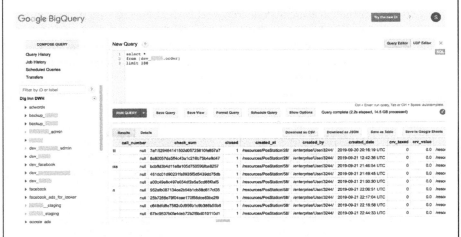

EXHIBIT 2 Screenshot of Dig's *BigQuery* environment

Note: Confidential details have been obscured.
Source: Dig

EXHIBIT 3 Screenshot of Dig's *Looker* instance

Note: Confidential details have been obscured.
Source: Dig.

Beyond the technical hurdles, culture can also get in the way of these efforts. Launching a project too early, based on a faulty data foundation, can backfire if it comes face to face with savvy executives who know their data inside out. As soon as they detect issues with initial results, their trust in the entire project is likely to vanish.

"We're so fortunate at Dig," Asmat said,

> in that the whole company is on board with making the company more data driven, from our CEO Adam Eskin down. Everyone understands it's an incremental process, and that there will be hiccups along the way, and they're very supportive of our push to build a solid data foundation first. I've personally found we've built a lot of goodwill by being fully transparent with the entire company. Instead of going away and working in isolation, we focus on small, achievable goals like producing dashboards that will be immediately useful, and we keep everyone up to date on our progress.

This is often a winning strategy. From a theoretical perspective, it is tempting to attempt an ambitious top-down redesign of every system and every dataset from the start. Such approaches often fail for a number of reasons. First, it is easy to underestimate the amount of work that will be required from the outset, which can result in multiple costly delays. Second, a top-down redesign sometimes requires tearing up current systems and starting from scratch—this means there is little to show until the very end of the project, which can exacerbate the impact of delays. Third, a company's operations and corresponding data collection frameworks are rarely static—with a time-consuming top-down approach, the reality on the ground is likely to change before the project is complete, and by the time it is delivered, it is likely to be out of date. Finally, in implementing a top-down approach, it can be tempting to silo the efforts from the rest of the company after the initial project-planning phase. This is invariably a bad idea—even the most thorough project plans are unlikely to capture every complexity in a business.

Dig's approach was designed to avoid these pitfalls. By focusing on specific, pressing goals, Asmat and her team would be forced to maintain tight contact with relevant teams, and to produce directly actionable work at every step. Of course, the overall project from start to finish might take longer, but the results are guaranteed to produce value every step of the way.

Asked for examples, Asmat's eyes lit up.

> For a start, one of our most important decisions is what to put on our menu. We love rolling with the seasons—we change our menu seasonally, and often run short specials driven by what our farmers produce. Historically, we've always relied on our sales data to issue a weekly report tracking each product's performance. Unfortunately, these were static reports produced by one-off analyses, and over the years they grew into a mess of spreadsheets and *Google Docs*. So when it came to making decisions for the future based on year-on-year data, we just had to rely on our intuition, which could be biased by our preferences.

For example, we're a pretty healthy bunch at Dig, and there's a running joke in the office that we eat conspicuously less mac and cheese than the rest of America! Using our new data foundation, we can pull up historical product performance data, and I've lost track of all the times we've used this to make smarter decisions about what special to run (sometimes nixing things that sounded fun to us, but that the data revealed wouldn't perform very well). I can even think of one instance where what we discovered affected our marketing efforts—our customers *loved* our Thanksgiving special, and so we really leaned in to the concept.

Or here's another example, in a completely different area. One of our priorities at Dig is training our staff and helping them grow in their careers. One of the key indicators that a member of staff might be struggling is if they often fail to show up for their shifts. In the past, calculating the number of no-shows was a deeply laborious process, because it involved combining datasets from two sources—first, data from our scheduling system to check if the employee was *supposed* to show up, and then data from our payroll system to see if they *actually* showed up. Now that we've put the systems on the same footing, it's amazing how granular we can get. Not only can we identify individual employees of concern, we can also use a restaurant's performance as an indicator of the culture there and take remedial action if any location is lagging. Finally, we can provide valuable insights to our training team—if some specific roles tend to lead to more no-shows, perhaps we need to re-frame the role or how we train for it.

Oh, and how could I forget food waste? We obviously want to make sure we use every last bit of food we order, but figuring out how much food a restaurant is wasting used to be such a headache. We had to combine sales data from every ordering system—in-store, delivery, catering, etc.—use it to figure out how much we *should* have ordered and then compare it to data from our ordering system to figure out how much we *did* order (you won't be surprised to hear we have multiple ordering systems too). And don't even get me started on how hard it was to compare these metrics across restaurants. Now, we can quickly rank our restaurants in order of how wasteful they are, and help our struggling restaurants learn from our efficient ones.

Exhibit 4 shows an example of one of the dashboards Asmat's team built as part of this effort, to track the performance of Dig's supply chain over time. Before this latest effort, producing the dashboard might have taken an analyst the better part of a week. Now that the team has unified the datasets from which this dashboard feeds, it constantly updates and provides valuable insights to Dig's management team in real-time.

EXHIBIT 4 Screenshot of Dig's weekly supply chain report

Note: Parts of the image have been blurred and units have been obscured to hide confidential information. These plots do *not* simply represent item demand.

Source: Dig.

As Dig embarked on its expansion, Asmat's eyes were firmly set on empowering everyone at Dig—from management to team members in restaurants—with the wealth of data she and her team had available. There was a lot of work left to do, but given the payoff so far, she was confident her approach of working hand-in-hand with the business would produce results that would be worth the effort. "Come back next year and let's have this conversation again; you won't be able to stop me after just three examples!"

5.4 THE DATA

The files you downloaded in section 5.2 contain a year's worth of simulated data at Dig's New York City restaurants. Note that to protect Dig's proprietary information, the data are synthetic—you may notice that the restaurants therein are based on real Dig locations but do not match up exactly. Let's go through each of the datasets and understand their contents. Some of these datasets are too large to open in Excel, so you'll have to trust us that they do indeed contain the columns we say they do; you'll see this for yourself in section 5.6.1.

- The Restaurants.csv dataset contains data pertaining to each restaurant. It contains the following columns:
    - RESTAURANT_ID: the unique ID of the restaurant
    - NAME: the restaurant name
    - ADDRESS: the restaurant address
    - LAT: the restaurant latitude
    - LONG: the restaurant longitude
    - OPENING_DATE: the date on which the restaurant opened
    - DELIVERY_START: the date on which the restaurant started processing delivery orders

- The Items.csv dataset lists the items sold by Dig. These include items that might be in bowls as well as items that might be bought separately (like sides and desserts). Note that all items that can be ordered as part of a bowl can also be ordered separately as a side. This file contains the following columns:
    - ITEM_ID: the unique ID of the item
    - ITEM_NAME: the name of the item
    - ITEM_TYPE: the type of the item (main/side/sauce/cold side/dessert/drink)

- The Simplified orders.csv file is the largest of all the files you downloaded. It contains one line per order in the one-year period spanned by the dataset; as you can imagine, this file is quite large; so large, in fact, that it is difficult to ascertain how many lines it contains. You'll have to wait until section 5.6.1 to learn how to figure that out.

  Most orders in this file will contain a bowl (Dig's main offering). Each bowl contains the following components:

  - A base (salad, farro, or rice)
  - A main (chicken, beef, etc.)
  - Two sides (mac and cheese, carrots, etc.)

  In addition, each order might also contain one or more cookies, and one or more drinks. Sometimes, orders will *only* contain cookies and drinks, if no bowl is ordered.

  Note that this is a considerably simplified account of the way orders truly work at Dig (hence, the "Simplified" in the file name). In reality, some bowls may contain multiple servings of a given item, some items can be ordered separately as sides, and some orders may contain more than one bowl. We shall not consider these complexities for the purposes of this book.[3]

  The dataset contains the following columns:

  - ORDER_ID: the unique ID of the order
  - DATETIME: the date and time the order was placed
  - RESTAURANT_ID: the unique ID of the restaurant at which the order was made. Corresponds to RESTAURANT_ID in the Restaurants.csv table.
  - TYPE: the type of the order (IN_STORE, PICKUP, or DELIVERY)
  - DRINKS: the number of drinks in the order
  - COOKIES: the number of cookies in the order
  - MAIN: the ITEM_ID of the main in the bowl in this order. Corresponds to ITEM_ID in the Items.csv table. If the bowl contains two mains, this column will contain one of those two mains at random. If the order does not include a bowl, this value will simply be missing.
  - BASE: the ITEM_ID of the base of the bowl in this order. Corresponds to ITEM_ID in the Items.csv table. If the bowl contains two bases, this column will contain one of those two bases at random. If the order does not include a bowl, this value will simply be missing.
  - SIDE_1 and SIDE_2: the two sides in the bowl in this order. Corresponds to ITEM_ID in the Items.csv table. If the order does not include a bowl, these values will simply be missing.

- The `Summarized orders.csv` file aggregates the large order file to a daily level. It contains one row per restaurant per day on which the restaurant was open, and it contains the following columns:

    - `location`: the name of the location in question
    - `day`: the day this row pertains to
    - `number of orders`: the number of orders at that restaurant on that day
    - `percentage of deliveries`: the percentage of orders on that day that were delivery orders

As you might have surmised from the case study, one of the key data challenges at Dig (and, indeed, at any organization looking to do more with its data) is enabling key decision makers to query their data in the most efficient way possible. One way to do this is to summarize large datasets (like `Simplified orders.csv`) into smaller ones (like `Summarized orders.csv`) that can be analyzed more easily. By the time you're done with part 2, you will be equipped with all the skills you need to do this yourselves (see section 9.6 for details).

5.5 THE PANDAS LIBRARY

The main data analysis workhorse in Python is a library called `pandas`. It was developed by Wes McKinney, and now boasts an active community of users who constantly improve and expand on the library's functionality (and answer questions on Stack Overflow).

In part 2 of this book, we will no longer be using Python's command line interface. Instead, we will be creating a *Jupyter Notebook* for each chapter and run our code therein. The book's website contains one *Jupyter Notebook* for each chapter that contains the code for that chapter. As we learned in section 5.3.4, code in later cells can sometimes rely on code in earlier cells, so you should run the code in each notebook in order. For now, create a *Jupyter Notebook* in the folder in which you downloaded this chapter's file in section 5.2 (likely the code folder you created on your desktop in part 1).

Once you have your notebook, begin by importing `pandas` into Python as follows:

```
import pandas as pd
```

As a reminder, the second part of this expression will enable us to refer to pandas as pd in the future, instead of having to type pandas every time.

The pandas library makes two new data types available to us that will form the basis of our work with data:

- The Series, which can store *columns*.
- The DataFrame, which collects multiple series (columns) together with their column titles to give us a full table.

The following figure illustrates the structure of a DataFrame:

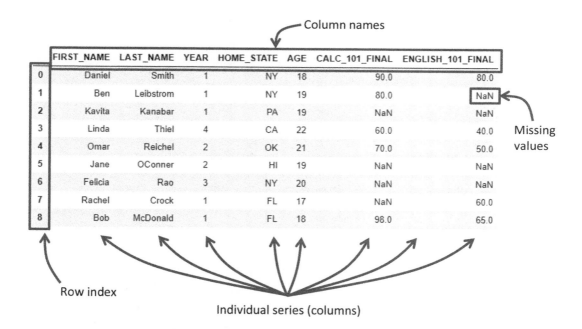

Each column is stored in a series with an associated column title. The row index (which we will discuss in more detail in section 5.5.3) contains the name of every row; by default, the row index starts at 0 and increases by 1 for each row, but the rows could be given other names. NaN denotes missing values in pandas (this stands for "not a number"); we shall later discuss how to handle missing data.

5.5.1 pandas DataFrames

We usually will read DataFrames directly from files (e.g., Excel files, or CSV files) and we will learn how to do that in section 5.6. Before we get into that, let's begin with a simpler example—it is possible to create a DataFrame directly in pandas using a dictionary of lists, in which each entry in the dictionary corresponds to a column and contains a list of entries. Create a new cell in *Jupyter*, type the following code (this is a lot to type; you can copy this text from https://www .pythonformbas.com/df_students), and run it:

```
students = (
    {'FIRST_NAME': ['Daniel', 'Ben', 'Kavita', 'Linda',
                    'Omar','Jane', 'Felicia', 'Rachel',
                    'Bob'],
     'LAST_NAME': ['Smith', 'Leibstrom', 'Kanabar', 'Thiel',
                   'Reichel', 'OConner', 'Rao', 'Crock',
                   'McDonald'],
     'YEAR': [1, 1, 1, 4, 2, 2, 3, 1, 1],
     'HOME_STATE': ['NY', 'NY', 'PA', 'CA', 'OK', 'HI',
                    'NY','FL', 'FL'],
     'AGE': [18, 19, 19, 22, 21, 19, 20, 17, 18],
     'CALC_101_FINAL': [90, 80, None, 60, 70, None, None,
                        None, 98],
     'ENGLISH_101_FINAL': [80, None, None, 40, 50, None,
                           None, 60, 65]} )
df_students = pd.DataFrame(students)
```

The first statement creates a dictionary in which each entry corresponds to a column and provides every value in that column. Notice that because the statement is so long, we split it over the first fifteen lines of the code snippet. How do we tell Python these lines are all part of the same statement? We can simply put an opening parenthesis at the end of the first line, and a closing parenthesis at the end of the last line. Python then ignores any line break between these two parentheses.

The second statement goes into the pandas package (which, remember, we can refer to as pd) and creates a DataFrame from the dictionary. It then stores the result in a variable called df_students.

Finally, create a new cell and run the following code therein to display the DataFrame:

```
df_students
```

	FIRST_NAME	LAST_NAME	YEAR	HOME_STATE	AGE	CALC_101_FINAL	EI
0	Daniel	Smith	1	NY	18	90.0	
1	Ben	Leibstrom	1	NY	19	80.0	
2	Kavita	Kanabar	1	PA	19	NaN	
3	Linda	Thiel	4	CA	22	60.0	
4	Omar	Reichel	2	OK	21	70.0	
5	Jane	OConner	2	HI	19	NaN	
6	Felicia	Rao	3	NY	20	NaN	
7	Rachel	Crock	1	FL	17	NaN	
8	Bob	McDonald	1	FL	18	98.0	

Notice pandas and *Jupyter Notebook* work together to display your DataFrame in a nice, tidy fashion.

5.5.2 Accessing Columns as Series

Now that we have created a DataFrame, we can access the individual series in this DataFrame in two ways. The first is to simply put the name of the column in square brackets:

```
df_students['FIRST_NAME']
```

```
0        Daniel
1           Ben
2        Kavita
3         Linda
4          Omar
5          Jane
6       Felicia
7        Rachel
8           Bob
Name: FIRST_NAME, dtype: object
```

The second is to simply put a dot after the name of the DataFrame, followed by the name of the column. (Note that to simplify formatting, we'll sometimes print code without displaying it in a *Jupyter Notebook* cell. Nevertheless, you should still run the code in *Jupyter* as shown earlier.)

```
df_students.FIRST_NAME
```

Which method you use is mostly a matter of preference. In some situations, however, the first method works better. For example, suppose we wanted to access a column whose name was another variable—we would do this as follows:

```
i = 'HOME_STATE'
df_students[i]
```

Trying to get an analogous result using `df_students.i` would not work, because `pandas` would look for a column called `i` instead of looking at the string inside that variable. Similarly, if a column name contains spaces, the second method can't be used.

Notice that when retrieving a single series, the output is not formatted as a pretty table as it was when we printed out a whole DataFrame—instead, it is printed out as plain text. This is a telltale sign that you are printing a series (a single column) instead of a DataFrame (multiple columns).

Having said that, consider the following code:

```
df_students[['FIRST_NAME']]
```

	FIRST_NAME
0	Daniel
1	Ben
2	Kavita
3	Linda
4	Omar
5	Jane
6	Felicia
7	Rachel
8	Bob

Notice the key difference between the two outputs. In the first case, we were putting a string inside the square brackets, and telling pandas to "select the column with the name in the string and return the series." Because the result is a series, it is printed as plain text. In the second case, we are providing a *list* inside the square brackets, and telling pandas "give me another DataFrame, that contains only the columns in the list." Because the result is a DataFrame (albeit one with a single column), it gets printed in a pretty format.

The following figure might clarify these two modes. The expression on the left selects a single column from a DataFrame and extracts it as a series. The expression on the right selects a subset of the existing columns and returns them as a DataFrame. How does pandas know what you're trying to do? It looks at the *type* of the object you put in between square brackets—on the left, the bit in between the square brackets is a string, and pandas can recognize you want a series with a single column. On the right, the bit between the square brackets is a list, and pandas can recognize you want a DataFrame.

```
df_students[ 'FIRST_NAME' ]          df_students[ [ 'FIRST_NAME' ] ]
              String                              List
```

With this newfound knowledge, we can select *two* columns instead of one. Can you guess how? ◆ (Remember, when you see a diamond in part 2 of the book, put down the book for a second and see whether you can figure out what to do before reading on):

```
df_students[['FIRST_NAME', 'LAST_NAME']]
```

	FIRST_NAME	LAST_NAME
0	Daniel	Smith
1	Ben	Leibstrom
2	Kavita	Kanabar
3	Linda	Thiel
4	Omar	Reichel
5	Jane	OConner
6	Felicia	Rao
7	Rachel	Crock
8	Bob	McDonald

A COMMON ERROR

A common **pandas** error occurs when you try to select multiple columns in a **pandas** DataFrame but forget to put a *list* inside the square brackets. Consider, for example, the following code:

```
df_students['FIRST_NAME', 'LAST_NAME']
```

The code should give you an error. Because this is the first **pandas** error we're encountering, it's worth acknowledging that **pandas** errors are usually rather long and intimidating. Here's our tip for reading them—scroll all the way to the bottom. The most relevant part is usually at the very end.

In this case, looking to the end of the error, we see the following:

```
KeyError: ('FIRST_NAME', 'LAST_NAME')
```

pandas has identified that the error comes from the column names—the argument in the square brackets is a *string*, and so **pandas** looks for a single column with the name (`'FIRST_NAME'`, `'LAST_NAME'`). This column, of course, doesn't exist, and so **pandas** throws an error. The correct thing to do is to include *two* square brackets (i.e., put a list in between the square brackets) to let **pandas** know we want to find multiple columns.

5.5.3 Row Index and Column Names

Every column in a pandas DataFrame has an associated name; this should be a familiar concept. Perhaps less familiar is the fact that every pandas *row* also has an associated *row name* (collectively called the *row index*). By default, the row name is simply equal to the row number, but it will sometimes be useful to use different names.

Altering the column names or row index is easy. Suppose we wanted to change the name of the ENGLISH_101_FINAL column to ENGLISH_101_FINAL_SCORE—we can run:

```
df_students.columns = ['FIRST_NAME', 'LAST_NAME', 'YEAR',
        'HOME_STATE', 'AGE', 'CALC_101_FINAL',
        'ENGLISH_101_FINAL_SCORE']
```

Run this line of code and look at the DataFrame. You will find the column names have changed accordingly. Similarly, suppose we wanted the row index to number rows starting from 1 instead of 0, we could run:

```
df_students.index = [1,2,3,4,5,6,7,8,9]
```

Look at the `df_students` DataFrame now—you will see the row index has changed.

It is quite inconvenient to have to specify the name of *every* column to change a single one. Thankfully, there's a way to modify the name of one column only. Suppose we wanted to revert the change we made above, we could run the following:

```
df_students.rename(columns={'ENGLISH_101_FINAL_SCORE':'ENGLISH_101_FINAL'})
```

LAST_NAME	YEAR	HOME_STATE	AGE	CALC_101_FINAL	ENGLISH_101_FINAL
Smith	1	NY	18	90.0	80.0
Leibstrom	1	NY	19	80.0	NaN
Kanabar	1	PA	19	NaN	NaN

This is our first time applying a function to a DataFrame, so it is worth taking stock of what we did. First, we type `df_students.rename` to access the `rename()` function, and apply it to `df_students`. (This is similar to the way you would type `a.upper()` to apply the `upper()` function to a string a.) Next, we pass a single argument to that function called `columns`. This argument is a dictionary, in which the keys are the old column names you'd like to change, and the values are the corresponding new column names. The output reflects the new column name.

Let's take another look at the DataFrame:

```
df_students
```

AME	YEAR	HOME_STATE	AGE	CALC_101_FINAL	ENGLISH_101_FINAL_SCORE
Smith	1	NY	18	90.0	80.0
strom	1	NY	19	80.0	NaN
nabar	1	PA	19	NaN	NaN

You may wonder why the old column name is back. What happened? It turns out that the `rename()` function (and indeed most other pandas functions we will look at) does not change the underlying DataFrame. These functions simply return a *new* version of the DataFrame, leaving the original underlying DataFrame unchanged. This is similar to the behavior in the following code:

```
name = 'Daniel'
name.upper()
```

```
'DANIEL'
```

```
name
```

```
'Daniel'
```

The line `name.upper()` returns the string in uppercase, but it doesn't actually modify the variable.

Often, you *do* want to modify the original DataFrame. In this book, we shall always do this by assigning the result of the function back to the original DataFrame:[4]

```
df_students = (
    df_students.rename(columns={'ENGLISH_101_FINAL_SCORE'
                                : 'ENGLISH_101_FINAL'}) )
```

`df_students` will now contain the new DataFrame with the new column name.

One final point—we will sometimes want to reset the row index (the names of the rows) back to the default (0 upwards). We can do this using the following code:

```
df_students = df_students.reset_index(drop = True)
```

Once again, we need to assign the result of the function to `df_students` to make sure we alter the original DataFrame. Why do we need `drop = True`? Without this argument, a new column will be created in the resulting DataFrame containing the *old index* (the one being replaced). Give it a try to see it in action.

5.5.4 .head() and .shape

When a large dataset is loaded into `pandas`, it is often useful to be able to look at the first few rows only. We can do this using the `head()` function:

```
df_students.head()
```

	FIRST_NAME	LAST_NAME	YEAR	HOME_STATE	AGE	CALC_101_FINAL	EI
0	Daniel	Smith	1	NY	18	90.0	
1	Ben	Leibstrom	1	NY	19	80.0	
2	Kavita	Kanabar	1	PA	19	NaN	
3	Linda	Thiel	4	CA	22	60.0	
4	Omar	Reichel	2	OK	21	70.0	

It is also useful to find the size of a DataFrame. We can do this using the shape attribute:

```
df_students.shape
```

```
(9, 7)
```

The result of this expression is a Python tuple (which you can think of as a read-only list; for details, see the box "Tuples" in section 3.5.1) in which the first component is the number of rows, and the second component is the number of columns. To access only the number of rows, for example, you can use `df_students.shape[0]`. (You could also simply use `len(df_students)` to find the number of rows.)

TO USE OR NOT TO USE PARENTHESES

You might have noticed an inconsistency in the features we discussed. In some cases, like `head()` and `reset_index()`, we need to include parentheses (round brackets). In others, like `shape`, or when we retrieve a column as a series, we do not include parentheses.

There are underlying reasons for this, but they don't really help us figure out when to use parentheses and when not to. Instead, we want to teach you to recognize what happens when you've made a mistake, so you can fix it.

Try the following two lines of code, in which parentheses are *not* required, but you include them:

```
df_students.FIRST_NAME()
df_students.shape()
```

In both cases, you will get an error. Using our earlier tip and scrolling to the end of the error, you will find the key words "`is not callable`" in both cases. These words are the key indicator that you have included parentheses when they are not required. By including parentheses, you are asking Python to *call* a function, but `df_students.FIRST_NAME` and `df_students.shape` are not functions—they are a series and a tuple, respectively. Thus, Python tells you they are not *call*able.

What about the other way around? Try the following line:

```
df_students.reset_index
```

Python does *not* give you an error, but it also doesn't produce the expected result (a DataFrame). Instead, you get a load of text that begins "**bound method . . .**" In this context, you can think of "method" as being another word for "function," and this is Python's way of telling you that you have a function but have not included parentheses.

A lack of parentheses can manifest in one last way. Suppose you wanted to first reset the index, and then access the `FIRST_NAME` column. The correct way to do this is as follows:

```
df_students.reset_index(drop = True).FIRST_NAME
```

We first reset the index on the DataFrame, which results in a DataFrame, and then access the `FIRST_NAME` column. This is called *chaining* pandas commands, and it is a strategy we'll be using again and again.

What happens if we forget the parentheses in this chained statement? Run this code:

```
df_students.reset_index.FIRST_NAME
```

We get an error that begins as follows:

```
'function' object has no attribute . . .
```

This is another telltale sign you have forgotten parentheses somewhere in your chained statement.

5.5.5 Code Completion in *Jupyter Notebook*

As we promised earlier, we will now discuss a final feature of *Jupyter Notebook*—code completion—that will quickly become one of your favorites.

To see this feature at work, create a new cell, type the letters df_s into the cell, and press the Tab key on your keyboard. Notice how *Jupyter Notebook* magically completes the name of the variable automatically, saving you the need to type the rest. *Jupyter* automatically figures out df_students is the only variable that starts with the characters df_s, and it automatically completes the variable name.

What happens if multiple variables start with these characters? Let's create a variable called df_surfboard to test this:

```
df_surfboard = 1
```

Then, type df_s and Tab in a new cell:

```
df_s
df_students
df_surfboard
```

You will notice *Jupyter Notebook* brings up a dropdown menu with all the variables that might fit the bill. You can use your arrow keys to navigate the list, and press Enter when you've found the one you want.

In case you're not yet rubbing your hands in glee and singing a chorus of "hail to *Jupyter Notebook*," don't worry—there's more.

Not only will *Jupyter* autocomplete variable names, it will also look *inside* pandas DataFrames to autocomplete code. To see this in action, create a new cell and type df_students.E and press Tab. Notice how *Jupyter* automatically realizes you are trying to access the ENGLISH_101_FINAL column and autocompletes it for you. If multiple columns fit the bill, the same kind of dropdown would appear.

Not singing yet? Don't worry, we're not done yet.

Jupyter Notebook will also autocomplete function names. Suppose, for example, you wanted to rename the columns in df_students. Create a new cell, type df_students.re and Tab. The following will appear:

```
df_students.re
    reindex
    reindex_like
    rename
    rename_axis
    reorder_levels
    replace
    resample
    reset_index
```

Notice that you can apply a number of functions to DataFrames that start with a lowercase re (if there were column names that started with re, they would also appear in the list).

One final feature we'll mention before we close. Create a new cell, type df_students.rename, hold down the Shift key, and press Tab twice in quick succession. The following dialog will pop up:

This contains the full documentation for the function; it turns out you can do this for *any* function in Python, which can come in handy if you ever need a quick reminder. (Note that the full documentation will probably seem a little intimidating at this point, so we're not expecting you to read the whole thing from start to finish; as you get more comfortable with pandas, you'll understand more and more of it.)

DOCUMENTING YOUR OWN FUNCTIONS WITH DOCSTRINGS

In part 1, we discussed how you could create your own functions. You might wonder what would happen if you used *Jupyter* to view the documentation for a function you created. First, create the following simple function, which simply adds two numbers:

```
def add_numbers(a, b):
    return a+b
```

Now, create a new cell, type add_numbers, and press Shift, Tab, Tab. The following will appear:

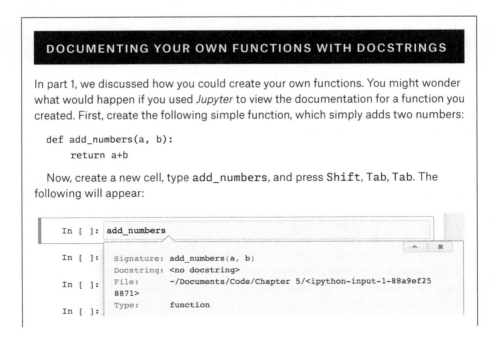

> Unsurprisingly, no documentation appears because you didn't include any. Including it is quite easy; you just need to include it between sets of triple quotes at the start of the function (this is called a *docstring* in Python):
>
> ```python
> def add_numbers(a, b):
>     '''
>     This function takes two numbers, a and b, and returns
>     the sum
>     '''
>     return a+b
> ```
>
> Now run that cell again to redefine the function with the new comment, and try to bring up the documentation again—you'll notice your docstring will appear there.

5.6 READING AND WRITING DATA

Thus far, we have been using the `df_students` DataFrame, which we created using a dictionary. It will sometimes be useful to create a DataFrame in this way, but in most business applications, the data need to be read from files and saved back to files that can be shared as required. In this section, we consider how to carry out these reading and writing operations in pandas.

5.6.1 Reading Data

Let's start simple—the `Students.xlsx` file contains an Excel version of the dataset we created in section 5.5. To load it into `pandas`, we can use the `read_excel()` function. Note that this will only work if you correctly created your *Jupyter Notebook* in the part 2 folder. If not, you have to list the full path of the file in the quotes:[5]

```python
df_students = pd.read_excel('raw data/Students.xlsx')
```

Running this line won't produce any output, but `df_students` will now contain the DataFrame that was read from the file. If an Excel workbook has multiple sheets, `pandas` also will allow you to specify which sheet to read. In this case, the only sheet in the workbook is `Sheet 1`, so we didn't need to specify this. But we could have written the following:

```python
df_students = pd.read_excel('raw data/Students.xlsx',
                            sheet_name='Sheet 1')
```

As with many other `pandas` functions, `read_excel()` provides a dizzying number of options, and covering them all could take up an entire chapter of this book. Thankfully, the `pandas` documentation is very informative. Google "pandas read_excel" (or use the feature we discussed in section 5.5.5 to display the documentation)—you will find instructions for reading data from Excel files with multiple sheets, no headers, and much more.

Another file format you might encounter is the CSV format. Let us, for example, move to the Dig case study and consider the summarized order data file, which is provided as a CSV. We can load this using the `read_csv()` function, and look at a few rows using `head()`:

```
df_summarized_orders = pd.read_csv('raw data/Summarized orders.csv')
df_summarized_orders.head()
```

	location	day	number of orders	percentage of deliveries
0	Bryant Park	2018-01-01	373	0.0
1	Bryant Park	2018-01-02	789	0.0
2	Bryant Park	2018-01-03	818	0.0
3	Bryant Park	2018-01-04	782	0.0
4	Bryant Park	2018-01-05	719	0.0

You'll notice the column names include spaces and are rather long. It would be cumbersome to type the entire name every time you wanted to refer to one of these columns. We therefore rename them to something more manageable:

```
df_summarized_orders.columns = ['RESTAURANT_NAME',
                                'DATE', 'NUM_ORDERS',
                                'PERC_DELIVERY']
```

We can similarly load the restaurant and items datasets as follows:

```
df_items = pd.read_csv('raw data/items.csv')
df_restaurants = pd.read_csv('raw data/restaurants.csv')
```

Finally, let us load the order dataset from the Dig case study. The data are provided in a CSV format but compressed in a zip file. You might be pleasantly surprised to hear that you won't even need to unzip the file—pandas can read data directly from a compressed file. Try the following code, which will load the file and print the size of the dataset.

```
df_orders = pd.read_csv('raw data/Simplified orders.zip')
df_orders.shape
```

This dataset is large and might take up to thirty seconds to load. We see, however, that it contains more than 2.38 million rows. We're starting to see the power of pandas.

We have discussed Excel and CSV files, but pandas can read many other formats. If you encounter a new kind of file you need to read, the likelihood is that pandas has a function that will let you read it—creative Googling will help you find it. In fact, we will introduce a third kind of file (the *pickle*) in the next section.

5.6.2 Writing Data

In later chapters, we will be using pandas to transform, modify, and summarize our dataset. Doing this in pandas will not modify the underlying file from which we loaded the data. Sometimes, we will want to export our data back to files so that we can keep them for future analysis or share them with others; pandas makes this easy.

Let's consider exporting a pandas DataFrame to a CSV file—this is useful if you want to share the file with someone who will open it in Excel. Let's export the summarized order dataset with its new column names:

```
df_summarized_orders.to_csv('Chapter 5/Summarized orders new.csv')
```

The string in the function is the file path, followed by the name of the file the DataFrame will be saved to. Notice that we are saving the file in the "Chapter 5" folder. If you open the resulting Excel file, you will notice that the file is saved with the row index in the first column. This is often unnecessary, especially if the row index is just the row number. To tell pandas to save the file without this row index, use the following:

```
df_summarized_orders.to_csv(
            'Chapter 5/Summarized orders new.csv', index=False)
```

One of the downsides of saving a file as a CSV is that it loses a lot of the work we might have done in Python. For example, in section 5.7, we will discuss how to specify the type of each column in our pandas DataFrame. If we do this and then save the file as a CSV, we would lose all that work and have to do it again the next time we load the CSV.

Thankfully, Python provides a different file type—the pickle—that allows us to preserve any Python variable, including a DataFrame, and reload it exactly as it was. (Get it? Like a pickle is a preserved cucumber.) To save a DataFrame as a pickle, we simply use the to_pickle() function as follows:

```
df_students.to_pickle('Chapter 5/df_students.pickle')
```

You will notice the file df_students.pickle will have been created in the location that you specified in the function—in this case, your "Chapter 5" folder. This file cannot be opened in Excel. It can only be read back into Python, using the pd.read_pickle() function:

```
pd.read_pickle('Chapter 5/df_students.pickle')
```

	FIRST_NAME	LAST_NAME	YEAR	HOME_STATE	AGE	CALC_101_FINAL	El
0	Daniel	Smith	1	NY	18	90.0	
1	Ben	Leibstrom	1	NY	19	80.0	
2	Kavita	Kanabar	1	PA	19	NaN	
3	Linda	Thiel	4	CA	22	60.0	
4	Omar	Reichel	2	OK	21	70.0	
5	Jane	OConner	2	HI	19	NaN	
6	Felicia	Rao	3	NY	20	NaN	
7	Rachel	Crock	1	FL	17	NaN	
8	Bob	McDonald	1	FL	18	98.0	

The resulting DataFrame will be *exactly* the same DataFrame that was saved to the pickle.

> ### PICKLES AND PANDAS VERSIONS
>
> If you try to open a new Excel file in an old version of Excel, you might come across some issues. The same is true of a pickle file. If you save a pickle and try to open it in a new version of pandas, you might encounter some cryptic errors. There are ways to fix this, but they are far beyond the scope of this book. For our purposes, make sure you stick to the same versions of Python and pandas when saving and loading your pickle files. If you encounter any error with the pickle files on this book's website, please let us know. We will be sure to include versions that work with all recent version of pandas.

5.7 COLUMN TYPES

In section 2.7.1, you were introduced to the concept of data types. Python keeps track of the *kind* of data each variable contains, whether it be a float, an integer, or a string. The same is true in pandas—each column has a type, and pandas keeps track of what it is.

To see the type of each column, we can use the info() function:

```
df_orders.info()
```

```
<class 'pandas.core.frame.DataFrame'>
RangeIndex: 2387224 entries, 0 to 2387223
Data columns (total 10 columns):
 #   Column         Dtype
---  ------         -----
 0   ORDER_ID       object
 1   DATETIME       object
 2   RESTAURANT_ID  object
 3   TYPE           object
 4   DRINKS         float64
 5   COOKIES        float64
 6   MAIN           object
 7   BASE           object
 8   SIDE_1         object
 9   SIDE_2         object
dtypes: float64(2), object(8)
memory usage: 182.1+ MB
```

Each column has an associated type—the object type is shorthand in pandas for "I have no idea what this is." Strings show up as having the object data type.

pandas is generally pretty good at figuring out what the type of each column is. You'll notice, in the previous example, that pandas automatically figured out that the DRINKS and COOKIES columns were numeric. In theory, it should have made those columns integers rather than floats (because the number of cookies and drinks is always a whole number), but for various complicated reasons related to missing values, pandas generally doesn't like storing columns as integers. Instead, it uses floats, which will work just fine for our purposes.

One column, however, pandas has *not* correctly identified: the DATETIME column. According to the previous output, this column is being treated as a simple string column, much like the TYPE column. This can't be right—a date is surely much more structured than a simple string column.

When pandas gets the type of a column wrong, we need to help it out. In the case of a datetime column, we can do this using the to_datetime() function, as follows:

```
df_orders.DATETIME = pd.to_datetime(df_orders.DATETIME)
```

Let's dissect this statement. We first extract the DATETIME column from the df_orders dataset as a series, and then we pass it to the pd.to_datetime() function. This will take the series and convert every entry to a datetime (note that this is a new datatype that we did not encounter in part 1). The column is then replaced by this new, formatted column. We have not yet discussed editing columns (we'll cover this formally in section 6.8.3), but the syntax is pretty self-explanatory.

Now run df_orders.info() again. You'll notice that the type of the DATETIME column is now datetime64[ns].

Looking at the actual DataFrame, however (using df_orders.head()), you might notice that nothing has changed. So, what was the point of going through this? You'll have to wait to section 6.7.5 to find out. For a quick preview, consider the following line of code:

```
df_orders.DATETIME.dt.day_name().head()
```

```
0       Thursday
1       Thursday
2       Saturday
3       Saturday
4         Sunday
Name: DATETIME, dtype: object
```

Now that pandas realizes that the DATETIME column is a date, it is able to extract information about that date, like the day of the week. We couldn't have done this on the original string column. We'll see much more of this shortly.

This discussion might leave you with many questions. What kind of date and time formats can the pd.to_datetime() accept? In the previous DataFrame, the original strings we loaded looked like this: 2018-10-11 17:25:50. What if our dates came in the following format instead: 11Oct18 05:25:00pm? We will let you investigate these other formats on your own, but you will find that pd.to_datetime() is surprisingly versatile.

To illustrate this versatility, let's convert the DATE column in df_summarized_orders to a date. Let's first remember what the table looks like:

```
df_summarized_orders.head()
```

	RESTAURANT_NAME	DATE	NUM_ORDERS	PERC_DELIVERY
0	Bryant Park	2018-01-01	373	0.0
1	Bryant Park	2018-01-02	789	0.0
2	Bryant Park	2018-01-03	818	0.0
3	Bryant Park	2018-01-04	782	0.0
4	Bryant Park	2018-01-05	719	0.0

Notice that the date is in a different format—it doesn't include a time. Nevertheless, the pd.to_datetime() function can easily handle it (the table won't look any different, but a key change will have happened—instead of being stored as a string, the DATE column will now be stored as a datetime):

```
df_summarized_orders.DATE = (pd.to_datetime(df_summarized_orders.DATE) )
df_summarized_orders.head()
```

	RESTAURANT_NAME	DATE	NUM_ORDERS	PERC_DELIVERY
0	Bryant Park	2018-01-01	373	0.0
1	Bryant Park	2018-01-02	789	0.0
2	Bryant Park	2018-01-03	818	0.0
3	Bryant Park	2018-01-04	782	0.0
4	Bryant Park	2018-01-05	719	0.0

5.8 WRAPPING UP

In this chapter, we introduced pandas as Python's primary data processing library. We discussed pandas series and DataFrames, and we looked at their structure. Finally, we discussed how files can be read and written from various files.

So far so good, but perhaps you found this to be slightly unimpressive. At this stage, the only real benefit we have reaped from using pandas is the ability to open large datasets. Other than that, it looks like a lot of overhead and a lot of trouble for not much benefit. In the next chapter, we'll begin reaping the real benefits of data analytics in Python, and you'll see how Dig could use these features to answer some key business questions.

Before we close, let us save the files we worked on in this chapter to pickle files, so that we can use them in the next chapter.

Run the following code to save these files to your "Chapter 5" folder:

```
df_students.to_pickle('Chapter 5/students.pickle')
df_orders.to_pickle('Chapter 5/orders.pickle')
df_summarized_orders.to_pickle(
    'Chapter 5/summarized_orders.pickle')
df_items.to_pickle('Chapter 5/items.pickle')
df_restaurants.to_pickle('Chapter 5/restaurants.pickle')
```

6

EXPLORING, PLOTTING, AND MODIFYING DATA IN PYTHON

WE'VE INTRODUCED pandas and discussed how it stores, reads, and writes data. But we haven't yet discussed how to do anything with the data once we've loaded it. The story of Dig, which you read about in chapter 5, is brimming with questions: both about Dig's data and, more broadly, about Dig's business.

In this chapter, we will finally reap the rewards of using pandas. We will use it to explore Dig's data, plot it, and, if needed, modify it, and we will use these techniques to answer a number of questions using the Dig dataset. For example, we will find out how many of Dig's orders are delivery orders, versus pickup orders, versus in-store orders; which of Dig's restaurants are most popular; how order volumes vary by day of week and time of year. Recall that the dataset we will be using to answer these questions is enormous. Yet, we will obtain the answers to most of these questions in mere seconds.

To ensure that we can focus on learning the relevant parts of pandas, most of the questions we'll be discussing in this chapter will be simple ones, formulated directly in terms of Dig's data. In chapter 9, we will consider more complex questions formulated in terms of Dig's business.

6.1 WHAT YOU'LL LEARN IN THIS CHAPTER

By the end of this chapter, you will have mastered most of pandas' basic functionality. We begin by discussing how to sort pandas DataFrames and how to plot them.

We consider the functionality pandas makes available for exploring your data and filtering it. The next part of the chapter will look at operating on columns and editing pandas DataFrames. Finally, we give you some practice with more examples based on specific business questions introduced in Dig's story.

6.2 WHAT YOU'LL NEED FOR THIS CHAPTER

Before we start, begin by creating a new *Jupyter Notebook* for this chapter in the part 2 folder you created in section 5.2 (see section 5.3.1 for a reminder on how to create a notebook). The first thing we'll do is load the files we saved at the end of chapter 5. To do this, paste the following code in the first cell, and run it (you might also want to name the file appropriately, and add a title to it, as we discussed in section 5.3.3):

```
import pandas as pd
df_students = pd.read_pickle('Chapter 5/students.pickle')
df_orders = pd.read_pickle('Chapter 5/orders.pickle')
df_summarized_orders = (
    pd.read_pickle('Chapter 5/summarized_orders.pickle') )
df_items = pd.read_pickle('Chapter 5/items.pickle')
df_restaurants = (
    pd.read_pickle('Chapter 5/restaurants.pickle') )
```

As ever, the *Jupyter Notebook* for this chapter, as well as the files from the last chapter, are available on the book's website.

6.3 SORTING DATA IN PANDAS

We begin by discussing a simple but crucial operation: sorting data in pandas.

We begin with the simplest form of sorting. Let's recall what the df_students DataFrame looked like:

```
df_students.head()
```

	FIRST_NAME	LAST_NAME	YEAR	HOME_STATE	AGE	CALC_101_FINAL
0	Daniel	Smith	1	NY	18	90.0
1	Ben	Leibstrom	1	NY	19	80.0
2	Kavita	Kanabar	1	PA	19	NaN
3	Linda	Thiel	4	CA	22	60.0
4	Omar	Reichel	2	OK	21	70.0

Suppose we wanted to sort df_students by HOME_STATE. We can write the following:

```
df_students.sort_values('HOME_STATE')
```

	FIRST_NAME	LAST_NAME	YEAR	HOME_STATE	AGE	CALC_101_FINAL
3	Linda	Thiel	4	CA	22	60.0
7	Rachel	Crock	1	FL	17	NaN
8	Bob	McDonald	1	FL	18	98.0
5	Jane	OConner	2	HI	19	NaN
0	Daniel	Smith	1	NY	18	90.0

Notice that the output is now sorted in increasing alphabetical order. To reverse this order, we can simply pass the ascending=False argument to the sort_values() function, like this: ◆

```
df_students.sort_values('HOME_STATE', ascending=False)
```

	FIRST_NAME	LAST_NAME	YEAR	HOME_STATE	AGE	CALC_101_FINAL
2	Kavita	Kanabar	1	PA	19	NaN
4	Omar	Reichel	2	OK	21	70.0
0	Daniel	Smith	1	NY	18	90.0
1	Ben	Leibstrom	1	NY	19	80.0
6	Felicia	Rao	3	NY	20	NaN

A few important notes on the output:

- The row index is shuffled when the data are sorted. Each row *keeps* its initial name. Often, it is useful to relabel the rows of the new DataFrame to number from zero upward. You can do this using the `reset_index()` function, with `drop=True` to ensure that the initial index is not added as an extra column (see section 5.5.3 for a reminder):

```
df_students.sort_values('HOME_STATE').reset_index(drop=True)
```

- Running the `sort_values()` function does *not* alter the underlying DataFrame. If you look at `df_students` after running the previous operations, you will find that it has maintained its original order. To permanently sort the DataFrame, you need to assign the result back to the DataFrame as follows:

```
df_students = ( df_students.sort_values('HOME_STATE')
               .reset_index(drop=True) )
```

Sorting by two columns is just as simple; we simply pass a list of columns to the `sort_values()` function. ◆

```
df_students.sort_values(['HOME_STATE', 'LAST_NAME'])
```

	FIRST_NAME	LAST_NAME	YEAR	HOME_STATE	AGE	CALC_101_FINAL
0	Linda	Thiel	4	CA	22	60.0
1	Rachel	Crock	1	FL	17	NaN
2	Bob	McDonald	1	FL	18	98.0
3	Jane	OConner	2	HI	19	NaN
5	Ben	Leibstrom	1	NY	19	80.0

Notice that within each HOME_STATE, the rows are sorted by LAST_NAME.

When sorting a *series* (a single column), there's no need to specify a column name—sort_values() can be used by itself:

```
df_students.CALC_101_FINAL.sort_values()
```

```
0      60.0
7      70.0
5      80.0
4      90.0
2      98.0
1      NaN
3      NaN
6      NaN
8      NaN
Name: CALC_101_FINAL, dtype: float64
```

One last note—sometimes, instead of sorting by one of the columns, you will want to sort by the row index (the row names). You can easily do this using the sort_index() function:

```
df_students.sort_index()
```

	FIRST_NAME	LAST_NAME	YEAR	HOME_STATE	AGE	CALC_101_FINAL	EↃ
0	Linda	Thiel	4	CA	22	60.0	
1	Rachel	Crock	1	FL	17	NaN	
2	Bob	McDonald	1	FL	18	98.0	
3	Jane	OConner	2	HI	19	NaN	

At this point, this might not seem so useful to you. Why would we ever seek to sort a DataFrame by row numbers? We will later consider situations in which the row index contains much more than row numbers, and this operation will become very useful indeed.

6.4 PLOTTING DATA IN PANDAS

Plotting in Python is an enormous topic. In this book, we cover what you'll need to build some impressive plots without focusing on too much of the technical details. Bear in mind that what we cover in this book is only a fraction of what's available. This section focuses on the mechanics of creating plots, but it might seem a little dry until we are able to apply these mechanics to the Dig case in the rest of the chapter.

Begin by loading Python's plotting libraries as follows:

```
import matplotlib.pyplot as plt
```

The easiest way to produce a plot is directly from a pandas series.[1] Try the following:

```
df_students.CALC_101_FINAL.plot(kind='bar')
```

```
<matplotlib.axes._subplots.AxesSubplot at 0x1312c0350>
```

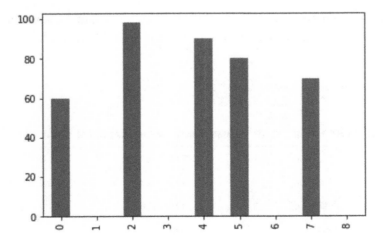

Let's understand what is happening. First, we write df_students.CALC_101_ FINAL, which returns a *series* containing the CALC_101_FINAL column. The index of this series is simply the same as the index of the DataFrame it comes from. Finally, we call plot(kind='bar') on this series. Python will plot a bar chart in which the *x*-axis is the row index, and the *y*-axis corresponds to the values. Notice that missing values simply lead to missing bars.

Of course, bar charts are not the only available plots, and we'll introduce a number of others in what follows.

By itself, this plot is of dubious use, because the index doesn't mean much. Try the following code, however:

```
df_students.index = df_students.LAST_NAME
df_students.CALC_101_FINAL.plot(kind='bar')
df_students = df_students.reset_index(drop=True)
```

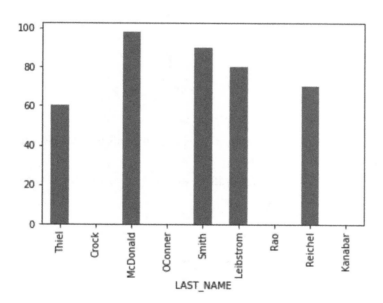

The first line sets the index of the DataFrame to be the last name (see section 5.5.3). The second line plots the CALC_101_FINAL column, using the new index as the *x*-axis. Finally, we use reset_index() to reset the index back to what it was originally—the row number.

Having to alter the index every time we want to produce a plot with a meaningful *x*-axis seems cumbersome, and indeed, pandas allows us to apply plot() directly to a DataFrame to make the process more seamless:

```
df_students.plot(x='LAST_NAME',
                 y='CALC_101_FINAL', kind='bar')
```

`<matplotlib.axes._subplots.AxesSubplot at 0x124622250>`

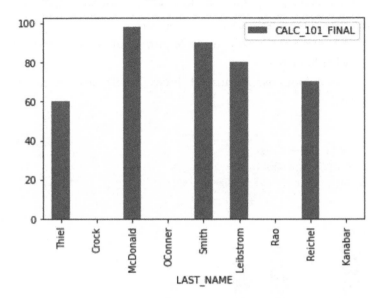

When `plot()` is applied to a DataFrame, it accepts arguments for the columns that should be used on the *x*- and *y*-axis.

This covers the basics of plotting in `pandas`—we'll return to this topic again and again throughout the rest of the chapter.

6.5 EXPLORING DATA IN PANDAS

We spent a great deal of time, in our introduction to Dig, discussing the importance of creating a dataset that provides a single source of truth—a basis upon which our analysis can lie. In creating this dataset, the first step is to take stock of our data, explore it, and understand it inside out. `pandas` makes many tools available to do this.

6.5.1 The value_counts() Function

The first function we'll explore—and one of the functions we use most often in pandas—is the `value_counts()` function. It can be applied to any series and will tell you how often each value occurs in the series. For example, let's return to the orders table in the Dig case:

```
df_orders.head()
```

	ORDER_ID	DATETIME	RESTAURANT_ID	TYPE	DRINKS	COOKIES	M/
0	O1820060	2018-10-11 17:25:50	R10002	IN_STORE	1.0	2.0	N
1	O1011112	2018-05-31 11:35:00	R10003	IN_STORE	0.0	0.0	N
2	O752854	2018-04-21 18:12:57	R10001	DELIVERY	0.0	2.0	

Suppose we would like to find out what values the TYPE column contains, and how many of each value it contains. We can use the following piece of code:

```
df_orders.TYPE.value_counts()
```

```
IN_STORE     1713136
PICKUP        401440
DELIVERY      272648
Name: TYPE, dtype: int64
```

We first refer to the `df_orders` DataFrame and then access the TYPE column. Finally, we call the `value_counts()` function.

This result tells us that there are three values in the TYPE column, and it tells us how often each one appears. We immediately see that most orders are in-store orders, but we do have a fair number of pickup and delivery orders.

The `value_counts()` function also can display these frequencies as proportions. Try adding `normalize=True` as an argument: ◆

```
df_orders.TYPE.value_counts(normalize=True)
```

```
IN_STORE      0.717627
PICKUP        0.168162
DELIVERY      0.114211
Name: TYPE, dtype: float64
```

Thus, we see that 72 percent of orders are in-store orders.

TECHNICAL REMINDERS

First, recall that there are two ways to access columns in **pandas** (see section 5.5.2 for a reminder). Here, we used the dot notation, but we could have used the following alternative notation:

```
df_orders['TYPE'].value_counts()
```

The results are identical.

Second, carefully look at the output of the **value_counts()** function. You might have noticed it is not formatted as a pretty table. This is a telltale sign the output is a series, not a DataFrame. The row index of this series contains the unique entries in the column, and the value in each row is the number of times this unique entry occurs.

Just to solidify our understanding, try to carry out a **reset_index()** on the resulting series. Before you do, try and figure out what the output will be. ◆

```
df_orders.TYPE.value_counts(normalize=True).reset_index()
```

	index	TYPE
0	IN_STORE	0.717627
1	PICKUP	0.168162
2	DELIVERY	0.114211

The result is now a DataFrame, with the index added as a column in that DataFrame.

Using the plotting functionality we learned in section 6.4, we can visualize these data in a graph: ◆

```
( df_orders.TYPE.value_counts(normalize=True)
 .plot(kind='bar') )
```

`<matplotlib.axes._subplots.AxesSubplot at 0x131c07290>`

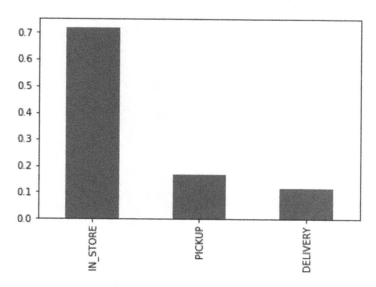

Make sure you understand every step of this expression. We first access the TYPE column as a series; we then apply `value_counts()` to it, which returns a series with a row index corresponding to the unique entries in that column; and, finally, we plot this series. The row index appears on the *x*-axis, and the frequency on the *y*-axis. It might be helpful to run each part of this chained command individually before you run the whole thing to understand what each part is doing.

Let's now move on to another question: Which of our restaurants achieves the highest sales volume? And which lags behind? Can you figure out how to answer this before looking at our solution? ◆

One way to answer this question is to run a `value_counts()` on the RESTAURANT_ID column in the `df_orders` dataset. This will count the number of orders at each restaurant in the timescale spanned by our data: ◆

```
df_orders.RESTAURANT_ID.value_counts().plot(kind='bar')
```

`<matplotlib.axes._subplots.AxesSubplot at 0x121484c10>`

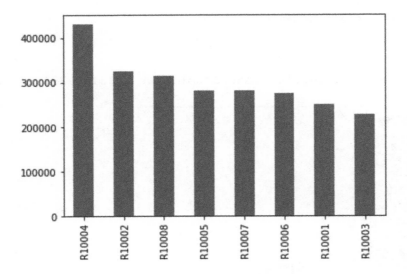

It looks like restaurant R10004 is the most active, whereas restaurant R10003 is the least active. Looking at the df_restaurants table, we find that these are the NYU and Bryant Park restaurants, respectively. In chapter 7, we will see how to obtain those restaurant names automatically without needing to look them up manually.

As a final exercise, let's find out how many times each restaurant appears in the df_summarized_orders table. ♦ Let's recall what the table looks like:

```
df_summarized_orders.head()
```

	RESTAURANT_NAME	DATE	NUM_ORDERS	PERC_DELIVERY
0	Bryant Park	2018-01-01	373	0.0
1	Bryant Park	2018-01-02	789	0.0

Luckily, we see the table already includes restaurant names. Now let's see how often each restaurant appears: ♦

```
df_summarized_orders.RESTAURANT_NAME.value_counts()
```

```
Upper West Side     365
NYU                 365
Flatiron            365
Midtown             365
Williamsburg        365
Columbia            365
Upper East Side     355
Bryant Park         261
Name: RESTAURANT_NAME, dtype: int64
```

Most restaurants appear 365 times in this table, which we would expect, because the table should contain one row for each day of the year for each restaurant. How are we to explain the number of rows for the Upper East Side and Bryant Park restaurants, then?

For the Bryant Park restaurant, we note that the number of rows is 365 − (52 × 2) = 261. Because there are fifty-two weekends every year, and two days per weekend, it seems that Bryant Park might be closed on weekends. How might we verify whether this is indeed what is happening? We would have to ensure that the dataset contains no rows for Bryant Park on weekends. Unfortunately, we don't have the tools to do that yet, but we will very soon (section 6.7.5).

It is worth taking stock of the process we just went through—we first ran `value_counts()` to see whether the data looked reasonable. In so doing, we found an inconsistency. We then hypothesized where the inconsistency might come from, and finally, we identified another option we could carry out to verify whether our hypothesis was correct. This process is a fundamental part of working with data, and we encourage you to apply this approach to any new dataset you encounter.

Before we close, how might we explain the 355 rows for the Upper East Side restaurant? We might posit that this restaurant is closed on national holidays, and we will later see how to verify this.

6.5.2 Describing Numerical Columns and Plotting Histograms

The `value_counts()` function is invaluable, but it's not particularly useful for numerical columns. For example, consider the NUM_ORDERS column in the summarized order data, and run `value_counts()` on it:

```
df_summarized_orders.NUM_ORDERS.value_counts()
```

You should find that the result includes more than 797 rows; in fact, we can find the number of rows ♦ using shape:

```
df_summarized_orders.NUM_ORDERS.value_counts().shape
```

```
(797,)
```

Why so many? The NUM_ORDERS column can contain many different unique values, since any store may observe many possible numbers of orders on any given day, and each of these unique values occupies a row in the value_counts() series.

Instead, pandas makes a describe() function available, which calculates some summary statistics for a numerical column:

```
df_summarized_orders.NUM_ORDERS.describe()
```

```
count    2806.000000
mean      850.756949
std       195.490367
min       200.000000
25%       739.000000
50%       833.000000
75%       949.000000
max      1396.000000
Name: NUM_ORDERS, dtype: float64
```

Thus, we see that the mean of the NUM_ORDERS column is 851 orders per day, with a standard deviation of 195 orders. If you have taken a statistics class, you know that most of the time, values lie within two standard deviations of the mean. This could provide a useful mechanism that Dig could use to check whether orders are abnormally high or low on any given day at a given restaurant. Alarms might ring if orders dropped below 461 orders per day or went above 1,241 orders per day.[2]

What if we want to produce a plot describing a numerical column?

The first, perhaps simplest plot is a boxplot, which you can produce as follows:

```
df_summarized_orders.NUM_ORDERS.plot(kind='box')
```

`<matplotlib.axes._subplots.AxesSubplot at 0x10d9de990>`

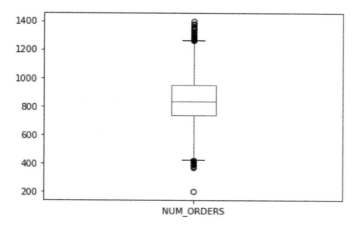

For those unfamiliar with these plots, the line in the middle represents the median of the column (in this case, just over 800). The upper and lower parts of the box represent the upper and lower quartiles of the data. The two whiskers extend one and a half times the width of the box either side of the box. Finally, any points outside the whiskers are *outliers*, which are plotted separately.

Box and whisker plots can be useful, but we also might be looking for a more detailed plot that actually shows the distribution of values the variables can take. A histogram does exactly that—it plots values of the numerical column on the *x*-axis, and the frequency of those values on the *y*-axis. Try this:

```
df_summarized_orders.NUM_ORDERS.plot(kind='hist')
```

`<matplotlib.axes._subplots.AxesSubplot at 0x131af09d0>`

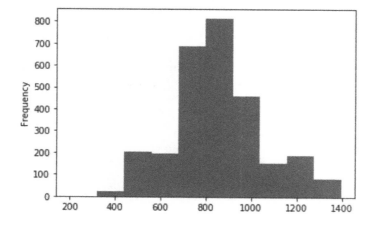

We see that most days experience around 800 sales per day, with some outliers either side of that average. We shall explore this later.

To make the histogram finer, we can use the `bins` argument, which controls the number of individual bins, or bars, in the histogram: ♦

```
df_summarized_orders.NUM_ORDERS.plot(kind='hist', bins=30)
```

`<matplotlib.axes._subplots.AxesSubplot at 0x121706b10>`

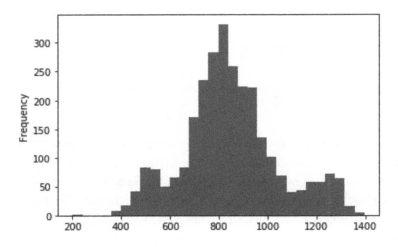

This finer histogram makes it even clearer that there seems to be three "groups" of days: those with around 500 orders, those with around 800 orders, and those with around 1,300 orders.

One thing you might have noticed about these histograms is that their *y*-axes have different scales—the numbers are much lower in the second one. This is because the height of each bar simply counts the number of points in that bucket. It stands to reason that when the buckets get narrower (as in the second histogram), there are fewer observations in each one.

This seems suboptimal. How are we to compare different histograms to each other if they have very different scales? Thankfully, by passing the `density=True` to the `plot()` function, we can change the scale so that all the bars sum to one:

```
df_summarized_orders.NUM_ORDERS.plot(kind='hist', density=True)
```

```
<matplotlib.axes._subplots.AxesSubplot at 0x1218a1790>
```

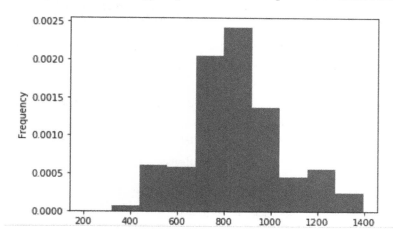

This allows different histograms to be compared.

One might also wonder whether similar insights are available based on the PERC_DELIVERY column (which, you will remember, indicates the percentage of orders in that day at that store that were delivery orders). How might you explore that column? ♦

```
df_summarized_orders.PERC_DELIVERY.hist(bins=40)
```

```
<matplotlib.axes._subplots.AxesSubplot at 0x1218af690>
```

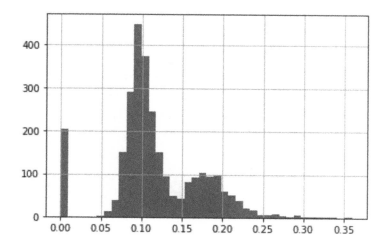

What does this histogram imply? First, we find a large peak at zero—this implies that there is a significant number of days at some restaurants on which no deliveries occur at all. There is another cluster of days on which around 10 percent of orders are deliveries, and finally a cluster on which around 17 percent of orders are deliveries.

At this point, you might be itching with questions: Are all the "o delivery" days at the same restaurants (i.e., do some restaurants just not do deliveries)? Are the number of deliveries related to the weather in any way? Worry not—we shall address these questions and more in what follows.

One last question you might have is whether there is somehow a relationship between these two variables. Perhaps days with more orders tend to also be days with more deliveries, or perhaps these days are driven by greater foot traffic. We can answer these questions using a *pair plot*, as follows:

```
import seaborn as sns
sns.jointplot(x='NUM_ORDERS', y='PERC_DELIVERY',
              data=df_summarized_orders, kind='kde')
```

```
<seaborn.axisgrid.JointGrid at 0x1219d9a50>
```

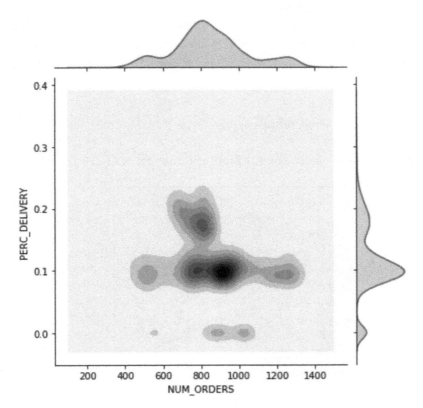

Notice that to produce this plot, we had to import the seaborn library, which adds advanced plotting functionality to Python. The plots in the margins are *density plots*, which you can think of as a continuous version of the histograms in the previous two figures,[3] and the main plot represents cooccurrences of these two variables. The darkness of the figure at any point indicates how many points occur in that area. For example, the very light area at the top-right-hand corner of the plot implies there are almost no days with around 1,400 orders and around 40 percent deliveries.

What do we learn from the plot? It's frankly quite difficult to tell. You certainly could look at the darkest spot on the plot and conclude that the most common combination of these two variables is stores with around nine hundred orders per day, 10 percent of which are deliveries. But it's difficult to conclude much more with any degree of reliability—partly because the very dark spot overwhelms the rest of the plot.

This example illustrates one of the reasons we introduce this kind of pair plot— to encourage caution when using more complex visualization techniques. At the risk of generalizing too broadly, the more complex a visualization is, the more skill is required to use it properly. When you look at the previous plot, would you be able to describe exactly how Python produced it? What determines the height and width of the density plots? How is the distance between the contours calculated? What if you wanted a more granular plot? The more details you don't precisely understand, the more likely something is to go wrong. Compare this to the simple bar charts and histograms we had produced thus far, which were far more straightforward. As a beginner, I'd suggest you follow Mr. Weasley's advice from *Harry Potter and the Chamber of Secrets*: "Never trust anything that can think for itself if you can't see where it keeps its brain." If you're not confident you know how a plot was produced, think twice before using it.

6.5.3 Aggregations

Every function we've considered in this section so far involves *aggregating* the data in some way—both the value_counts() and describe() functions take every value in their respective column—and combine them in some way to produce a result.

There are, of course, many other ways to aggregate data, and pandas is flexible in what it allows us to do. Following are some of the most useful aggregation functions in pandas:[4]

- sum() : sum every value in the column
- max() : find the maximum value in the column
- min() : find the minimum value in the column
- mean() : find the mean (average) of the values in the column
- median() : find the median value in the column
- std() : find the standard deviation of values in the column
- unique().tolist() : return a list that contains the unique elements in that column

For example, we can find the average number of drinks per order in the Dig data as follows: ◆

```
df_orders.DRINKS.mean()
```

```
0.09649031678635939
```

Similarly, to find all the unique restaurants in the df_summarized_orders table, we could simply run the following: ◆

```
df_summarized_orders.RESTAURANT_NAME.unique().tolist()
```

```
['Bryant Park',
 'Columbia',
 'Flatiron',
 'Midtown',
 'NYU',
 'Upper East Side',
 'Upper West Side',
 'Williamsburg']
```

Note that, strictly speaking, we do not need the tolist() at the end of this expression. The unique() function returns something called an *array*, which behaves similarly to a list in Python. Rather than introduce a whole new data type, however, we convert it to a list, which we're more familiar with.

Another useful aggregation function is worth mentioning here—the correlation between two variables. (As a reminder, the correlation between two variables is a number between –1 and 1. A 0 implies no relationship exists between the two variables. A positive number implies that when one variable is high, the other also tends to be high. A negative number implies that when one variable is high, the other tends to be low.) It is slightly different from the previous functions in that it uses *two* columns (and finds the correlation between them) rather than one column. The following code snippet illustrates how to use this function:

```
df_summarized_orders.NUM_ORDERS.corr(
    df_summarized_orders.PERC_DELIVERY)
```

```
-0.1966740921641795
```

You might be wondering whether it is possible to aggregate only *some* of the data in a DataFrame. For example, instead of finding the average number of drinks per order *overall*, we might want to find this average *by restaurant*. pandas is able to carry out these kind of grouped aggregations, which we return to in chapter 8.

6.6 FILTERING DATAFRAMES

Now that we've touched on exploring DataFrames, let's consider another crucial operation—*filtering* DataFrames. We might, for example, want to apply `value_counts()` only to orders at one specific restaurant. This would require first filtering down `df_orders` to orders at that restaurant, and then running a `value_counts()`.

Filtering is actually quite simple. All you need to do is create a list of `True`/ `False` values with as many rows as the DataFrame: `True` for those rows you want to keep, and `False` otherwise. You then put this list between square brackets after the DataFrame name. For example:

```
df_students[ [True, True, False, False, True, False, False, False, True] ]
```

	FIRST_NAME	LAST_NAME	YEAR	HOME_STATE	AGE	CALC_101_FINAL	EI
0	Linda	Thiel	4	CA	22	60.0	
1	Rachel	Crock	1	FL	17	NaN	
4	Daniel	Smith	1	NY	18	90.0	
8	Kavita	Kanabar	1	PA	19	NaN	

Notice that this returns a new DataFrame with the first, second, fifth, and ninth rows from the original DataFrame.

A few things to note:

- Looking at the row index in the resulting table, you will notice that the row index is not reset. Every row keeps the row index it had in the original Data-Frame. If this is undesirable, you can always use reset_index(drop=True).
- Sometimes pandas uses the same notation for different things. In this case, putting square brackets after a DataFrame can mean several things:
  - If the square bracket contains a string, for example, df_orders['DRINKS'], pandas will return a single series corresponding to that column.
  - If the square bracket contains a list, for example, df_orders[['DRINKS', 'COOKIES']], pandas will return a DataFrame containing the columns in the list.
  - If the square bracket contains a list of True/False values (as in the previous example), it will return a filtered DataFrame.
  - Additional ways to use [] notation can cause undue confusion, so we won't go into them here.
- The previous operation does not modify the DataFrame directly, it simply *returns* a filtered version.

That's really all there is to it! We've managed to filter a DataFrame.

Of course, this isn't particularly useful unless we are also able to create interesting lists of True/False values. For example, to filter down to orders at the Columbia restaurant, we would need a list of values that are True if orders in that row were at that restaurant, and `False` otherwise. This might seem a little abstract right now, but will make more sense in section 6.7.3.

6.7 OPERATING ON COLUMNS

In section 6.5, we learned how to explore data in `pandas`. Each of the operations we discussed involved *aggregation*—combining every value in a column to obtain some sort of result.

In this section, we consider operations that apply to every row in a column. For example, how can we add one to each row, or multiply each row by five, or search for a specific string in each row? These operations will underscore many of our analyses.

6.7.1 Arithmetic

Arithmetic is the first, and simplest, kind of operation you might want to carry out on numeric columns in `pandas`. In this respect, `pandas` replicates Python notation almost exactly—you can treat a `pandas` series (column) as if it were a single number and carry out operations accordingly.

For example, suppose Dig buys paper bowls for food service in packs of one hundred and you wanted to figure out the number of packs each restaurant used on each day. You could run the following line of code: ◆

```
(df_summarized_orders.NUM_ORDERS / 100).head()
```

```
0    3.73
1    7.89
2    8.18
3    7.82
4    7.19
Name: NUM_ORDERS, dtype: float64
```

(Notice that we use `head()` on the result to ensure that the result does not take up too much of our screen.)

In addition to carrying out arithmetic between a column and a number like one hundred, we can carry out operations between columns. For example, suppose we want to find the total number of "extras" (cookies or drinks) per order. We can do the following: ♦

```
(df_orders.COOKIES + df_orders.DRINKS).head()
```

```
0    3.0
1    0.0
2    2.0
3    1.0
4    0.0
dtype: float64
```

As another example, suppose we want to calculate the number of nondelivery orders from each store on each day, we would need to multiply the number of orders by the proportion of nondelivery orders, as follows: ♦

```
(df_summarized_orders.NUM_ORDERS *
    (1 - df_summarized_orders.PERC_DELIVERY)).head()
```

```
0    373.0
1    789.0
2    818.0
3    782.0
4    719.0
dtype: float64
```

The comparison to standard Python extends beyond numbers. Just as you can "sum" two strings in Python to combine them, you can do the same thing in pandas. For example, suppose we wanted to create a new series containing—for each order—the order ID followed by a colon followed by the order type (e.g., 01279827:PICKUP). We could do this as follows: ♦

```
(df_orders.ORDER_ID + ':' + df_orders.TYPE).head()
```

```
0    01820060:IN_STORE
1    01011112:IN_STORE
2     0752854:DELIVERY
3     02076864:PICKUP
4    01988898:IN_STORE
dtype: object
```

This operation takes the ORDER_ID column, combines it with the single string containing a colon, and then combines it with the TYPE column.

(Note that if you are trying to do this with columns from two *different* datasets, things can get a little hairy; we'll discuss this in section 7.6.1.)

6.7.2 Missing Values

Let's recall what df_students looks like:

```
df_students.head()
```

	FIRST_NAME	LAST_NAME	YEAR	HOME_STATE	AGE	CALC_101_FINAL	EI
0	Linda	Thiel	4	CA	22	60.0	
1	Rachel	Crock	1	FL	17	NaN	
2	Bob	McDonald	1	FL	18	98.0	
3	Jane	OConner	2	HI	19	NaN	
4	Daniel	Smith	1	NY	18	90.0	

Looking at the CALC_101_FINAL column, we notice that some entries are NaN. This is the way pandas denotes *missing values*. For these specific students, no values exist in that column, presumably because they didn't take the class.

What happens when you try to do arithmetic on columns with missing values? As you might expect, if *any* of the entries are missing, the result also will be missing. Consider the following:

```
df_students.CALC_101_FINAL + df_students.ENGLISH_101_FINAL
```

```
0    100.0
1      NaN
2    163.0
3      NaN
4    170.0
5      NaN
6      NaN
7    120.0
8      NaN
dtype: float64
```

Rows 0, 2, 4, and 7 each had calculus scores *and* English scores; therefore, they have a result in the series. The remaining rows were missing entries in one series, the other, or both; therefore, they appear as missing in the result.

What if we wanted to handle these missing values differently? For example, if we wanted to treat them as zeros? The pandas function called `fillna()` allows us to fill in missing values. For example, recall the content of the CALC_101_ FINAL column:

```
df_students.CALC_101_FINAL
```

```
0     60.0
1      NaN
2     98.0
3      NaN
4     90.0
5     80.0
6      NaN
7     70.0
8      NaN
Name: CALC_101_FINAL, dtype: float64
```

Now, consider this piece of code:

```
df_students.CALC_101_FINAL.fillna(0)
```

```
0     60.0
1      0.0
2     98.0
3      0.0
4     90.0
5     80.0
6      0.0
7     70.0
8      0.0
Name: CALC_101_FINAL, dtype: float64
```

Every missing value has simply been replaced by a zero.

Thus, if we want to perform the previous sum, but with every missing value replaced by a zero, we could run the following code:

```
df_students.CALC_101_FINAL.fillna(0) + (
    df_students.ENGLISH_101_FINAL.fillna(0) )
```

```
0      100.0
1       60.0
2      163.0
3        0.0
4      170.0
5       80.0
6        0.0
7      120.0
8        0.0
dtype: float64
```

Finally, one last function that will be useful is the isnull() function; it returns a series that is as long as the original one. It contains True whenever the corresponding value is missing, and False otherwise. For example:

```
df_students.CALC_101_FINAL.isnull()
```

```
0      False
1       True
2      False
3       True
4      False
5      False
6       True
7      False
8       True
Name: CALC_101_FINAL, dtype: bool
```

The notnull() function does the opposite:

```
df_students.CALC_101_FINAL.notnull()
```

```
0       True
1      False
2       True
3      False
4       True
5       True
6      False
7       True
8      False
Name: CALC_101_FINAL, dtype: bool
```

You might want to do this for two reasons. The first is that this series of True/False values can be used to filter down DataFrames, as we saw in section 6.6. For example, if we wanted to keep only those rows with non-null CALC_101_ FINAL values, we could do the following: ◆

```
df_students[df_students.CALC_101_FINAL.notnull()]
```

	FIRST_NAME	LAST_NAME	YEAR	HOME_STATE	AGE	CALC_101_FINAL	EN
0	Linda	Thiel	4	CA	22	60.0	
2	Bob	McDonald	1	FL	18	98.0	
4	Daniel	Smith	1	NY	18	90.0	
5	Ben	Leibstrom	1	NY	19	80.0	
7	Omar	Reichel	2	OK	21	70.0	

Notice that the DataFrame produced keeps the original index, as we discussed earlier.

The second way this kind of series can be used is by summing it. When you sum a series of True/False values, pandas will interpret all True values as one, and all False values as zero. So for example, to find the number of non-null entries in the CALC_101_FINAL column, you could do the following:

```
df_students.CALC_101_FINAL.notnull().sum()
```

```
5
```

Can you figure out how you might use this to find the total number of orders *with* bowls in the dataset? You will remember that orders *with* bowls are the ones with non-null values in the MAIN column. So, we can try this: ◆

```
df_orders.MAIN.notnull().value_counts()
```

```
True     2275639
False     111585
Name: MAIN, dtype: int64
```

More than two million orders are *with* bowls and around one hundred thousand are *without* them.

Note that we also could have obtained this result by first filtering down the DataFrame to those rows *with* bowls, and then finding the number of rows in the resulting table: ♦

```
df_orders[df_orders.MAIN.notnull()].shape
```

```
(2275639, 10)
```

6.7.3 Logic

The next set of operations we will consider is *logical* operations. These operations will return a series with as many entries as the original series containing True if a certain condition is met, and False otherwise.

We already met an operation of this kind—the isnull() function. You can do the same thing with every comparison operation you learned in section 3.3. For example, suppose we wanted to check whether each order has at least one drink. You could do the following:

```
(df_orders.DRINKS >= 1).head()
```

```
0      True
1      False
2      False
3      True
4      False
Name: DRINKS, dtype: bool
```

Looking back at the original table, you will find that the first and fourth rows have at least one drink, whereas the others do not.

We could similarly figure out whether each order has *exactly* two drinks:

```
(df_orders.DRINKS == 2).head()
```

```
0      False
1      False
2      False
3      False
4      False
Name: DRINKS, dtype: bool
```

Looking at the original table (`df_orders`), we do indeed find that none of the first few rows has exactly two drinks.

At this point, you might be rubbing your hands in glee. Using these capabilities, we can start doing much more interesting filtering on our DataFrames. For example, if we wanted to filter down our DataFrame to orders with cookies, we could do this: ◆

```
df_orders[df_orders.COOKIES > 0].head()
```

	ORDER_ID	DATETIME	RESTAURANT_ID	TYPE	DRINKS	COOKIES	N
0	O1820060	2018-10-11 17:25:50	R10002	IN_STORE	1.0	2.0	
2	O752854	2018-04-21 18:12:57	R10001	DELIVERY	0.0	2.0	
27	O1566571	2018-09-02 18:01:47	R10006	IN_STORE	1.0	1.0	
33	O902238	2018-05-14 13:10:44	R10008	IN_STORE	0.0	1.0	
44	O1085575	2018-06-11 21:11:04	R10004	IN_STORE	0.0	1.0	

Similarly, to find the *number* of orders with cookies, we can proceed in one of two ways. We can either find the shape of the filtered DataFrame or find the sum of the `True/False` series: ◆

```
df_orders[df_orders.COOKIES > 0].shape
```

```
(476507, 10)
```

```
(df_orders.COOKIES > 0).sum()
```

```
476507
```

Similarly, to find the percentage of orders with exactly two drinks, we could do the following: ◆

```
(df_orders.DRINKS == 2).value_counts(normalize=True)
```

```
False      0.988726
True       0.011274
Name: DRINKS, dtype: float64
```

It looks like only 1.1 percent of orders contain exactly two drinks.

In addition to carrying out simple comparisons, we also can combine them with each other. For example, suppose you wanted to find the percentage of orders with at least one drink and *exactly* two cookies. To obtain the former, you would use df_orders.DRINKS >= 1, and to obtain the latter, you would use df_orders. COOKIES == 2. But how might you combine them? You might be tempted to use the and operator, which you encountered when discussing if statements in section 3.2.1. Unfortunately, this is one way in which pandas diverges from standard Python notation; instead of and, it uses the ampersand symbol &. Thus, in this case, the correct line is as follows:

```
( ((df_orders.DRINKS >= 1) & (df_orders.COOKIES == 2))
                   .value_counts(normalize=True) )
```

```
False      0.995318
True       0.004682
dtype: float64
```

In other words, we find 0.5 percent of orders satisfy our conditions. (As we will shortly explain in the box "A Common Bug," note that both parts of the statement must be in parentheses.)

Finally, how would we find all orders with *either* more than one drink *or* two cookies exactly? By analogy, you might be tempted to use the or keyword from if statements, but here as well, pandas differs slightly—you need to use the pipe symbol |, which looks like a vertical line. Thus, the correct line here is as follows:

```
( ((df_orders.DRINKS >= 1) | (df_orders.COOKIES == 2))
                   .value_counts(normalize=True) )
```

```
False      0.866356
True       0.133644
dtype: float64
```

Thus, 13.36 percent of orders satisfy *at least* one of these conditions.

A COMMON BUG

A bug that commonly plagues Python beginners is forgetting to put the right number of parentheses around their multiple logical statements. For example, try this:

```
( (df_orders.DRINKS >= 1 & df_orders.COOKIES == 2)
                  .value_counts(normalize=True) )
```

Compare this carefully to the code in the main body of the text—notice two sets of parentheses are missing. The statement will give you an error, and it will be a completely unintelligible one. What is actually happening is that the ampersand & is evaluated *first*, and so Python understands the previous line as follows:

```
( (df_orders.DRINKS >= (1 & df_orders.COOKIES) == 2)
                  .value_counts(normalize=True) )
```

This makes no sense, of course, and so Python complains. Thus, if you ever get an inexplicable error when using & or |, check to ensure that you have parentheses around each individual statement.

6.7.4 The isin() function

In the previous section, we saw how to check whether each entry is equal to a particular value. Another common operation is to check whether each entry is *one of several* values. You could do this, of course, using multiple pipes (|), but it would get pretty cumbersome. For example, suppose you wanted to check whether each restaurant is either restaurant ID R10001 or restaurant ID R10002 (these are the Columbia restaurants and Midtown restaurants, respectively). You could do this:

```
((df_orders.RESTAURANT_ID == 'R10001') |
    (df_orders.RESTAURANT_ID == 'R10002')).head()
```

```
0        True
1       False
2        True
3       False
4       False
Name: RESTAURANT_ID, dtype: bool
```

The `isin()` function allows you to do all of this in one fell swoop, as follows:

```
df_orders.RESTAURANT_ID.isin(['R10001', 'R10002']).head()
```

```
0       True
1       False
2       True
3       False
4       False
Name: RESTAURANT_ID, dtype: bool
```

You simply pass a list to the `isin()` function, and it will check whether each entry in the series is included in that list. This is analogous to the `in` keyword in Python, which you encountered in section 3.3.7.

6.7.5 Datetime Columns

In chapter 5, we went to great lengths to make sure that the columns in our datasets that contained dates and times were formatted in Python. We're about to reap the benefits of that work.

Before we start, it's worth mentioning that dates get a bad rap with people who work with data, and for good reason—they can be a pain to work with. The fastest way to see a data scientist turn green is to give them a dataset with dates in several different time zones. The good news is that `pandas` actually makes it a cinch to handle dates. The one thing you'll need to remember is that all datetime functionality in `pandas` is accessed using `dt`.

It will be useful to ground ourselves in some specific business questions as we go through this section. In particular, we will address the following questions:

1. Are some weekdays busier than others when it comes to sales? Do we tend to observe more sales on weekdays and fewer on weekends, or vice versa?
2. How do order patterns vary throughout the year? Do we find higher sales in the summer and a dip in the winter, or vice versa?
3. How can we find the number of sales on any given day?

Let's begin. The first (and simplest) thing we can do with DATETIMES in pandas is extract specific parts of the timestamp. For example, suppose we wanted to find the minute past the hour at which each order was placed, we could do this:

```
df_orders.DATETIME.dt.minute.head()
```

```
0     25
1     35
2     12
3     50
4     37
Name: DATETIME, dtype: int64
```

Looking at the original DataFrame, you will find the result is correct. Any part of a timestamp can be extracted in this manner, including year, month, day, hour, minute, and second. So far, this is nothing particularly groundbreaking—give those a quick try.

Where pandas really shines is in its ability to extract more complicated information about dates. Following are some of the more useful examples:

- dt.weekday returns the day of the week, from zero (Monday) to six (Sunday). For example, try df_orders.DATETIME.dt.weekday. You can also use day_name(), which returns the name of the day of the week (note, confusingly, that it requires parentheses whereas weekday does not).
- weekofyear and dayofyear return the number of weeks and days since the start of the year respectively.
- quarter returns the quarter in which the date falls.
- normalize() returns the timestamp, but with the time set to midnight. So, for example, a timestamp of "January 1, 2019, 1:20pm" would be transformed to "January 1, 2019, 12:00am." This can be useful, for example, when you want to combine all orders by day.

These functions are most useful when you combine them with the methods discussed earlier. To see this, let's attempt to answer the first question, and find sales patterns by day of week: ♦

```
( df_orders.DATETIME.dt.weekday.value_counts()
          .sort_index().plot(kind='bar') )
```

`<matplotlib.axes._subplots.AxesSubplot at 0x132ce2b90>`

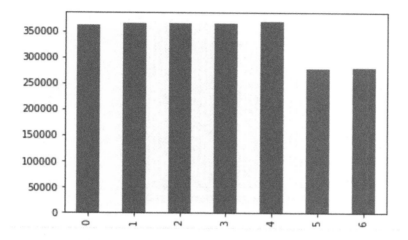

We're conscious, by the way, that we're starting to do a lot in a single Python statement. Here, for example, we are accessing the DATETIME column, extracting the weekday from it, applying `value_counts()`, sorting it to ensure we start with Monday and end with Sunday, and plotting it. The ability to do so much in a Python statement results in powerful and elegant code, but if you find yourself getting confused by these longer statements, try to evaluate each part of the statement one by one and see what it does. In this case, you might first run `df_orders.DATETIME`, then `df_orders.DATETIME.dt.weekday`, and then `df_orders.DATETIME.dt.weekday.value_counts()`, until you've recreated the full statement..

This plot should make it clear that sales are roughly constant throughout the week, but significantly lower on weekends.

As a second example, let's consider the second question. Do orders tend to peak in the summer? Or perhaps people are drawn to Dig's food in the winter? How would you do this? ◆

```
( df_orders.DATETIME.dt.weekofyear.value_counts()
              .sort_index().plot(kind='bar') )
```

`<matplotlib.axes._subplots.AxesSubplot at 0x1250a2e10>`

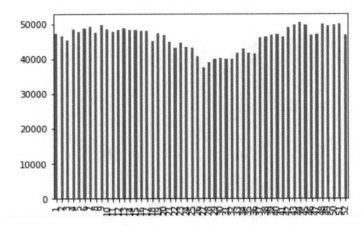

This code first extracts the week of the year for each date, and then finds the number of orders in each week of the year. Again, we encourage you to try each statement one by one to understand what it's doing. We clearly see orders are lowest in weeks twenty to thirty (in the middle of the summer) and higher in the winter.[5]

Although this plot does the job, it does look a little awkward—the many bars crowd each other out, and the plot starts at zero, which obscures the variation. To fix this, we can use a different kind of plot—a line graph. To obtain this plot, we simply change the kind argument:

```
( df_orders.DATETIME.dt.weekofyear.value_counts()
              .sort_index().plot(kind='line') )
```

`<matplotlib.axes._subplots.AxesSubplot at 0x1320c1790>`

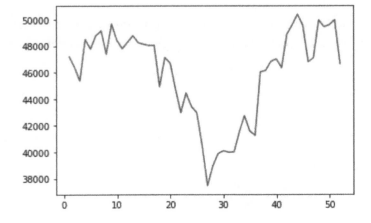

Notice that the *y*-axis no longer starts at zero, making the pattern far clearer. Furthermore, the use of lines instead of bars makes the plot far easier to read.

The last feature we shall consider is logic using dates, which is best illustrated by example. Consider the following statement:[6]

```
(df_orders.DATETIME >= '2018-06-01').head()
```

```
0        True
1       False
2       False
3        True
4        True
Name: DATETIME, dtype: bool
```

This produces a series equal to True if the date in that row is after June 1, 2018, and False otherwise.

One place this feature wouldn't work as you might expect is if you try to find all the orders on one specific date. For example, to find the number of orders placed on June 1, 2018, you might be tempted to do the following:

```
(df_orders.DATETIME == '2018-06-01').sum()
```

```
0
```

Why is the result zero? When pandas converts the string on the right-hand-side to a DateTime, it needs to figure out what time to use. Because no time is provided, it simply uses midnight. Thus, the previous statement counts the number of orders that happened at *exactly* midnight on June 1, 2018. Unsurprisingly, the result is zero!

Can you figure out the right way to do this? (Hint: Go back and remind yourself what the dt.normalize() function does.) ◆

```
(df_orders.DATETIME.dt.normalize() == '2018-06-01').sum()
```

The normalize function sets the time in every date to midnight, so now the equality comparison works. You could also have done the following:

```
( (df_orders.DATETIME >= '2018-06-01') &
    (df_orders.DATETIME < '2018-06-02') ).sum()
```

```
6748
```

This finds the number of orders between midnight on June 1, 2018, and midnight on June 2, 2018—unsurprisingly, the same number.

6.7.6 String Columns

In part 1, we discussed a number of operations you could carry out on strings—for example, you could make them uppercase or lowercase, or extract parts of them. Here, we discuss how to carry out these operations on pandas series rather than individual values. The first thing to know is that, just like all of the date functions are hidden behind the dt keyword, string functions are hidden behind the str keyword.

Let's look at a simple function that takes a series of text and converts it to uppercase:

```
df_items.ITEM_NAME.str.upper().head()
```

```
0            FARRO WITH SUMMER VEGETABLES
1                        SPINDRIFT LEMON
2                     CLASSIC BROWN RICE
3                               KOMBUCHA
4    CAULIFLOWER WITH GARLIC AND PARMESAN
Name: ITEM_NAME, dtype: object
```

Similarly, a lower() function is available.

Now, suppose we want to find the number of menu items that contain the word "lemon." You could do this as follows:

```
( df_items.ITEM_NAME.str.lower().str
        .contains('lemon').sum() )
```

3

Study this statement carefully, there's a lot going on. In the first line, we take the ITEM_NAME column and make all values lowercase—this is to ensure that we catch every instance of "lemon," whether it's uppercase or lowercase. Note that this operation will return a series, so to access the string functions again, we need to use the str keyword again. We then call the contains() function to find the word "lemon" (making sure to use lowercase because we've lowercased every string in the series). This will return a series with True if that line's ITEM_NAME contains "lemon," and False otherwise. Finally, we sum them to find that three lines in total contain the word.

Let's now consider accessing parts of a string. In section 3.5.3, you saw that you could do things like "Hello"[1:4] to access the second, third, and fourth characters in the string. You can do the same thing for every row in a series by simply using square brackets after the str keyword. For example:

```
df_items.ITEM_NAME.str[1:4].head()
```

```
0    arr
1    pin
2    las
3    omb
4    aul
Name: ITEM_NAME, dtype: object
```

When might this actually be useful? Recall that every order ID begins with the letter "O." As you're checking the quality of your data, you might want to make sure this is indeed the case: ♦

```
df_orders.ORDER_ID.str[0].value_counts()
```

```
O    2387224
Name: ORDER_ID, dtype: int64
```

First, we extract the first character in every string, and then we find every possible value this first character can take. Thankfully, "O" is the only option here, so every ID works as we expect.

The last operation we studied in section 3.5.2 that we might want to replicate is splitting strings. Suppose that for some reason, we wanted to separate every word in each item name; we could do the following:

```
df_items.ITEM_NAME.str.split(' ').head()
```

```
0              [Farro, with, Summer, Vegetables]
1                             [Spindrift, Lemon]
2                           [Classic, Brown, Rice]
3                                    [Kombucha]
4      [Cauliflower, with, Garlic, and, Parmesan]
Name: ITEM_NAME, dtype: object
```

We can then access each of the individual elements using the str keyword again. For example, find the second word in each item name as follows: ♦

```
df_items.ITEM_NAME.str.split(' ').str[1].head()
```

```
0       with
1      Lemon
2      Brown
3        NaN
4       with
Name: ITEM_NAME, dtype: object
```

Notice that the fourth item in the series is NaN (a missing value), because that item name contains only one word. Thus, finding the second word in that item name returns a missing value.

6.7.7 The apply() function

We should consider one final operation before we close. The apply() function can take any function you define and apply it sequentially, row by row, to an entire series.

Let's consider the simple example of finding whether each order was placed at the Columbia restaurant (restaurant R10001). We already know how to do this, as follows:

```
(df_orders.RESTAURANT_ID == 'R10001').head()
```

```
0      False
1      False
2       True
3      False
4      False
Name: RESTAURANT_ID, dtype: bool
```

Suppose, instead, that we defined a function called `is_columbia()`:

```
def is_columbia(restaurant_id):
    return restaurant_id == 'R10001'

is_columbia('R10001')
```

```
True
```

The last line simply tests our function; it should return `True` if the restaurant is Columbia, and `False` otherwise.

We then can perform the same operation by simply applying this function to every row in the RESTAURANT_ID column:

```
df_orders.RESTAURANT_ID.apply(is_columbia).head()
```

```
0      False
1      False
2       True
3      False
4      False
Name: RESTAURANT_ID, dtype: bool
```

Magic! We have automatically applied our function to every row in the series. Note, by the way, that we do not need to include parentheses after the function name when using `apply()`.

At this stage, you might wonder why you wouldn't just use `apply()` all the time. Why worry about all the functions we discussed in the previous sections when we can simply define a function that does what we want and use `apply()`?

It turns out that `apply()` is *almost* always much slower than the equivalent native pandas operation. We can time how long a cell takes to run in *Jupyter Notebook* by adding the `%%time` directive at the start of the cell. In this case, we can do this:

```
%%time
df_orders.RESTAURANT_ID.apply(is_columbia).head()
```

```
CPU times: user 378 ms, sys: 16.7 ms, total: 395 ms
Wall time: 395 ms

0      False
1      False
2       True
3      False
4      False
Name: RESTAURANT_ID, dtype: bool
```

We find that it takes 395 milliseconds (or thousandths of a second) to run (you might get a slightly different runtime when you run it). Let's now try this without apply():

```
%%time
(df_orders.RESTAURANT_ID == 'R10001').head()
```

```
CPU times: user 161 ms, sys: 1.29 ms, total: 162 ms
Wall time: 164 ms

0    False
1    False
2     True
3    False
4    False
Name: RESTAURANT_ID, dtype: bool
```

We now find that it only takes 162 milliseconds to run. That's almost three times faster. When you're operating on the scale of milliseconds, it doesn't really matter—we doubt you even noticed the difference in running time in these two statements. But if you embedded these statements in a loop, for example, or were running them on far larger datasets, a factor of three speedup can make the difference between getting the answer immediately and having to wait overnight.

In addition to using apply() on a series, we also can use it on a full DataFrame. Consider this example (warning: this will take more than a minute to run):

```
%%time
def total_extras(row):
    return row.COOKIES + row.DRINKS

df_orders.apply(total_extras, axis=1).head()
```

```
CPU times: user 2min 13s, sys: 2.17 s, total: 2min 16s
Wall time: 2min 53s

0    3.0
1    0.0
2    2.0
3    1.0
4    0.0
dtype: float64
```

Let's consider the last line first. We are using the apply() function directly on the DataFrame. Notice that we need to provide the function with an axis argument:

- If axis=1, the function will loop through every row. It will then take each row and pass it to the total_extras function. This is what we do here—every time the function is called, it gets a row.
- If axis=0, the function will loop through every column. It will then take each column and pass it to the function. We might do this if, for example, we wanted to find the average of each column. This is clearly not what we want to do in this instance.

The function itself is quite simple. For each row, it just adds the number of cookies and drinks in that row. Notice how this operation takes a whopping 136 seconds to complete. (In fact, this takes so long you might want to comment out the line once you've run it by putting a # in front of it, so that it doesn't take so long to run if you ever rerun the notebook.)

You might wonder how long it would take if we just did it directly. Let's see:

```
%%time
(df_orders.COOKIES + df_orders.DRINKS).head()
```

```
CPU times: user 12.9 ms, sys: 11.4 ms, total: 24.3 ms
Wall time: 16.4 ms

0    3.0
1    0.0
2    2.0
3    1.0
4    0.0
dtype: float64
```

This time it took only 24 milliseconds! In other words, it was almost ten *thousand* times faster!

Long story short—always use built-in functions if you can. In the few cases this isn't possible, apply() is a powerful tool.

LAMBDA FUNCTIONS

Another way to define functions, called a *lambda function*, can be particularly useful together with `apply()`. It does not introduce any new functionality—it simply provides a shorter, more elegant way to define single-line functions. We introduce it here to make sure you understand it if you see this technique in someone else's code.

Recall the code we used to define the `total_extras()` function:

```
def total_extras(row):
    return row.COOKIES + row.DRINKS
```

The following would have been an identical way to define this function:

```
total_extras = lambda row : row.COOKIES + row.DRINKS
```

This really doesn't match anything we've seen so far, so let's dissect it step by step:

- First, the lambda keyword tells Python we're about to define a one-line function.
- Second, the name of the arguments to the function follows (in this case, just row). If there is more than one argument, they need to be separated by commas.
- Third, these arguments are followed by a colon.
- Fourth, write the expression we want the function to return.

Most puzzlingly, we then take the whole thing and assign it to the variable `total_extras`. Having done this, the variable `total_extras` is now a function and can be used in the same way as if it was defined using the first method.

This might be useful simply because it allows us to run the entire `apply()` sequence in the main text in one line, as follows:

```
df_orders.apply(lambda row: row.COOKIES
                        + row.DRINKS, axis=1).head()
```

```
0    3.0
1    0.0
2    2.0
3    1.0
4    0.0
dtype: float64
```

Instead of defining the function, we pass a lambda function directly to `apply()`.

We're not expecting you to have mastered lambda functions after this quick introduction, but we hope you at least will know what you're looking at if you see this in someone else's code.

6.8 EDITING DATAFRAMES

You might have noticed that our discussion so far has focused almost exclusively on operating on *existing* DataFrames. With one or two exceptions, we have said nothing about editing, or otherwise changing a DataFrame. If you come from Excel, this might seem peculiar—editing a cell is the most natural operation in Excel (you just type in a cell), and we haven't even touched on it yet.

Part of the reason for this is that when you use pandas, it usually will be in the context of very large datasets like the Dig dataset. In those contexts, editing the dataset doesn't really make much sense. The dataset will have been retrieved from a database, and it is the *analysis* of the dataset that is of greater interest.

Nevertheless, in some situations, you will want to edit a DataFrame, and we discuss this here.

6.8.1 Adding Columns

The first, and simplest operation you might want to perform on a DataFrame is adding a column. For example, suppose we wanted to add a column to the df_orders table containing True if the order contains a drink, and False otherwise.

First, we need to obtain the series we want to put in the new column. Using our discussion from section 6.7.3, we can do this using df_order.DRINKS > 0. Adding it to the DataFrame really couldn't be easier. We just do this:

```
df_orders['HAS_DRINK'] = (df_orders.DRINKS > 0)
```

We simply refer to the column on the left-hand-side and set it equal to the series we want it to contain. This is similar to creating a new key/value pair in a dictionary.

One crucial warning at this point—this *only works* using the square-bracket notation—if you were to try to add a column using the dot notation, for example using df_orders.HAS_DRINK = (df_orders.DRINKS > 0), the column would not be added.

6.8.2 Removing Columns

Removing columns is equally simple. You can simply use the drop() function with the name of the column. For example, if we wanted to remove the HAS_DRINK column, we could do the following:

```
df_orders = df_orders.drop(columns='HAS_DRINK')
```

Three quick notes:

- Applying the function itself on the right-hand-side does not change the DataFrame—it simply returns a DataFrame without that column. You need to set df_orders equal to that result to "save" it.
- drop('HAS_DRINK') wouldn't work; you need to specify the name of the columns argument.
- If you want to drop multiple columns, you can pass a list to the columns argument of the function instead of a string.

6.8.3 Editing Entire Columns

Editing entire columns is so simple that it barely deserves its own section. For example, suppose you wanted to replace the NUM_ORDERS column in df_summarized_orders with that same number divided by ten. You could do the following:

```
df_summarized_orders['NUM_ORDERS'] =(
        df_summarized_orders.NUM_ORDERS / 10 )
```

We simply "overwrite" the existing column with its new value. We can then reverse the change as follows:

```
df_summarized_orders['NUM_ORDERS'] =(
        df_summarized_orders.NUM_ORDERS * 10 )
```

Note that when *editing* a column (rather than adding one), the dot notation *does* work on the left-hand side of the equal sign.

6.8.4 Editing Specific Values in a DataFrame; loc[]

We have left the most complex topic for last: how do you edit specific values in a DataFrame (i.e., the equivalent of typing in a cell in Excel)?

Let's begin with a simple example. Suppose we wanted to add a column to the df_summarized_order DataFrame called ORDER_VOLUME that contains "LOW" if under 600 orders were placed that day, "MEDIUM" if between 600 and 1,200 orders were placed, and "HIGH" otherwise.

One way to do this is as follows:

1. Create a column that contains the word "HIGH".
2. Replace the values in that column with the word "MEDIUM" for all days with fewer than 1,200 orders.
3. Replace the values in that column with the work "LOW" for all days with fewer than 600 orders.

The first step is relatively simple. We can simply do this:

```
df_summarized_orders['ORDER_VOLUME'] = 'HIGH'
```

For the second step, you might be tempted to do this":

```
df_summarized_orders[df_summarized_orders.NUM_ORDERS
              <= 1200]['ORDER_VOLUME'] = 'MEDIUM'
```

The logic behind this statement would be to first filter down the DataFrame to only those days with fewer than 1,200 orders, and then to set the ORDER_VOLUME column for those rows to "MEDIUM." Why doesn't this work?

The answer is quite subtle. Under the hood, when you filter down the DataFrame, pandas sometimes creates a *copy* of the DataFrame in memory and returns that copy to you—not the original DataFrame. This copy exists as a completely separate object. Thus, when you then select the ORDER_VOLUME column and set it to "MEDIUM," it carries out that operation only on the *copy* and not on the original DataFrame, which remains unchanged.[7]

Try running the previous code in pandas. Thankfully, pandas gives you a big ugly error. The error text reads as follows:

```
A value is trying to be set on a copy of a slice from a DataFrame.
```

We now understand the error—pandas tells you you're trying to set a value on a *copy* of a DataFrame.

How do we solve this problem? Pandas makes a loc keyword available, which allows you to filter and change a DataFrame *at the same time*. The correct version of the previous statement follows:

```
df_summarized_orders.loc[df_summarized_orders.NUM_ORDERS
                <= 1200, 'ORDER_VOLUME'] = 'MEDIUM'
```

When you run loc, you use square brackets, specify the rows you want to filter by (in the same way as when filtering a DataFrame), type a comma, and then specify the name of the column you want to edit.

So our last statement in our "to-do" list looks like this:

```
df_summarized_orders.loc[df_summarized_orders.NUM_ORDERS
                <= 600, 'ORDER_VOLUME'] = 'LOW'
```

Note that this error doesn't just arise in the previous context. Consider the following code:

```
df_new = df_summarized_orders[
        ['DATE', 'NUM_ORDERS', 'PERC_DELIVERY']]
df_new['NUM_DELIVERY'] = ( df_new.NUM_ORDERS *
                df_new.PERC_DELIVERY )
```

The first line simplifies the df_summarized_orders DataFrame by selecting three of its columns. The second creates a new column containing the total absolute number of delivery orders (by multiplying the number of orders by the percentage of delivery orders). Believe it or not, this will give you the same error as before. What's happening? You're not even filtering the DataFrame!

The error occurs because the first step selects some columns from the DataFrame. The DataFrame that is returned might be a copy, but it might refer to the original DataFrame, and so it's unclear whether df_new is a whole new (i.e., separate) DataFrame, or whether it simply refers to the original one. When you later edit it by adding a column, pandas doesn't know whether you want to edit the new DataFrame or the original one.

Luckily, it is simple to avoid this kind of situation. When you select a subset of an original DataFrame and you think you will want to edit the resulting

DataFrame later, you need to create a *copy* using the copy() function to explicitly let pandas know a copy is what you want. The correct code follows:

```
df_new = df_summarized_orders[
    ['DATE', 'NUM_ORDERS', 'PERC_DELIVERY']].copy()


df_new['NUM_DELIVERY'] = ( df_new.NUM_ORDERS *
                df_new.PERC_DELIVERY )
```

We realize this all seems a little technical, and it might seem a bit opaque upon first reading. If nothing else, remember that if you ever see an error message that reads "A value is trying to be set on a copy of a slice from a DataFrame," the explanation is in this chapter.

6.9 MORE PRACTICE

We already have covered *a lot*! The examples we chose in this chapter, however, may have seemed a bit contrived; we chose them to ensure that we could focus on the Python techniques themselves. In this section, we return to the story of Dig and apply what we've learned to answer some more realistic questions.

6.9.1 Miscellaneous Analyses

It is worth verifying the hypothesis we came up with in section 6.5.1. You will recall that we noticed the Bryant Park location appeared only 261 times in the df_summarized_orders DataFrame, and we hypothesized that this was because the restaurant was closed on weekends. We mentioned that to check this, we would want to make sure none of the days for which Bryant Park was listed in the dataset were weekends. Try to figure out how you would do this by yourself before reading the solution; you might want to review sections 6.5.1 and 6.7.5. ◆

Here's our solution:

```
( df_summarized_orders
  [df_summarized_orders.RESTAURANT_NAME == 'Bryant Park']
  .DATE
  .dt.day_name()
  .value_counts() )
```

```
Monday       53
Wednesday    52
Thursday     52
Tuesday      52
Friday       52
Name: DATE, dtype: int64
```

Let's carefully take stock of what we're doing here (each number in the list corresponds to a line number in the code):

1. We start with `df_summarized_orders` (you might want to remind yourself of the DataFrame's structure by looking at the first few rows)
2. We filter down the DataFrame to rows pertaining to Bryant Park
3. We extract the `DATE` column
4. We use the `dt` keyword to pull up the datetime functions, and extract the name of the weekday in each row
5. We use `value_counts()` to find the number of times each weekday appears in the subset of rows we have selected

The results quite conclusively confirm our hypothesis—Bryant Park only has weekdays (Monday to Friday) in our dataset.

Here's another miscellaneous analysis we could run: Suppose we wanted to identify the day in our data with the most sales. How would we do it? ♦

The easiest way to do this is simply by sorting the `df_summarized_orders` DataFrame by the `NUM_ORDERS` column and looking at the first row.

```
df_summarized_orders.sort_values('NUM_ORDERS',
                        ascending=False).head()
```

	RESTAURANT_NAME	DATE	NUM_ORDERS	PERC_DELIVERY	ORDE
1530	NYU	2018-06-24	1396.0	0.063754	
1397	NYU	2018-02-11	1381.0	0.099203	
1406	NYU	2018-02-20	1371.0	0.068563	
1410	NYU	2018-02-24	1361.0	0.085966	
1683	NYU	2018-11-24	1353.0	0.105691	

We find that all five of the top-selling days are at the NYU store and that the most popular day was on June 24, 2018. This was the weekend of the New York Pride parade, which passes near NYU, so this isn't so surprising.

How would you find the day in our data with the highest sales *at a particular restaurant*? Or the highest-selling weekday? We'll leave these challenges to you, although we do provide the solution in the *Jupyter Notebook* for this chapter.

6.9.2 Delivery Percentages by Restaurant

One of the most exciting aspects of Dig's growth is its expansion beyond its main restaurant offering to delivery, pick-up orders, and catering. We will discuss this in much more detail in chapter 9. For now, note that in deciding how to invest in its delivery service, it is crucial for Dig to understand exactly how the service is being used at each of its restaurants. For our next analysis, we shall find the percentage of sales at each restaurant that comes from deliveries.[8]

Let's warm up by finding the average number of delivery orders across *all* restaurants. How would you do this? ♦

You might first be tempted to try this:

```
df_summarized_orders.PERC_DELIVERY.mean()
```

```
0.11669955062317698
```

This is *almost* right, but not quite. Can you figure out why? ♦ The answer is quite subtle, and to understand it, consider two days—one with one thousand orders, of which 20 percent were deliveries, and one with five hundred orders, of which 10 percent were deliveries. What is the average percentage of deliveries? The method above would say it's $(10 + 20)/2 = 15$ percent. But that isn't quite right, because the first day had more orders, and so it should be weighted more heavily. ♦

What is the correct calculation here? ♦ We would need to find the total number of delivery orders $(1{,}000 \times 0.2) + (500 \times 0.1) = 250$, and divide it by the total number of orders (1,500), to get a percentage of 16.7 percent. Not massively different, but still different.

How would you translate this to our DataFrame? ♦

```
n_deliveries = (df_summarized_orders.NUM_ORDERS
                *df_summarized_orders.PERC_DELIVERY).sum()
n_deliveries / df_summarized_orders.NUM_ORDERS.sum()
```

```
0.11421131825082187
```

In the first two lines, we find the number of deliveries by multiplying the delivery percentage by the number of orders for each row, and summing the result. We then divide it by the total number of orders. The result is thankfully very similar.

How would we do this for a specific restaurant? ♦ You might initially think of taking every instance of `df_summarized_orders` in the code and filtering it down to that restaurant. Rather than doing that, however, why not create a function that will do this for us? ♦

```
def percent_delivery(df):
    n_deliveries = (df.NUM_ORDERS * df.PERC_DELIVERY).sum()
    return n_deliveries / df.NUM_ORDERS.sum()

percent_delivery(df_summarized_orders)
```

```
0.11421131825082187
```

Given a DataFrame `df`, this function will find the average delivery percentage. In the last line, we apply this to the full DataFrame to the check the function works and we get the same result as before.

We now can apply this to a DataFrame containing Columbia orders only: ♦

```
columbia_orders = ( df_summarized_orders
                    [df_summarized_orders.RESTAURANT_NAME
                                         == 'Columbia'] )
percent_delivery(columbia_orders)
```

```
0.10066185558789521
```

So it looks like the Columbia restaurant observes *fewer* delivery orders than other restaurants.

In the *Jupyter Notebook* for this chapter, we show you how to use a loop to do this for every restaurant and plot the results. You will find that delivery is significantly more popular on the Upper East Side and Upper West Side. For those not familiar with Manhattan, these are residential neighborhoods, and so the higher proportion of delivery orders makes sense. You will also find that Bryant Park and Midtown have particularly low delivery numbers. Can you think why? As is often the case, there is a simple explanation that is not particularly insightful—Bryant

Park and Midtown only started delivering halfway through 2018, and so the delivery percentage was zero for these restaurants for much of the year.

6.9.3 Staffing Analysis

Our last analysis on this dataset will concern staffing. This is another topic we'll return to in more detail in chapter 9, but you'll remember that this issue was a crucial one in the story of Dig. In deciding how to allocate its staff across restaurants, it is important for Dig to understand the kinds of demands it observes at its restaurants, both on weekdays and weekends. Before you read on, you might want to stop for a second and ask yourself what plots you might produce to help Dig plan these schedules. ◆

The solution we adopted was to plot two histograms for each restaurant—one showing the distribution of the number of orders on weekdays, and one showing the number of orders on weekends. These histograms will provide a rich impression of the kinds of demands we might face at each restaurant.

As we did in the previous section, let's begin by plotting a histogram of all order amounts for all days in our dataset:

```
df_summarized_orders.NUM_ORDERS.plot(kind='hist', bins=30)
```

```
<matplotlib.axes._subplots.AxesSubplot at 0x1a693ae850>
```

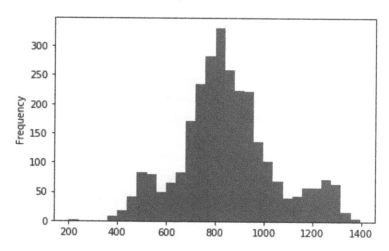

Now suppose we want to produce one histogram for weekdays, and one for weekends, what would we do? We can try this: ◆

```
( df_summarized_orders
    [df_summarized_orders.DATE.dt.weekday < 5]
    .NUM_ORDERS
    .plot(kind='hist', bins=30) )

( df_summarized_orders
    [df_summarized_orders.DATE.dt.weekday >= 5]
    .NUM_ORDERS
    .plot(kind='hist', bins=30) )
```

`<matplotlib.axes._subplots.AxesSubplot at 0x1a9b2768d0>`

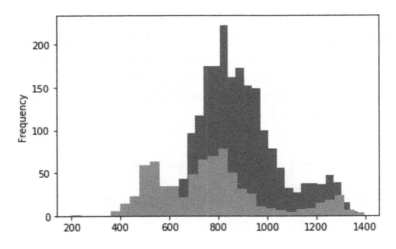

These two statements are identical to the first, with one exception—the first filters orders down to weekdays (days with numbers less than five) and the second to weekends (days with numbers greater or equal to five). Notice how we use `dt.weekday` to get the weekday for each date.

This is almost what we want, but we have three issues with the plot. The first is that they are clearly on different scales, which makes them difficult to compare. Can you figure out why that is? ◆ It is simply because there are far fewer weekend days than weekdays, thus making the number of orders "per bar" in the plot lower for weekends. We can fix this simply by using the `density=True` argument, which we discussed in section 6.5.2. ◆

The second issue is that the second plot masks and obscures parts of the first. We can fix this using the `alpha` argument (which we haven't seen before); by passing `alpha=0.5` to the `plot()` function, we can make the plot slightly transparent.

The final issue is that the plot has no legend, so it's hard to know which plot shows weekdays and which shows weekends. We can add one using `plt.legend(['Weekdays', 'Weekends'])`; notice that the order of the items in the list matches the order in which the plots were produced. The final code looks like this:

```
( df_summarized_orders
    [df_summarized_orders.DATE.dt.weekday < 5]
    .NUM_ORDERS
    .plot(kind='hist', bins=30, density=True) )

( df_summarized_orders
    [df_summarized_orders.DATE.dt.weekday >= 5]
    .NUM_ORDERS
    .plot(kind='hist', bins=30, density=True, alpha=0.5) )

plt.legend(['Weekdays', 'Weekends'])
```

```
<matplotlib.legend.Legend at 0x1a6925dd50>
```

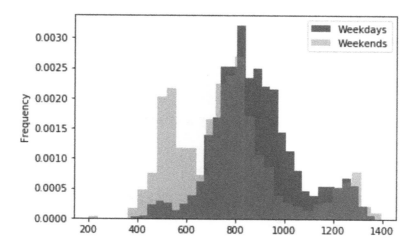

Finally, we use a loop to plot this result for every restaurant individually. If you want a challenge, try this yourself before reading on: ◆

```
# Rename the df_summarized_order DataFrame to shorten
# our code
df_so = df_summarized_orders

# Loop through each restaurant
for r in df_so.RESTAURANT_NAME.unique().tolist():
    # Print the restaurant name
    print(r)

    # Filter the orders down to this restaurant
    df = df_so[df_so.RESTAURANT_NAME == r]

    # Plot weekday and weekend histogram
    ( df[df.DATE.dt.weekday < 5]
        .NUM_ORDERS.plot(kind='hist', bins=30,
                                  density=True) )

    weekend_rows = (df.DATE.dt.weekday >= 5)
    if weekend_rows.sum() > 0:
        ( df[weekend_rows]
            .NUM_ORDERS.plot(kind='hist', bins=30,
                                  density=True, alpha=0.5) )

    # Create a legend
    plt.legend(['Weekday', 'Weekend'])

    # Show the plot at each stage of the loop
    plt.show()
```

Let's go through this line by line (again, the following numbers refer to line numbers in the code):

3. `df_so = df_summarized_orders`
   This line simply "renames" the `df_summarized_orders` DataFrame to something shorter, so as to shorten the code—it's purely aesthetic.
6. `for r in df_so.RESTAURANT_NAME.unique().tolist():`
   This line first creates a list with every unique restaurant, and loops through it. We call the variable that will contain the name of every restaurant r. So r will first contain Bryant Park, then Columbia, then Flatiron, and so on.

8. `print(r)`

   This simply prints the name of the restaurant so that we know which one we're looking at.

11. `df = df_so[df_so.RESTAURANT_NAME == r]`

    This line takes the full summarized orders DataFrame, and filters it down to those rows pertaining to restaurant `r`. We will base the rest of our code on this filtered DataFrame `df`.

14. This line filters down `df` to weekday rows—specifically, those for which `df.DATE.dt.weekday < 5` (Monday-Friday), and then plots the histogram as we did earlier.

18. This line creates a series called `weekend_rows` with as many lines as rows in `df_so_filtered` that contains `True` if the row corresponds to a weekend, and `False` otherwise.

19. This line is one we didn't have to use before. It checks that there is at least one weekend row for the restaurant and that it plots the weekend histogram only if there are any. This is required because, unfortunately, plotting a histogram based on a DataFrame with no rows leads to a `pandas` error.

20. Plot the weekend histogram, as we saw previously.

25. Display a legend.

28. `plt.show()`

    Finally, the last line immediately displays the plots we created. We need this because if we don't include this line, Python will plot *all* of these histograms on top of each other in one plot, instead of plotting them one by one. Try it without that last statement to see what it would look like.

We won't reproduce every resulting histogram here for the sake of space, but let's look at the first three histograms produced:

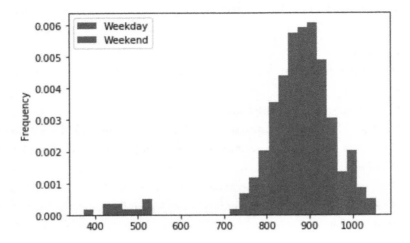

Columbia

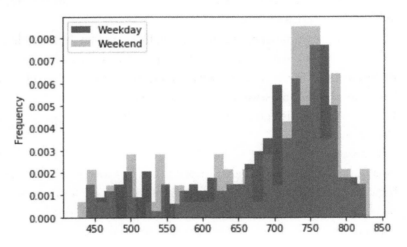

Flatiron

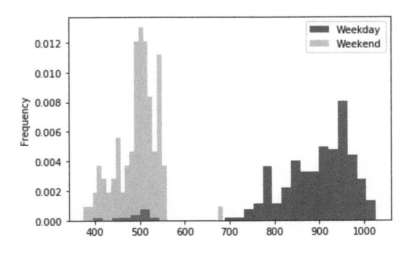

These histograms provide a rich view of ordering patterns at each restaurant. Spend some time reviewing them in detail and figuring out what these plots imply. ◆ Here are a few things that struck us:

- Bryant Park only has one histogram (for weekdays) and none for weekends— this makes sense, as we earlier found that Bryant Park is closed on weekends.
- For some stores (like Columbia), the distributions on weekdays and weekends is identical—it seems the store observes as many customers on weekdays as it does on weekends. For others, like Flatiron and Midtown, the distributions are strikingly different. Weekdays have many more orders than weekends. This is, again, unsurprising, given these two neighborhoods are in business districts, which might experience smaller volumes on weekends.
- For the Flatiron restaurant, it is interesting to note that the weekend distribution is far narrower than the weekday distribution, which is wider and flatter. This implies that there is more certainty around order volumes on weekends than on weekdays, which might make weekends easier to staff in advance at those restaurants.

6.10 WRAPPING UP

This chapter covered a lot of ground. We introduced the bulk of basic pandas functionality that we'll be using in the book, and we found that even these basic tools could lead to significant business insights.

Our analyses thus far, however, have involved only *one* dataset. In practice, many of the questions you might have to answer will require querying multiple datasets in combination with each other. In the next chapter, we'll discuss how to use pandas to combine multiple datasets to carry out more complex analyses.

7

BRINGING TOGETHER DATASETS

WE NOW HAVE a well-rounded understanding of the various operations you can do in pandas. We have discussed how pandas stores, reads, and writes data, and we have discussed the various ways you can explore, manipulate, and modify data in Python.

Something's missing, though. Think back to the case study of Dig in chapter 5—a key theme that comes up again and again in the story is the importance of being able to combine *multiple* datasets to carry out meaningful analyses. Recall, for example, the fact that Dig uses multiple systems to keep track of each set of human resources data, and the datasets produced by these systems need to be combined to carry out meaningful analyses.

In this chapter, we discuss why and how you might want to combine multiple datasets. We then look at the methods pandas makes available to carry out these kinds of operations.

7.1 WHAT YOU'LL LEARN IN THIS CHAPTER

This chapter has two aims. The first is to teach you how to think of operations that involve multiple datasets. What are the different ways to combine datasets? Which should you pick when? The second is to introduce you to the pandas syntax to actually carry out these various joins. Once we have talked about both topics, we will conclude by applying them to the Dig order dataset.

7.2 WHAT YOU'LL NEED FOR THIS CHAPTER

Before we start, begin by creating a new *Jupyter Notebook* for this chapter, as well as a folder called "Chapter 7" to save your in-progress files throughout the chapter. You should create both the notebook and the folder in the part 2 chapter folder you created in section 5.2.

The first thing we'll do is import some of the packages we'll need. Paste the following code in the first cell and run it:

```
import pandas as pd
import matplotlib.pyplot as plt
```

Next, we'll load some files we saved at the end of chapter 5. To do this, paste the following code in the next cell and run it (we won't use these files until section 7.9):

```
df_orders = pd.read_pickle('Chapter 5/orders.pickle')
df_items = pd.read_pickle('Chapter 5/items.pickle')
df_restaurants = (
    pd.read_pickle('Chapter 5/restaurants.pickle') )
```

As ever, the *Jupyter Notebook* for this chapter, and the files from last chapter, are available on the book's website.

7.3 COMBINING DATASETS: AN INTRODUCTION

Before we begin, it is worth asking what we mean by "combining datasets" and why this is an operation that could be important. This is best illustrated by example, so let's consider a few:

- In the Dig orders dataset, each order contains the ID of each item in the order but does not contain the *name* of the item. A separate dataset contains the IDs together with the relevant names. Producing a list of every item in an order will require combining these two datasets.

- Consider a university database with the following three tables:

    ○ One table containing the names of full-time students and their details (e.g., the name of their faculty advisers)

    ○ One table containing the names of part-time students and their details (e.g., the name of their faculty advisers)

    ○ One table containing the grades of students in a given class (e.g., "Introduction to Python")

These three datasets are useful in their own right, but the answers to many questions would require the *combination* of these datasets. For example, suppose you wanted to identify all students who scored a B or below in "Introduction to Python" together with their faculty advisers? Or, what if you wanted to give each faculty adviser a report about all of the students under their supervision? Or what, if you wanted to find out whether any faculty advisers had a disproportionate share of underperforming students?

- Consider a ridesharing company with three datasets—one listing every driver, one detailing each driver's driving history last month (for drivers that drove), and one containing a record of push notifications sent to driver's devices, encouraging them to use the app and pick up riders (for those who received such notifications). We might be curious on the impact of push notifications on a driver's driving frequency—these insights would require combining data from both datasets.

- Consider an e-commerce company with several tables:

    ○ One listing every order made on the company's website

    ○ One listing every customer and their details

    ○ One listing every product and its characteristics

The company might want to know whether products with certain characteristics are more popular than others, or how customer characteristics relate to ordering patterns (e.g., whether customers on the east coast order more often than those on the west coast?) Answering these questions would require combining data from all these datasets.

- Consider a call center with several tables:

    ○ One containing the name of each employee at the call center

    ○ One with payroll details, listing the payments that were made to each employee

    ○ One with a record of each call made, and the length of the call

A number of questions might require combining these datasets. For example, correlating the number of calls made by each employee with their salary.

The ability to combine datasets in the manner just described is one of the most useful features of `pandas`, but it can be a little finicky to apply correctly. Doing this topic full justice would require a book in its own right, which might be called *Databases for MBAs* (watch this space . . .). In this chapter, we will provide the basics to get you going, and explain how they can be applied in `pandas`.

7.4 SOME TOY DATASETS

Before we "graduate" to using the Dig dataset, we will practice the mechanics of joining datasets on some simple "toy" datasets, inspired by the previous university example. These datasets are available in an Excel workbook with one dataset per tab. We downloaded this workbook in section 5.2, and we can load these datasets as follows:

```
df_full_time = pd.read_excel('raw data/university.xlsx',
                             sheet_name='full_time')
df_part_time = pd.read_excel('raw data/university.xlsx',
                             sheet_name='part_time')
df_grades = pd.read_excel('raw data/university.xlsx',
                          sheet_name='grades')
```

Let's have a look at each of those datasets. First, the `df_full_time` DataFrame, which contains details of full-time students (in general, we would use `head()` to print only the first rows, but in what follows, it will be useful to have the entire table):

`df_full_time`

	student_id	first_name	last_name	adviser
0	1	Melvin	Ware	Prof Duncan
1	2	Thomas	Moore	Prof Brown
2	3	Joseph	Paul	Prof Alvarez
3	4	Sarah	Cruz	Prof Duncan

Second, the df_part_time DataFrame, which contains details for the part-time students:

df_part_time

	student_id	first_name	last_name	adviser
0	5	David	Freeman	Prof Duncan
1	6	Elizabeth	Brown	Prof Duncan
2	7	Amanda	Schultz	Prof Kennedy
3	8	Tanner	Perkins	Prof Alvarez
4	9	Ashley	Gonzales	Prof Kennedy
5	10	Latonya	Porter	Prof Alvarez
6	11	Jacinda	Peterson	Prof Alvarez

Finally, the df_grades DataFrame, which contains the grades of all students who took "Introduction to Python":

df_grades

	student_id	final_grade
0	1	95
1	3	71
2	6	76
3	7	91
4	8	75
5	11	59
6	15	86

For now, let's focus on a simple task—producing a dataset that, for each student that has taken "Introduction to Python," lists their name, adviser, and final grade. You might notice a few problems from the get-go. ♦ First, the students are split across two files. Second, the grades are in a separate file. Third, a student included in the grades file doesn't exist in the student file (student ID 15).

This last error might seem bizarre at first sight—how could a student have been assigned a grade without existing in the student information table? Unfortunately, this kind of error occurs all the time in real datasets for all kinds of reasons (e.g., a student might have left the school and been removed from the student tables, or someone might have just made a mistake when entering the grade). We not only need to handle this gracefully but also need to be able to detect this problem so that we can be aware of errors that can exist in our data.

7.5 THE FIVE TYPES OF JOINS

We are now ready to begin combining tables. One quick disclaimer: there is a truly bewildering number of different ways to combine tables in pandas, all of which do more or less the same thing (in some sense, this is a testament to how important these operations are). For a beginner, these topics are complex enough without the additional confusion of many alternative competing methods. In this section, therefore, we made the deliberate choice of picking only one method for each kind of join—the one we consider the most general. As you work with data more and more, you'll become familiar with other available methods.

7.5.1 The Union

The first—and simplest—method for combining two tables is called a *union*. This method is useful when two tables are basically two parts of one table that has been split in half. This can happen for a number of reasons—sometimes, a table is too large to be transmitted all at once and needs to be split into a few pieces. In other situations—as the example here—the table is split into logical parts: full-time students in one table, part-time students in the other. A union will simply bring those disparate parts together into one large table. To perform a union in pandas, simply use the `pd.concat()` function, and pass a *list* of the DataFrames you want to join to the function:

```
df_students = pd.concat([df_full_time, df_part_time])
df_students
```

	student_id	first_name	last_name	adviser
0	1	Melvin	Ware	Prof Duncan
1	2	Thomas	Moore	Prof Brown
2	3	Joseph	Paul	Prof Alvarez
3	4	Sarah	Cruz	Prof Duncan
0	5	David	Freeman	Prof Duncan
1	6	Elizabeth	Brown	Prof Duncan
2	7	Amanda	Schultz	Prof Kennedy
3	8	Tanner	Perkins	Prof Alvarez

A few points are worth noting:

- A common bug is to forget to put the DataFrames in a list, and instead of what is shown here, to type pd.concat(df_full_time, df_part_time)—this will give you an error.
- The row index from each of the original DataFrames being combined is maintained in the final DataFrame. This can result in a duplicated index. For example, notice that in the previous table, Daniel Smith and Linda Thiel both have row index 0. We don't use row indexes much in this book, so in theory, nothing is wrong with that, but you might want to reset the index to make sure the index is unique:

```
df_students = ( pd.concat([df_full_time, df_part_time])
                         .reset_index(drop=True) )
df_students
```

	student_id	first_name	last_name	adviser
0	1	Melvin	Ware	Prof Duncan
1	2	Thomas	Moore	Prof Brown
2	3	Joseph	Paul	Prof Alvarez
3	4	Sarah	Cruz	Prof Duncan
4	5	David	Freeman	Prof Duncan
5	6	Elizabeth	Brown	Prof Duncan
6	7	Amanda	Schultz	Prof Kennedy

- You might want the final table to track the origin of the initial row. We can do this by simply adding an indicator column to each constituent table before joining the tables:

```
df_full_time['student_type'] = 'full_time'
df_part_time['student_type'] = 'part_time'
pd.concat([df_full_time, df_part_time]).reset_index(drop=True)
```

	student_id	first_name	last_name	adviser	student_type
0	1	Melvin	Ware	Prof Duncan	full_time
1	2	Thomas	Moore	Prof Brown	full_time
2	3	Joseph	Paul	Prof Alvarez	full_time
3	4	Sarah	Cruz	Prof Duncan	full_time

- For tables to be combined using a union, they need to have the same columns.

7.5.2 Inner, Outer, Left, and Right Joins

We now look at a second problem. Suppose we wanted to combine df_grades and df_students to produce something like this:

	student_id	final_grade	first_name	last_name
0	1	95	Melvin	Ware
1	3	71	Joseph	Paul
2	6	76	Elizabeth	Brown
3	7	91	Amanda	Schultz
4	8	75	Tanner	Perkins
5	11	59	Jacinda	Peterson

This seems easy, right? Alas, when it comes to joins, the devil is in the details!

The first thing we need is a way to tell pandas how to match rows from one table to rows in the other. This is easiest illustrated by example. How is pandas to know that a row in df_students matches a row in df_grades? In this case, it's quite simple—it will look for rows that have the same value of student_id. This column is the *join key* for this particular join, and it is the first ingredient of every join. Often, the join key will be a column that uniquely identifies every row—sometimes even two columns, as we'll later see.

Once we've figured this out, there is, alas, a complication—what happens if a student_id occurs in one table but not in the second, or vice versa? In this case, as we just saw, student_id 15 appears in df_grades but not in df_students, and student_id 2 did not take "Introduction to Python," and therefore, the student does not appear in df_grades. When this happens, there are three things we could do:

- Include only those rows that appear in *both* tables—if a row is missing from one table or the other, drop it. This is called an *inner join*, and for our tables, it would look like this:

	student_id	final_grade	first_name	last_name
0	1	95	Melvin	Ware
1	3	71	Joseph	Paul
2	6	76	Elizabeth	Brown
3	7	91	Amanda	Schultz
4	8	75	Tanner	Perkins
5	11	59	Jacinda	Peterson

- Include *all rows*, regardless of whether they appear in one table, the other, or both. This is called an *outer join*. The result would look like this:

	student_id	final_grade	first_name	last_name	adviser
0	1	95.0	Melvin	Ware	Prof Duncan
1	3	71.0	Joseph	Paul	Prof Alvarez
2	6	76.0	Elizabeth	Brown	Prof Duncan
3	7	91.0	Amanda	Schultz	Prof Kennedy
4	8	75.0	Tanner	Perkins	Prof Alvarez
5	11	59.0	Jacinda	Peterson	Prof Alvarez
6	15	86.0	NaN	NaN	NaN
7	2	NaN	Thomas	Moore	Prof Brown
8	4	NaN	Sarah	Cruz	Prof Duncan
9	5	NaN	David	Freeman	Prof Duncan
10	9	NaN	Ashley	Gonzales	Prof Kennedy
11	10	NaN	Latonya	Porter	Prof Alvarez

Notice that when an entry is missing from one of the tables, pandas simply fills the corresponding entry with the special value NaN, which denotes a missing value (see section 6.7.2 for a reminder). This is true, for example, of student ID 15's name, and student ID's 2 final grade.

- Include all rows in one table or the other. For example, we could keep all the rows in the df_grades table and obtain this:

	student_id	final_grade	first_name	last_name
0	1	95	Melvin	Ware
1	3	71	Joseph	Paul
2	6	76	Elizabeth	Brown
3	7	91	Amanda	Schultz
4	8	75	Tanner	Perkins
5	11	59	Jacinda	Peterson
6	15	86	NaN	NaN

Or keep all the rows in the df_students table and obtain this:

	student_id	final_grade	first_name	last_name
0	1	95.0	Melvin	Ware
1	2	NaN	Thomas	Moore
2	3	71.0	Joseph	Paul
3	4	NaN	Sarah	Cruz
4	5	NaN	David	Freeman
5	6	76.0	Elizabeth	Brown
6	7	91.0	Amanda	Schultz
7	8	75.0	Tanner	Perkins
8	9	NaN	Ashley	Gonzales
9	10	NaN	Latonya	Porter
10	11	59.0	Jacinda	Peterson

In doing this kind of join, we typically call one table the "left table" and one table the "right table." It doesn't matter which is which, but in this case let's call df_grades the "left table" and df_students the "right table." A *left join* is one in which we keep all the rows in the "left table". A *right join* is one in which we keep all the rows in the "right table".

7.6 JOINS IN PANDAS

To summarize, we have seen the five ways to combine tables in Python. The first is a union, which simply brings two parts of one table together.

The next four combine tables using a join key. These kinds of joins have five "ingredients":

- The left table (df_grades)
- The right table (df_students)
- The column in the left table containing the value to join on (student_id)
- The column in the right table containing the value to join on (student_id)
- The type of join

The following table summarizes these four kinds of joins, along with a representation of these joins as a Venn diagram, in which each circle represents a table:

Join type	Description
Left join	Keep all the rows in the left dataset. Bring in rows from the right dataset if they exist.
Right join	Keep all rows in the right dataset. Bring in rows from the left dataset if they exist.
Inner join	Only keep rows that exist in both the left and right datasets.
Outer join	Keep all rows.

In section 7.7, we return to the topic of how to pick the right kind of join, which can sometimes be tricky. In this section, we will focus on the mechanics of doing a join in Python.

Unions are done using the `concat()` function, as we discussed in section 7.5.1. The remaining joins are done using `pd.merge()`. Run the following code:

```
pd.merge(df_grades,
        df_students,
        left_on='student_id',
        right_on='student_id',
        how='left',
        validate='one_to_one')
```

	student_id	final_grade	first_name	last_name	adviser
0	1	95	Melvin	Ware	Prof Duncan
1	3	71	Joseph	Paul	Prof Alvarez
2	6	76	Elizabeth	Brown	Prof Duncan
3	7	91	Amanda	Schultz	Prof Kennedy
4	8	75	Tanner	Perkins	Prof Alvarez
5	11	59	Jacinda	Peterson	Prof Alvarez

The following figure illustrates how each of the ingredients of a join are specified in the function:

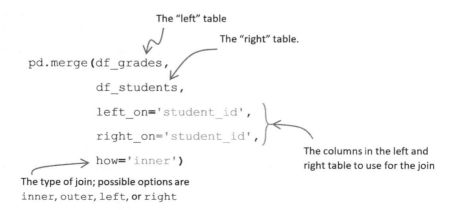

A few points are worth making here:

- `pd.merge()` will include every column in both tables. There's no way to tell it to just include some columns, but you can easily accomplish this by selecting columns in the tables before combining them. For example:

```
df_result = pd.merge(df_grades,
    df_students[['student_id', 'first_name', 'last_name']],
    left_on='student_id',
    right_on='student_id',
    how='left')
```

	student_id	final_grade	first_name	last_name
0	1	95	Melvin	Ware
1	3	71	Joseph	Paul
2	6	76	Elizabeth	Brown
3	7	91	Amanda	Schultz
4	8	75	Tanner	Perkins
5	11	59	Jacinda	Peterson
6	15	86	NaN	NaN

- You can get into trouble if both the left and right tables have columns with the same name—it wouldn't make sense for the resulting table to have two columns with the same name. If pandas detects this, it will try to de-conflict the names by adding the suffixes _x and _y to the column names from the left and right table, respectively. We strongly suggest, however, that you do not rely on that feature; having a function that might or might not change the names of your columns depending on the context in which it's called can result in confusing code. Instead, try using the rename() function (section 5.5.3) before doing the join.
- In the previous example, the join key includes only *one* column. In some cases, *two or more* columns might need to be used. For example, suppose full-time and part-time students each had their own sets of user IDs (i.e., full-time students were numbered 1, 2, 3, . . . and part-time students were numbered 1, 2, 3, . . .). Then we would need *both* the student ID *and* their full-time or part-time status to uniquely identify a student and perform the join. pd.merge() makes this easy—all you need to do is pass a list rather than a string to left_on and right_on. We will see examples of this later.

- If neither `left_on` or `right_on` is provided to `pd.merge()`, pandas will automatically look for any columns that exist in *both* tables and will use those columns to carry out the join. Furthermore, if the name of the column containing the join key is the same in both tables, we can use the on argument instead of specifying *both* `left_on` and `right_on`. In this book, we will always specify both arguments for clarity.

7.6.1 Index Alignment

One last completely different way to quickly do a left join in pandas can sometimes be useful as a shortcut and that is *index alignment*. For this method to work, the join key must be the row index of both tables.

Begin by creating a copy of `df_grades` and `df_students`, setting the index of both tables to `student_id`, and reminding yourself of what each table contains:

```
df_grades_2 = df_grades.copy().set_index('student_id')
df_grades_2.head()
```

	final_grade
student_id	
1	95
3	71
6	76
7	91
8	75

```
df_students_2 = df_students.copy().set_index('student_id')
df_students_2.head()
```

	first_name	last_name	adviser
student_id			
1	Melvin	Ware	Prof Duncan
2	Thomas	Moore	Prof Brown
3	Joseph	Paul	Prof Alvarez
4	Sarah	Cruz	Prof Duncan
5	David	Freeman	Prof Duncan

Now run the following line and look at `df_students_2`:

```
df_students_2['python_grade'] = df_grades_2.final_grade
df_students_2
```

	first_name	last_name	adviser	python_grade
student_id				
1	Melvin	Ware	Prof Duncan	95.0
2	Thomas	Moore	Prof Brown	NaN
3	Joseph	Paul	Prof Alvarez	71.0
4	Sarah	Cruz	Prof Duncan	NaN
5	David	Freeman	Prof Duncan	NaN
6	Elizabeth	Brown	Prof Duncan	76.0
7	Amanda	Schultz	Prof Kennedy	91.0
8	Tanner	Perkins	Prof Alvarez	75.0
9	Ashley	Gonzales	Prof Kennedy	NaN
10	Latonya	Porter	Prof Alvarez	NaN
11	Jacinda	Peterson	Prof Alvarez	59.0

What has happened? pandas automatically *aligned* the row indexes in the two tables. It has effectively carried out a *left join* with the row index as the join key and brought in the series we assigned. Any row in `df_students_2` that has no matching row in `df_grades` gets filled with a NaN, and any row in `df_grades` that has no matching row in `df_students_2` gets ignored.

This is something pandas does whenever you try to carry out operations that involve series with two different indices, but we won't explore this any further here.

7.7 PICKING THE RIGHT KIND OF JOIN

It is usually simple to figure out when a union is needed—the telltale sign is a table split into two parts. When one of the other kinds of joins is needed, though, it's a little harder to figure out whether the correct join is an inner join, an outer join, a left join, or a right join. In this section, we will first revisit the previous example, and then look at a few others and discuss which type of join is most appropriate in each case.

7.7.1 Revisiting Our First Example

Let's first consider the previous example (df_grades as the left table, and df_students as the right table). What is the right kind of join to produce a list of the names of students who have taken Python with their grades? ♦

You might initially be tempted to use an inner join, to include only students that exist in our database *and* who have taken introduction to Python. And you'd be more or less correct—an inner join would indeed work in this instance.

There also would be, however, an argument for doing a *left join*, which would keep every line in df_grades, regardless of whether a corresponding student exists in df_students. Why? Simply because if a student took "Introduction to Python" (and is therefore in df_grades) but is *not* in df_students, you'd probably want to know—it might reflect some database error. Doing an inner join would completely obscure these data issues.

If we do a left join, any students missing from df_students will be brought in with a value of NaN for first_name and last_name. We can count these and print a warning, and then drop these rows: ♦

```
df_result = pd.merge(df_grades,
        df_students[['student_id', 'first_name', 'last_name']],
        left_on='student_id',
        right_on='student_id',
        how='left')

if df_result.first_name.isnull().sum() > 0:
    print('Warning! df_students is missing some students.')

df_result = df_result[df_result.first_name.notnull()]
df_result
```

Warning! df_students is missing some students.

	student_id	final_grade	first_name	last_name
0	1	95	Melvin	Ware
1	3	71	Joseph	Paul
2	6	76	Elizabeth	Brown
3	7	91	Amanda	Schultz
4	8	75	Tanner	Perkins
5	11	59	Jacinda	Peterson

7.7.2 More Practice

Picking the right kind of join is an important—and sometimes tricky—topic, so let's get some more practice with the ridesharing example we briefly mentioned at the start of section 7.3. Suppose we have the following datasets:

- `df_drivers` lists every driver and their `driver_id`, `driver_name`, and `driver_age`.
- `df_driving` lists every driver that drove last month, their `driver_id`, and the `num_hours` they drove last month.
- `df_notifications` lists every driver that received a push notification last month, their `driver_id`, and `num_notifications` (i.e., the number of notifications they received).

The join we should use depends on the question we want to ask. Let's consider a few examples; as ever, we encourage you to give some thoughts to each of these before you rush to read the solution:

- "On average, how many hours did drivers drive last month?" ♦ This question could be interpreted in two ways:
  - ○ If we want to find the average number of hours *for drivers who drove at all last month*, all we need to do is ♦ `df_driving.num_hours.mean()`—we do not need any joins, because that table contains every driver who drove.
  - ○ If we want to find the average number of hours *for all drivers*, we can use a number of approaches, but because we're talking about joins, let's use that. We would do the following: ♦

```
df_res = pd.merge(df_drivers, df_driving,
                  left_on='driver_id',
                  right_on='driver_id',
                  how='left')
df_res.num_hours = df_res.num_hours.fillna(0)
df_res.num_hours.mean()
```

The first line does a left join between `df_drivers` and `df_driving`. A left join is appropriate because we want to obtain a table with *every driver* regardless of whether or not they drove.[1] This will result in a table with one row for every driver, and NaN values in the num_hours column for any drivers who did not drive in the last month. The second line fills these NaN values with zeros, because these drivers did not drive. Finally, the last line finds the average.

- "How many drivers were sent notifications *and* drove last month?" To answer this question, we would do the following: ♦

```
df_res = pd.merge(df_driving, df_notifications,
                  left_on='driver_id',
                  right_on='driver_id',
                  how='inner')
len(df_res)
```

The first line performs an inner join between df_driving and df_notifications. An inner join is appropriate in this case because we want drivers in *both* tables, those who drove *and* received notifications. The resulting table will contain only drivers in both tables, and so looking at the number of rows in this table will give us our desired result.

- "How many drivers were sent notifications *or* drove last month?" To correctly answer this question, we would do the following: ♦

```
df_res = pd.merge(df_driving, df_notifications,
                  left_on='driver_id',
                  right_on='driver_id',
                  how='outer')
len(df_res)
```

The first line performs an outer join between df_driving and df_notifications. An outer join is appropriate in this case because we want drivers in *either* table—either if they have driven, or if they have received a notification. The resulting table will contain those drivers we care about, and so the number of rows in that table is our desired result.

The topic of joins is complex, and it would take far more than one chapter to do it justice. These examples should provide a good starting point you can build on as you experiment with your own datasets.

7.8 PRIMARY KEYS AND JOINS

Before we close our introduction to joins, we need to discuss one last topic that we have thus far taken for granted—*primary keys*. This section is quite technical and can be skipped without any loss in continuity. It is, however, a crucial topic, and we encourage you to at least skim it.

A primary key is a column (or group of columns) that uniquely identifies a row in a table. Each row must have its own primary key, and it can be used to identify the row in another table.

For example, in the `df_full_time` table in section 7.5, the primary key is `student_id`—each student is uniquely identified by his or her ID. This ID can then be used in other tables (e.g., the `df_grades` table) to refer to a particular student.

The main requirement for a primary key is that it should be *unique*—no two rows can have the same primary key or else the key no longer represents that row uniquely. We can check whether a column is unique by using the `pandas` `duplicated()` function:

```
df_full_time_student_id.duplicated().sum()
```

```
0
```

The `duplicated()` function returns a series containing `False` if it is the first time the value in that row was encountered in that DataFrame, and `True` if this value has occurred before. We would expect the sum of that series to be zero if the column is unique and contains no duplicates.

In some cases, a table's primary key has *two* columns. For example, consider an online retailer with a number of independent websites in each country. In this situation, order ID "1" might not uniquely identify an order, because there might be an order ID "1" in the United States, an order ID "1" in Canada, and so on. A valid primary key in this case would be order ID *and* country. Thankfully, the `duplicated()` function works on DataFrames as well, so you could check that these two columns form a valid primary key using `df_orders[['ORDER_ID', 'COUNTRY']].duplicated().sum()`.

Why do we introduce primary keys in the context of joins? Simply because in every join we will be encountering in this book, at least *one* of the two join keys (in the left table or the right table) will be a primary key. For example:

- When we joined `df_grades` and `df_students` on `student_id`, that column was a primary key for `df_students`, because it uniquely identified each student (and, for that matter, was also a primary key in `df_grades`).
- In our ridesharing examples, we were always joining on `driver_id`, which was a primary key for both tables in question.

The reason this topic is crucial is that if you use `pd.merge()` and *neither* join column is a primary key, pandas won't give you an error (because in some cases outside the scope of this book, this is the right thing to do). The results, however, will be quite different from what you expect.

It is therefore important to ask yourselves—before every join—which of your join columns should be a primary key. You can check whether your expectation is met using the `duplicated()` method, but `pd.merge()` provides an easier way. It allows you to pass a `validate` argument to the function. If it is provided, the function will automatically check for primary keys before doing the merge. The argument can take one of the following three values:

- `one_to_one` will ensure that the join keys in *both* tables are unique
- `one_to_many` will ensure that the join key in the *left* table is unique
- `many_to_one` will ensure that the join key in the *right* table is unique

For example, in the university example, in which `student_id` is unique in both tables, you would run the following:

```
pd.merge(df_grades,
        df_students,
        left_on='student_id',
        right_on='student_id',
        how='left',
        validate='one_to_one')
```

If the uniqueness conditions you specified are not met, the function will throw an error.

7.9 CONSTRUCTING THE DIG ORDER DATASET

As in our previous chapter, we introduced the concept of joins using two toy datasets—df_grades and df_students. We are now ready to return to the Dig case study and to apply what we learned to produce a more useful version of the df_orders dataset.

Let's first remember what it looks like:

```
df_orders.head()
```

RESTAURANT_ID	TYPE	DRINKS	COOKIES	MAIN	BASE	SIDE_1	SIDE_2
R10002	IN_STORE	1.0	2.0	NaN	NaN	NaN	NaN
R10003	IN_STORE	0.0	0.0	NaN	NaN	NaN	NaN
R10001	DELIVERY	0.0	2.0	I0	I7	I15	I14
R10005	PICKUP	1.0	0.0	I0	I5	I9	I12

Notice that the columns listing the items in the bowl (MAIN, BASE, SIDE_1, and SIDE_2 only list the ID of the item, not its name). This makes it hard to read the orders. We might want to bring in item *names* rather than their IDs, using the df_items table:

```
df_items.head()
```

	ITEM_ID	ITEM_NAME	ITEM_TYPE
0	I7	Farro with Summer Vegetables	Bases
1	I39	Spindrift Lemon	Drinks
2	I5	Classic Brown Rice	Bases
3	I36	Kombucha	Drinks
4	I8	Cauliflower with Garlic and Parmesan	Market Sides

In particular, we might want to create columns called MAIN_NAME, BASE_NAME, SIDE_1_NAME, and SIDE_2_NAME, containing these names rather than IDs.

Before we dive into this, let's ask ourselves what the correct type of join would be here. Pause a second and see if you can figure it out. ♦ The answer is a left join, with `df_orders` on the left. Why? Simply because we want to use our list of orders as our "base dataset," (no pun intended) keep all those orders, and *bring in* item names. It is informative, in this case, to discuss each of the other kinds of joins in turn and understand why they would not be appropriate.

- An *inner join* should be identical to a left join as long as every item in `df_orders` exists in `df_items`. Why might this not be the case? Other than data errors, `df_orders` might refer to an old item that *used* to be sold on an old menu but has since been discontinued and removed from the database for some reason or other. In this situation, doing an inner join would delete any orders that involved these items. This is almost sure to be the wrong thing to do, because it would artificially make it look like we have *fewer* orders than we actually do. Even though the items in these orders have been discontinued, the orders still happened and should be counted.

- An *outer join* would certainly keep every order, but consider what happens if there are items in `df_items` that were never ordered. An outer join would create extra rows for these items, thus creating "phantom orders" that do not really exist.

- A *right join* would be the worst of all worlds. It would artificially create orders for items that were never ordered *and* drop any orders with items not in `df_items`.

Similarly, the orders table only contains restaurant IDs, not restaurant names. We might want to bring in the restaurant names into a column called `restaurant_name` using the `df_restaurants` table:

```
df_restaurants.head()
```

	RESTAURANT_ID	NAME	ADDRESS	LAT	LONG	OPENING_|
0	R10001	Columbia	2884 Broadway, New York, NY 10025	40.811470	-73.961230	8/9,
1	R10002	Midtown	1379 6th Ave, New York, NY 10019	40.763640	-73.977960	3/19,
2	R10005	Flatiron	40 W 25th St, New York, NY 10010	40.743600	-73.991070	11/14,

Which join should we use here? ◆ Again, for the same reason, we'll want a left join, with df_orders on the left.

We're now ready to dive in. Let's begin with the easier of the two problems—bringing in the restaurant name. It might help to review section 7.6 and ask yourself what the key "ingredients" of this join are, and how they fit into the pd.merge() function. ◆ The following line of code should do the trick:

```
df_res = ( pd.merge(df_orders,
        df_restaurants[['RESTAURANT_ID', 'NAME']],
                left_on='RESTAURANT_ID',
                right_on='RESTAURANT_ID',
                how='left')
        .rename(columns={'NAME': 'RESTAURANT_NAME'}) )
```

If your answer didn't look like this, take a second to see if you can understand our answer before we explain what we're doing. ◆

- First, we're specifying df_orders as the left table and df_restaurants as the right table. We are careful to select only the RESTAURANT_ID and NAME columns in df_restaurants, because we don't want to bring in the others (try to see what happens if you forget to do this).
- Second, we specify that the join key is in a column called RESTAURANT_ID in both tables.
- Third, we specify that we want a left join, as we just discussed.
- Fourth, we rename the NAME column that will have been brought in to call it RESTAURANT_NAME (try running this statement without the rename() function to understand its effect).
- Fifth, we save the result in df_res. We will use this as our final "results" DataFrame, which we will add columns to one by one.

Let's see what we have for our labor so far:

```
df_res.head()
```

TYPE	DRINKS	COOKIES	MAIN	BASE	SIDE_1	SIDE_2	RESTAURANT_NAME
STORE	1.0	2.0	NaN	NaN	NaN	NaN	Midtown
STORE	0.0	0.0	NaN	NaN	NaN	NaN	Bryant Park
IVERY	0.0	2.0	I0	I7	I15	I14	Columbia

Notice that we have successfully added a column with the restaurant name.

Let's now move to our second task—finding the name of the items in each order. Let's begin with the MAIN column by creating a column called MAIN_NAME. Take a second again and see if you can figure out what the ingredients of the join are here. ◆

- The left table is now going to be df_res, which is just our original df_orders but with our new RESTAURANT_NAME column. The right table will be df_items (and as above, we'll want to select the columns we care about—ITEM_ID and ITEM_NAME).
- For the first time, we encounter a join in which the join key is not the same in both tables. In the left table, the column containing the item ID we care about is MAIN. In the right table, it is ITEM_ID.
- The type of the join is left, as discussed previously.

Using these ingredients, our join looks like this. ◆ Notice that we are not yet saving the result in df_res but just looking at it. We'll make some final changes to the join before we're done:

```
( pd.merge(df_res,
           df_items[['ITEM_ID', 'ITEM_NAME']],
           left_on='MAIN',
           right_on='ITEM_ID',
           how='left')
    .rename(columns={'ITEM_NAME':'MAIN_NAME'}) ).head()
```

IES	MAIN	BASE	SIDE_1	SIDE_2	RESTAURANT_NAME	ITEM_ID	MAIN_NAME
2.0	NaN	NaN	NaN	NaN	Midtown	NaN	NaN
0.0	NaN	NaN	NaN	NaN	Bryant Park	NaN	NaN
2.0	I0	I7	I15	I14	Columbia	I0	Charred Chicken Marketbowl
0.0	I0	I5	I9	I12	Flatiron	I0	Charred Chicken Marketbowl
0.0	I1	I7	I9	I9	Williamsburg	I1	Spicy Meatballs Marketbowl

This table appears mostly as expected. There is one last annoyance, though. The result also contains a column called ITEM_ID. To understand where it came from, let's remind ourselves of the columns in each of the tables we're joining, and use a line to show the join keys in each table:

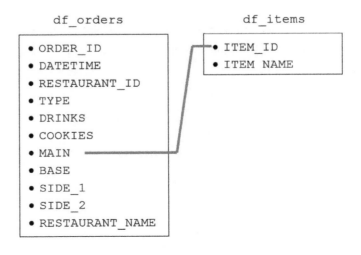

As we mentioned, pandas will always bring in *every* column in the second table—in this case, this includes the ITEM_ID column. We can hardly remove that column *before* joining when it's the column we're joining on! The easiest way to handle this is to simply drop the column at the end:

```
df_res = ( pd.merge(df_res,
            df_items[['ITEM_ID', 'ITEM_NAME']],
            left_on='MAIN',
            right_on='ITEM_ID',
            how='left')
        .rename(columns={'ITEM_NAME': 'MAIN_NAME'})
        .drop(columns='ITEM_ID') )
```

Our last step is to do this for the other columns (BASE, SIDE_1, and SIDE_2). An easy way to do this is to simply copy and paste the line above and modify it appropriately. Can you figure out which parts of the code will require modification? ◆ Only two short parts will require changing: the first is the left_on argument (e.g., you'd have to change it to BASE to specify that it is the base you want to bring in), and the second is what you are renaming the column *to* in the last line (the new name will be BASE_NAME). Finally, we repeat this process for SIDE_1 and SIDE_2 (see the *Jupyter Notebook* for this chapter for the code).

It might have occurred to you that this kind of repetitive copy-pasting of code is precisely what loops are for, and indeed, there is a way to do this using a loop. We won't print it here for the sake of space, but it's included as an optional cell in the *Jupyter Notebook* for this chapter. We highly recommend you give it a try yourself before looking. Here's a hint: to figure out the variable you should loop over, ask yourself what it is you are copy pasting here. ◆

We are finally ready to enjoy the fruits of our hard work:

```
df_res.head()
```

RESTAURANT_NAME	MAIN_NAME	BASE_NAME	SIDE_1_NAME	SIDE_2_NAME
Midtown	NaN	NaN	NaN	NaN
Bryant Park	NaN	NaN	NaN	NaN
Columbia	Charred Chicken	Farro with Summer	Snap Peas	Green Goddess Beans with

We can now produce far more meaningful plots. For example, suppose we wanted to figure out the most popular mains in bowls sold by Dig:

```
df_res.MAIN_NAME.value_counts().plot(kind='bar')
```

```
<matplotlib.axes._subplots.AxesSubplot at 0x109323750>
```

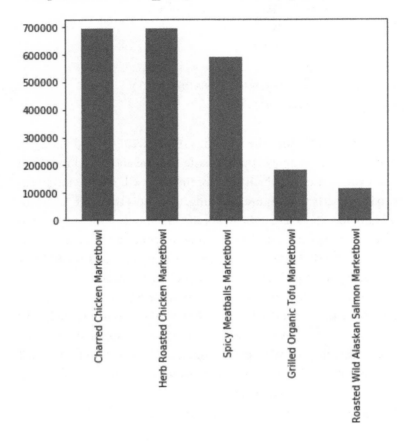

This plot is far more easily interpretable than it was with IDs.

7.10 WRAPPING UP

We began this chapter by discussing examples of situations in which datasets need to be combined and reviewing the various joins that can be used in these situations.

We then applied what we'd learned to create a more useful version of Dig's df_orders dataset. This combined dataset will form the basis of much of our work in future chapters. Let's save it, then, to make sure we can reload it later.

Run the following line:

```
df_res.to_pickle('Chapter 7/orders.pickle')
```

The concepts we covered in this chapter are complex—indeed, they could form the basis of an entire book on databases. Our discussion, however, should give you a strong foundation and prepare you to work with multiple datasets in Python. We will be using these concepts in the rest of the book to carry out useful analyses involving multiple datasets.

8

AGGREGATION

WE ARE NOW READY for our last major topic—aggregation. Together with joins, aggregations are some of the most useful operations pandas makes available. Aggregation is useful in any situation in which you need to combine multiple rows in pandas and calculate some summary statistics thereon. You can think of aggregation as Excel pivot tables on steroids.

We already encountered simple examples of aggregations in section 6.5.3 when we introduced the mean() function. For example, in the Dig df_summarized_ orders dataset, running the following code:

```
df_summarized_orders.NUM_ORDERS.mean()
```

combines (*aggregates*) every row in the dataset by finding the average value of the NUM_ORDERS column.

In this chapter, we extend our study of aggregation to more complex cases in which we want to aggregate on certain slices of the dataset. We will discuss a few examples of this later in this chapter, but to give one example, suppose we want to find the average number of orders *by restaurant*. We could do this, of course, by looping over the name of each restaurant, filtering the DataFrame to that restaurant, and separately finding the average number of orders in the remaining data. In this chapter, we will look at far more efficient techniques.

8.1 WHAT YOU'LL LEARN IN THIS CHAPTER

We begin this chapter by introducing the basics of aggregation—roughly equivalent to creating a simple pivot table in Excel. We then consider some more advanced topics, such as aggregating using multiple columns and aggregating on date and time columns.

8.2 WHAT YOU'LL NEED FOR THIS CHAPTER

Before we start, begin by creating a new *Jupyter Notebook* for this chapter, and the "Part 2" folder you created in section 5.2. We'll first import some packages that we'll need. Paste the following code in the first cell and run it:

```
import pandas as pd
import matplotlib.pyplot as plt
```

Next, we'll load some files we saved in previous chapters. To do this, paste the following code in the next cell and run it:

```
df_students = pd.read_pickle('Chapter 5/students.pickle')
df_summarized_orders = pd.read_pickle(
                'Chapter 5/summarized_orders.pickle')
df_orders = pd.read_pickle('Chapter 7/orders.pickle')
```

As ever, the *Jupyter Notebook* for this chapter, and the files from previous chapters, are available on the book's website.

8.3 THE BASICS OF AGGREGATION

We will begin our study of aggregation with the df_students dataset, which is small enough to be able to see exactly what each aggregation operation is doing and to understand how it works. Once we've mastered these basics, we will move to the larger, more realistic Dig datasets.

Let's first remind ourselves what the dataset looks like:

```
df_students.head()
```

	FIRST_NAME	LAST_NAME	YEAR	HOME_STATE	AGE	CALC_101_FINAL	E?
0	Daniel	Smith	1	NY	18	90.0	
1	Ben	Leibstrom	1	NY	19	80.0	
2	Kavita	Kanabar	1	PA	19	NaN	
3	Linda	Thiel	4	CA	22	60.0	
4	Omar	Reichel	2	OK	21	70.0	

For our first basic operation, suppose we wanted to find the average age of students in each academic year. We know enough, at this stage, to do this manually—you could look over every academic year, filter the DataFrame down to that academic year, and find the average age. But what a pain.

Luckily, there is an easier way. pandas' groupby() function allows us to carry out the operation above in one line:

```
df_students.groupby('YEAR').AGE.mean()
```

```
YEAR
1    18.2
2    20.0
3    20.0
4    22.0
Name: AGE, dtype: float64
```

Let's understand each part of this statement—we begin by applying the groupby() function to df_students. We pass the name of the YEAR column to specify we want to separate the dataset into multiple tables by that column. Next, we select the AGE column as the one we want to do calculations over. Finally, we apply the mean() function to find the average of that column.

A few points:

- Look at the structure of the result and—notice that this is not formatted as a table—as we saw earlier, this implies that output is a series, not a table. The structure of the series is such that the index gives the particular grouping category, and the value gives the aggregated function. As usual, we can always use `reset_index()` to turn this into a DataFrame:

```
df_students.groupby('YEAR').AGE.mean().reset_index()
```

	YEAR	AGE
0	1	18.2
1	2	20.0
2	3	20.0
3	4	22.0

Note that this is one of the cases in which we do *not* want to use `drop=True` on `reset_index()`. In this case, we *want* to keep the index, because it contains valuable information.

- In the previous example, we grouped on a single column—the YEAR column. The strength of the `groupby()` function is that it also allows us to group on multiple columns. For example, suppose we wanted to find the average AGE by YEAR *and* HOME_STATE, we could do this as follows:

```
df_students.groupby(['YEAR', 'HOME_STATE']).AGE.mean()
```

```
YEAR   HOME_STATE
1      FL              17.5
       NY              18.5
       PA              19.0
2      HI              19.0
       OK              21.0
3      NY              20.0
4      CA              22.0
Name: AGE, dtype: float64
```

Notice the syntax: instead of passing a single column name to groupby() as a string, we pass a list containing the two column names we want to group by. Again, the result is a series, the index contains the columns we group by, and the values contain the average age. Because we are now grouping by two columns, the structure of the index is a little more complicated—this is called a *multi-level index*, and it is outside the scope of this book. Instead, we'll simply reset the index to get a structure we're more familiar with:

```
df_students.groupby(['YEAR', 'HOME_STATE']).AGE.mean().reset_index()
```

	YEAR	HOME_STATE	AGE
0	1	FL	17.5
1	1	NY	18.5
2	1	PA	19.0
3	2	HI	19.0
4	2	OK	21.0
5	3	NY	20.0
6	4	CA	22.0

- Notice that we access the AGE column after the groupby() using .AGE. Just as in a DataFrame, we can also use ['AGE'] to access a column from groupby():

```
df_students.groupby('YEAR')['AGE'].mean()
```

```
YEAR
1    18.2
2    20.0
3    20.0
4    22.0
Name: AGE, dtype: float64
```

Because of the structure of the resulting series, we also can easily plot the results of a simple groupby() as follows:

```
df_students.groupby('YEAR').AGE.mean().plot(kind='bar')
```

`<matplotlib.axes._subplots.AxesSubplot at 0x1222f0e50>`

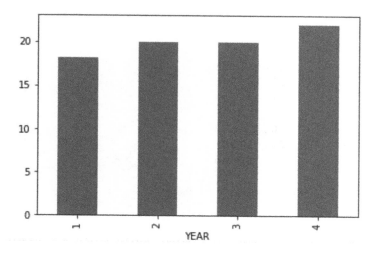

Let's practice what we've learned on the df_summarized_orders dataset to find the average number of daily orders at each restaurant:

```
( df_summarized_orders.groupby('RESTAURANT_NAME')
                      .NUM_ORDERS.mean() )
```

```
RESTAURANT_NAME
Bryant Park        871.436782
Columbia           687.150685
Flatiron           772.556164
Midtown            891.136986
NYU               1180.438356
Upper East Side    774.650704
Upper West Side    770.372603
Williamsburg       862.120548
Name: NUM_ORDERS, dtype: float64
```

It is interesting to compare these numbers to the ones we would get using a different method. Let's use the full orders dataset (the one that lists every order one by one rather than summarizing them by day). To find the total number of orders in our year's worth of data, we can count the number of times each restaurant appears in that dataset. Then we divide it by 365, the number of days in the year:

```
df_orders.RESTAURANT_NAME.value_counts() / 365
```

```
NYU                1180.438356
Midtown             891.136986
Williamsburg        862.120548
Flatiron            772.556164
Upper West Side     770.372603
Upper East Side     753.427397
Columbia            687.150685
Bryant Park         623.136986
Name: RESTAURANT_NAME, dtype: float64
```

Notice a very curious fact—for some restaurants (like NYU and Columbia), the numbers obtained using both methods are identical. For others, however (like Upper East Side and Bryant Park), the numbers obtained using both methods are different. Can you think why that might be? Pause for a second and see if you can figure it out. ◆

The key to the riddle is that the two methods are identical for restaurants at which sales occur on every day of the year (e.g., NYU and Columbia). For restaurants that close on some days, however (e.g., on weekends or on public holidays), the two methods are different. To understand why, consider what these methods are actually doing:

- As we saw in chapter 6, df_summarized_orders only lists days on which an order happened at a given restaurant. If *no order* happened on a given day (e.g., on a day when the restaurant was closed), the date does not even appear for that restaurant in that dataset. Thus, when we find an average, it gives us the average order per day *on which the restaurant was open*, not including days on which no sales occurred.
- The second method divides the number of days by 365, regardless of the number of days on which sales actually happened.

Neither one of these methods is necessarily right or wrong—each is appropriate to answer a different kind of question. For example:

- The first method might be appropriate to decide how much of a given perishable item to deliver to a restaurant every day (e.g., fresh vegetables). Because deliveries would occur only on days when the restaurant is open, the average orders per day *on which the restaurant is open* is appropriate.
- The second method might be appropriate for accounting and finance purposes. In deciding how much money a restaurant will collect over a year, every day counts.

We introduce this example to show that answering even a simple question using data can require a fair amount of subtlety and a real understanding of how the business operates. Luckily, if you've stuck with us this far, you have an understanding of pandas that is deep enough to equip you to really understand what every operation is doing and to figure out which is correct for a given situation.

8.3.1. Aggregating Functions

Each of the examples used the same aggregating operation—finding the mean of a column. There are a number of other functions pandas makes available that you can use in this way. Among them are the following:

- Statistics

    - mean() : find the average of each group
    - median() : find the median of each group
    - sum() : find the sum of each group
    - min() : find the minimum of each group
    - max() : find the maximum of each group
    - std(), sem() : find the standard deviation of each group, and the standard error of the group mean—the exact definition of the standard deviation and standard error is beyond the scope of this book, but we include this for those who might have heard of these concepts and are looking to implement them.

Note that every one of these methods *ignores* NaN missing values. For example, when calculating the mean, the function will sum all non-missing values, and then divide by the number of non-missing values, as if the missing values never existed. This is often the right thing to do, but not always. For example, if missing values represent zeros (e.g., days with no sales), you *must* first replace them with zeros using `fillna(0)` (see section 6.7.2). This is one of the most common sources of errors when aggregating in Python.

- Counting variables

  ○ `size()` : returns the number of rows in each group *including* NaN missing values

  ○ `count()` : returns the number of rows in each group *not including* NaN missing values

  ○ `nunique()` : returns the number of *unique* values in each group, ignoring any NaN missing values

Let's use aggregation to find the number of orders at each restaurant using the `df_orders` DataFrame. We already did this using `value_counts()`, but let's try using `groupby()`: ♦

```
df_orders.groupby('RESTAURANT_NAME').TYPE.size()
```

```
RESTAURANT_NAME
Bryant Park          227445
Columbia             250810
Flatiron             281983
Midtown              325265
NYU                  430860
Upper East Side      275001
Upper West Side      281186
Williamsburg         314674
Name: TYPE, dtype: int64
```

Notice that `size()` does not require a specific column to operate on—it just tallies up the number of rows. We picked TYPE, but we could have picked any other row, or indeed no row at all.[1]

```
df_orders.groupby('RESTAURANT_NAME').size()
```

```
RESTAURANT_NAME
Bryant Park          227445
Columbia             250810
Flatiron             281983
Midtown              325265
NYU                  430860
Upper East Side      275001
Upper West Side      281186
Williamsburg         314674
dtype: int64
```

Comparing these results to those of value_counts(), we find the results are identical:

```
df_orders.RESTAURANT_NAME.value_counts()
```

```
NYU                  430860
Midtown              325265
Williamsburg         314674
Flatiron             281983
Upper West Side      281186
Upper East Side      275001
Columbia             250810
Bryant Park          227445
Name: RESTAURANT_NAME, dtype: int64
```

The benefit of groupby(), of course, it that it allows us to create groups over more than one column. Let us, for example, find the number of orders of *each type* at each restaurant: ◆

```
df_orders.groupby(['RESTAURANT_NAME', 'TYPE']).size()
```

```
RESTAURANT_NAME   TYPE
Bryant Park       DELIVERY      15613
                  IN_STORE     171494
                  PICKUP        40338
Columbia          DELIVERY      25247
                  IN_STORE     182603
                  PICKUP        42960
Flatiron          DELIVERY      28859
                  IN_STORE     204607
                  PICKUP        48517
Midtown           DELIVERY      22380
                  IN_STORE     244980
                  PICKUP        57905
NYU               DELIVERY      43310
                  IN_STORE     314832
                  PICKUP        72718
Upper East Side   DELIVERY      52080
                  IN_STORE     180605
                  PICKUP        42316
Upper West Side   DELIVERY      53337
                  IN_STORE     184588
                  PICKUP        43261
Williamsburg      DELIVERY      31822
                  IN_STORE     229427
                  PICKUP        53425
dtype: int64
```

Hopefully, this example begins to show you the power of groupby().

8.3.2 Using unstack()

One additional feature can come in very handy when aggregating over multiple columns, and that is the unstack() function. Consider the last join in the previous section—because we aggregated over multiple columns, we ended up with a series with a two-column index—one with the first column we aggregated over (RESTAURANT_NAME) and one with the second (TYPE).[2] We previously saw how to use reset_index() to convert this series to a DataFrame:

```
( df_orders.groupby(['RESTAURANT_NAME', 'TYPE'])
                    .size().reset_index().head() )
```

	RESTAURANT_NAME	TYPE	0
0	Bryant Park	DELIVERY	15613
1	Bryant Park	IN_STORE	171494
2	Bryant Park	PICKUP	40338
3	Columbia	DELIVERY	25247
4	Columbia	IN_STORE	182603

Notice how each column of the index gets converted to a column in the DataFrame.

The unstack() function takes a different approach. It takes the last column in the index, and creates a column for every unique value in that index, thus "unstacking" the table::

```
df_orders.groupby(['RESTAURANT_NAME', 'TYPE']).size().unstack()
```

TYPE	DELIVERY	IN_STORE	PICKUP
RESTAURANT_NAME			
Bryant Park	15613	171494	40338
Columbia	25247	182603	42960
Flatiron	28859	204607	48517
Midtown	22380	244980	57905
NYU	43310	314832	72718
Upper East Side	52080	180605	42316
Upper West Side	53337	184588	43261
Williamsburg	31822	229427	53425

Notice how this table contains the same number as the series, but is reshaped to contain the order types as columns. This operation will be extremely useful in chapter 9 when we handle more complex questions.

8.4 CALCULATIONS ON MULTIPLE COLUMNS

The examples we have shown thus far have all considered aggregating one column only. Often, we want to aggregate *multiple* columns. As a simple example, suppose we wanted to find the average number of drinks per order *and* the average number of cookies per order at each restaurant.

When the aggregating function is the same for all columns (in this case, we are applying the `mean()` aggregation to the `DRINKS` column *and* to the `COOKIES` column), we can simply do this by selecting both columns after the `groupby()` (notice how similar this is to selecting multiple columns in a DataFrame):

```
( df_orders.groupby('RESTAURANT_NAME')[['DRINKS', 'COOKIES']]
                                                  .mean() )
```

RESTAURANT_NAME	DRINKS	COOKIES
Bryant Park	0.098138	0.261294
Columbia	0.066572	0.259049
Flatiron	0.097637	0.259161
Midtown	0.126128	0.260683
NYU	0.075769	0.258898
Upper East Side	0.118145	0.257603
Upper West Side	0.097032	0.260475
Williamsburg	0.096446	0.258750

Note that if you do *not* specify columns over which to aggregate, and just use `df_orders.groupby('RESTAURANT_NAME').mean()`, you would be finding the mean of every numerical column in the dataset.

When aggregation involves *different* aggregating functions on each column, things are a little more complicated.

In particular, suppose we want to create a DataFrame with the following data for each restaurant:

- The average number of drinks in each order
- The number of orders with non-missing values under MAIN (in other words, orders with bowls)

The first column requires the mean() transformation. The second requires count() (number of items excluding missing values). The cleanest way to do this is to use special syntax available in the agg() function in pandas:[3]

```
( df_orders.groupby('RESTAURANT_NAME')
        .agg(AV_DRINKS = ('DRINKS', 'mean'),
            N_W_MAIN = ('MAIN', 'count')) )
```

RESTAURANT_NAME	AV_DRINKS	N_W_MAIN
Bryant Park	0.098138	216767
Columbia	0.066572	239406
Flatiron	0.097637	268909
Midtown	0.126128	309502
NYU	0.075769	411253
Upper East Side	0.118145	261957
Upper West Side	0.097032	268023
Williamsburg	0.096446	299822

Notice how this function works:[4]

- It can be applied directly to the groupby(); there is no need to select a specific column.
- The function accepts one argument for every column you would like to produce in the output. Each argument should be the name of the output column (e.g., AV_DRINKS), and it should be equal to two terms in ()—the first should be the *input* column in the original table (e.g., 'DRINKS'), and the second should be the name of the function to apply, as a string (e.g., 'mean').

Using this function, we can carry out a truly dazzling number of aggregations to answer extremely complex business questions; we shall see some more examples in chapter 9.

One final point: when we discussed transforming columns in section 6.7, we noted that sometimes, no in-built function exists in pandas to do what we want. For those situations, we introduced the apply() function (see section 6.7.7). It is also possible to aggregate using custom functions. We cover this topic in an appendix available on the book's website.

8.5 MORE COMPLEX GROUPING

In this section, we consider two more advanced ways to group DataFrames: using a series and using datetime columns.

8.5.1 Grouping Using a Series

Suppose we wanted to determine whether people who order drinks are more likely to also add a cookie to their order.

One way to do this would be to add a column called HAS_DRINK to df_orders, and then to group by that column:

```
df_orders['HAS_DRINK'] = (df_orders.DRINKS > 0)
df_orders.groupby('HAS_DRINK').COOKIES.mean()
```

```
HAS_DRINK
False    0.259543
True     0.258149
Name: COOKIES, dtype: float64
```

The first line creates a column HAS_DRINK that—for each row—contains True if the order in that row contains a drink, and False otherwise. The second line takes all the rows for which HAS_DRINK=False, looks at the COOKIES column for those rows, and finds the average (0.26). It then does the same thing for rows with HAS_DRINK=True.

It looks like, no, buying a drink doesn't really affect propensity to buy a cookie, because the two numbers are similar.

However, pandas allows us to do this without even creating the new column, as follows:

```
df_orders.groupby(df_orders.DRINKS > 0).COOKIES.mean()
```

```
DRINKS
False     0.259543
True      0.258149
Name: COOKIES, dtype: float64
```

Consider what is happening here—the text inside the groupby() function, df_order.DRINKS > 0, is simply a series that contains True if the order has a drink, and False otherwise. We simply pass this series to the groupby() function, and pandas will automatically group by the result of that series. This leads to an identical result, but it can be convenient when implementing complex groupby() operations.

8.5.2 Grouping Using Dates and Times

One last kind of aggregation is worth discussing, and that is aggregating over dates and times. pandas has a function called resample(), which works exactly like groupby(), but for dates. There is one key difference, however—to be able to use resample(), you need to ensure that the datetime column is the index of the DataFrame, not just one of the columns.[5] Let's see this in action on the Dig dataset:

```
( df_orders.set_index('DATETIME')
        .resample('D')
        .DRINKS
        .mean()
        .reset_index()
        .head() )
```

	DATETIME	DRINKS
0	2018-01-01	0.064363
1	2018-01-02	0.083897
2	2018-01-03	0.069347
3	2018-01-04	0.076179
4	2018-01-05	0.080892

We begin by setting the index of the DataFrame to the DATETIME column. We then apply the `resample()` function and specify that we want to group by day using D. Finally, we treat the result as if we had done a `groupby()`. In this case, we find the average number of drinks on each day.

You won't be surprised to hear that D is not the only kind of frequency that can be used with this function. Options include the following:

- T—minutes
- H—hours
- D—days
- W—weeks
- M—months
- Y—years
- B—business day; this allows you to produce a time series only listing *business days*, excluding weekends. Any points that occur during weekends get lumped into Friday.
- BM—business month; same as business day, but for months

A full list of supported frequencies can be found in the pandas documentation.[5]

Of course, we're now free to plot the results of our analysis, which can lead to some powerful results. Let us, for example, plot the total number of orders per day at the Columbia restaurant. ◆ If you're having a little trouble figuring out how to do this, it might help to break down the task into steps:

- Filter the orders down to those at the Columbia restaurant.
- Set the index to be the DATETIME column.
- Resample.
- Find the number of orders (have a look back at section 8.3.1 if you can't remember which function to use).
- Plot it.

Here's how we would do it: ◆

```
( df_orders
  [df_orders.RESTAURANT_NAME == 'Columbia']
  .set_index('DATETIME')
  .resample('D')
  .size()
  .plot() )
```

`<matplotlib.axes._subplots.AxesSubplot at 0x10d8393d0>`

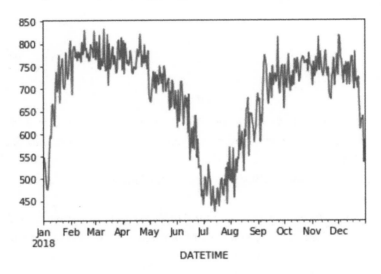

Let's consider each step (each number corresponds to the line number in the code):

2. Filter down `df_orders` to orders at the Columbia restaurant only.
3. Set the index of the DataFrame to the `DATETIME` column.
4. Resample it to a daily frequency.
5. Find the number of orders on each day.
6. Plot the result, using the index (in this case, the date) as the *x*-axis.

The result is highly informative. We see that there is clear seasonality at the restaurant: orders are lowest in the summer and winter, and highest during the semester.

We might wonder, whether this pattern holds generally? How would we modify the statement above to plot this result for *all* restaurants combined? ♦ All we'd need to do is remove line 2, which filters down to Columbia restaurants:

```
( df_orders
  .set_index('DATETIME')
  .resample('D')
  .size()
  .plot() )
```

`<matplotlib.axes._subplots.AxesSubplot at 0x11f974190>`

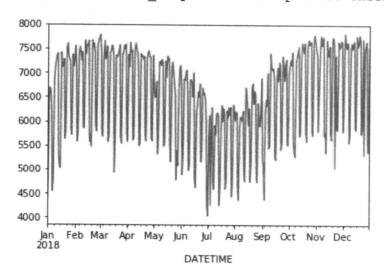

Looking at this plot, it does seem that the pattern persists even when looking at multiple restaurants, but the plot is rather hard to read because of those downward spikes. What do you think causes these to happen? ♦ The most likely explanation is that many restaurants are closed on weekends. So, every seven days, the number of orders drops considerably because only a small subset of the restaurants experience orders on those days.

How might we fix this plot? ♦ One way would be to simply plot by week rather than by day, and find the number of sales in each *week*. How would you do this in the previous code? ♦ You would simply replace the D with a W. One problem with this method is that it would result in a plot with only fifty-two points (for the fifty-two weeks in a year), and this plot might look a little jagged.

What could we do instead? ♦ One approach would be to plot a *moving average*, in which on each day, instead of plotting sales *on that day*, we plot the *average sales* for the two weeks before that day. This would have the effect of "smoothing out" any short-term changes in sales.

We can do this using the pandas `rolling()` function, which also acts like a `groupby()`. To understand how it works, it helps to look at the result of the previous `resample()` operation (this code is the same as the code that produced the Columbia plot, but without the `plot()` at the end):

```
( df_orders
  [df_orders.RESTAURANT_NAME == 'Columbia']
  .set_index('DATETIME')
  .resample('D')
  .size()
  .head() )
```

```
DATETIME
2018-01-01    519
2018-01-02    547
2018-01-03    532
2018-01-04    502
2018-01-05    477
Freq: D, dtype: int64
```

Now consider this code:

```
( df_orders
  [df_orders.RESTAURANT_NAME == 'Columbia']
  .set_index('DATETIME')
  .resample('D')
  .size()
  .rolling(3)
  .mean()
  .head() )
```

```
DATETIME
2018-01-01           NaN
2018-01-02           NaN
2018-01-03    532.666667
2018-01-04    527.000000
2018-01-05    503.666667
Freq: D, dtype: float64
```

In line 6, we are asking pandas to create a three-period rolling window ending with that date, and in line 7 we are finding the *average* sales over that entire window. Notice the nature of the result—values on January 1 and 2 are missing, because the original data does not contain three days of data before those two days. On January 3, we take January 1, 2, and 3 and average the number of orders on those days to get 532.7 (calculated as (519 + 547 + 532) / 3). The same is true for every other day. pandas gives you many ways to customize `rolling()`—the documentation is quite informative in that respect.

We now are finally ready to plot a smoother version of our overall sales graph. We'll use a fourteen-day moving average, but you can experiment with other numbers to vary the smoothness of the graph: ◆

```
( df_orders
    .set_index('DATETIME')
    .resample('D')
    .size()
    .rolling(14)
    .mean()
    .plot() )
```

```
<matplotlib.axes._subplots.AxesSubplot at 0x1201b4e90>
```

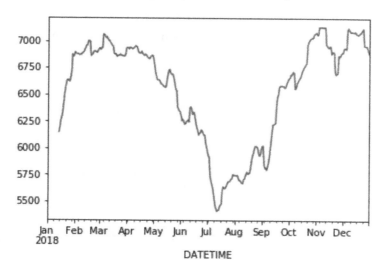

The seasonal variation pattern is now apparent across all stores.

We have one last point before we conclude this chapter. Both `resample()` and `rolling()` can be used in combination with the `groupby()` to carry out powerful analyses. For example, let's find the total number of sales by day in each store: ◆

```
( df_orders.set_index(df_orders.DATETIME)
        .groupby('RESTAURANT_NAME')
        .resample('D')
        .size()
        .reset_index()
        .head() )
```

	RESTAURANT_NAME	DATETIME	0
0	Bryant Park	2018-01-01	373
1	Bryant Park	2018-01-02	789
2	Bryant Park	2018-01-03	818
3	Bryant Park	2018-01-04	782
4	Bryant Park	2018-01-05	719

Here, we group by restaurant, and then resample by day, finding the number of rows in each group.

We have one last example to make sure we understand this concept. Suppose we wanted to find the total number of drinks bought at each restaurant in each month in 2018. We could do this as follows: ♦

```
( df_orders.set_index(df_orders.DATETIME)
        .groupby('RESTAURANT_NAME')
        .resample('M')
        .DRINKS
        .sum()
        .reset_index()
        .head() )
```

	RESTAURANT_NAME	DATETIME	DRINKS
0	Bryant Park	2018-01-31	1414.0
1	Bryant Park	2018-02-28	1336.0
2	Bryant Park	2018-03-31	1427.0
3	Bryant Park	2018-04-30	1478.0
4	Bryant Park	2018-05-31	2340.0

Looking at these numbers, orders seem to be ticking up in May, as the weather starts getting hotter. We will investigate this in greater detail in chapter 9.

One last caveat: the use of the `agg()` function that we discussed at the end of section 8.4 is a relatively new addition to pandas. Unfortunately, it does not yet work with DataFrames grouped using the `resample()` or `rolling()` function. As such, if you are trying to aggregate on multiple functions using a `resample()`, you will have to do each aggregation individually, and then join the resulting tables. We will see an example of this in section 9.9.

8.6 WRAPPING UP

In this chapter, we introduced the basics of aggregations. We saw how pandas can be used to reproduce the functionality of pivot tables in Excel, but on far larger datasets, and with far more flexibility. In particular, we looked at aggregation on generated columns and on columns containing dates and times.

This more or less wraps up our study of pandas. We've come a long way. In the last chapter, we will come full circle back to the Dig case study from chapter 5 and bring together everything we've learned to answer some questions pertaining to Dig's business.

9

PRACTICE

WE HAVE ALMOST REACHED the end of our time together (heartbreaking, we know…). This last chapter is a capstone of sorts. We will come full circle to the Dig case and answer a number of synoptic questions using everything we've learned so far.

We will consider a number of questions that will bring together many of the topics we discussed in part 2. We warn you, however, that some of these topics will be complex. That said, so are the real problems businesses face every day when working with data, and this section will give you practice tackling these kinds of problems. Even if you do not follow each line of code, reading through the solutions to these questions will expose you to some interesting ways datasets can be analyzed.

9.1 WHAT YOU'LL LEARN IN THIS CHAPTER

We have arranged the problems in this section in order of increasing difficulty, so that you can build up to the most complex analyses at the end of the chapter.

In Chapter 5, we introduced Dig and Shereen Asmat, senior manager, data and operational products at the company. We base the questions in this chapter on three parts of Dig's business that we discussed there:

- The launch of a new product or a new service (specifically, Dig's delivery-first service). We discuss this in sections 9.3, 9.4, 9.7, and 9.8.
- The staffing process Dig faces at its restaurants, which we discuss in sections 9.5 and 9.9.
- The process of becoming more data-driven as a company, which we discuss in section 9.6.

9.2 WHAT YOU'LL NEED FOR THIS CHAPTER

Before you start, begin by creating a new *Jupyter Notebook* for this chapter. The first thing you'll do is import some packages you'll need. Paste the following code in the first cell and run it:

```
import pandas as pd
import matplotlib.pyplot as plt
```

Next, you'll load some files you created in previous chapters. To do this, paste the following code in the next cell and run it:

```
df_summarized_orders = pd.read_pickle(
                'Chapter 5/summarized_orders.pickle')
df_orders = pd.read_pickle('Chapter 7/orders.pickle')
```

As ever, the *Jupyter Notebook* for this chapter, and the files from all previous chapters, are available on the book's website. If you skipped a previous chapter, make sure you download each of the files in the code above and put them in an appropriately named folder.

9.3 NEW PRODUCT ANALYTICS: CREATING FERTILE GROUND FOR SUCCESS

As you read in the story of Dig, one of the company's greatest sources of pride is that each restaurant prepares everything on site. Indeed, every one of its employees are trained to prepare food in its restaurants, in line with this ethos. There is, however, one exception—bottled and canned drinks. The infrastructure required to produce these items is usually prohibitive. Furthermore, a number of companies that produce these products share Dig's ethos for responsible sourcing and high-quality ingredients.

Therefore, it is perhaps unsurprising that, as you read, Dig does not produce its own bottled and canned drinks and instead stocks a number of products produced by other companies.

In this section, we consider a hypothetical future in which Dig *does* decide to launch a new line of drinks of its own. When a company launches a new product, it often decides to first launch at a single location and then to expand chain-wide. We will be asking how Dig might use its data to decide at which restaurant to launch this new product line, and when in the year to do it.

Notice a key difference between this question, and those we have considered thus far. In previous sections, the questions were phrased mostly in the context of the data, and it was clear how to use the data to answer them—the only question was what pandas code we would need to execute each step. This question is far more ambiguous, and we first need to figure out how to phrase this in the context of the data.

Before we begin, spend a few minutes thinking about this. What questions might you want to ask of the data? How might you want to get answers? We'll provide one proposed solution, but by all means, experiment with the data. ♦

Our first step might be to ask what we're trying to achieve. The answer is hopefully uncontroversial—we'd like to sell as much of the new drink as possible. How might we achieve this? Presumably, we'd like to find places where drinks are popular—launching the line in a restaurant where no one buys any drinks seems to be counterproductive. So perhaps our first question is whether some restaurants' customers tend to order more drinks than others. If this is the case, then we might expect those restaurants to be better candidates for our product launch. We can see if this is the case as follows: ♦

```
( df_orders.groupby('RESTAURANT_NAME').DRINKS
                    .mean().sort_values().plot(kind='bar') )
```

`<matplotlib.axes._subplots.AxesSubplot at 0x125abbbd0>`

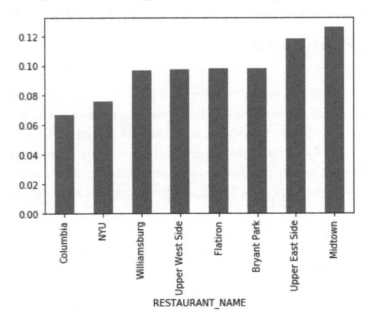

First, we group by the RESTAURANT_NAME (which we helpfully added to the dataset in chapter 7), and then we find the average of the DRINKS column, to find the average number of drinks per order at that restaurant. Finally, we sort the resulting series by its values, to plot the results in ascending order. Based on this plot, it seems like Midtown and the Upper East Side might be good places to launch.

Let's now turn our attention to time. As the product manager in charge of this launch, how might we decide when in the year to launch it? Following similar logic, we might want to look at the total number of drinks sold every month across Dig restaurants. We can do this as follows: ♦

```
( df_orders.set_index('DATETIME').resample('M')
                        .DRINKS.sum().plot() )
```

`<matplotlib.axes._subplots.AxesSubplot at 0x125d48890>`

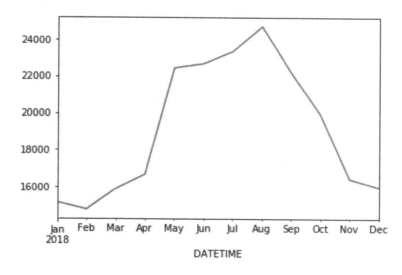

We first set the index of our DataFrame to the DATETIME column; we then resample over months and find the sum of drinks purchased at Dig in any given month. Perhaps unsurprisingly, the number of drinks purchased peaks in the summer, which would seem like a good time to launch our new product line.

What else could we try? ♦ Because we've decided the Midtown restaurant would be a good place to launch our product line, we might want to see whether this temporal pattern holds at that restaurant specifically. You could do this as follows: ♦

```
( df_orders[df_orders.RESTAURANT_NAME == 'Midtown']
        .set_index('DATETIME')
        .resample('M')
        .DRINKS.sum().plot() )
```

We won't print the results here for the sake of space, but they look similar.

Notice how we started with a question that seemed quite ambiguous, boiled it down to a more objective question, and then used the power of pandas to answer the question.

9.4 THE NEXT FRONTIER: DESIGNING DIG'S DELIVERY-SPECIFIC MENU

Dig is a young company entering a phase of exponential growth. One of the more exciting aspects of this growth is the company's expansion beyond its central restaurant offering to delivery, pick-up orders, and catering. These new lines of business were immediately popular when Dig launched them, with as many as 30 percent of orders coming from deliveries at some stores. As you read in our intro-duction to Dig, however, this success came with challenges. Dig initially treated delivery as a "bolt on" service to its primary restaurant offering, allowing custom-ers to order using the in-store menu, and contracting with third party services for delivery. This mirrored the approach taken by many of Dig's competitors, but it quickly became apparent to Dig's leadership that this led to a substandard cus-tomer experience. Among other problems, Dig's extensive menu meant that there were approximately 1,500 different possible Dig bowls, some of which were far better suited to delivery than others.

Dig realized an opportunity when it saw one, and it decided to heavily focus on ways to push the boundaries of how customers experienced Dig. In particular, it decided to create a brand-new, reimagined delivery service, with an entirely new menu and platform, built and optimized specifically for delivery. This would make it a trailblazer in the industry and put the company in a prime position to capture this increasingly large segment of the market.

As you can imagine, creating a brand-new delivery service is no small endeavor. There are some benefits to being the first mover, but it also means there's no rule-book to follow. In this section, and sections 9.7 and 9.8, we discuss questions Dig might answer using its data to support this effort. Before we get started, take a few minutes and think of the kinds of questions you might want to handle. ♦

Our first challenge will be around the design of Dig's new delivery menu. What options should Dig include in that menu? Part of the answer will center on which items "travel" better, but that's not something we can figure out based on the data we have. Another part of the answer will center on the options in Dig's *current* menu that are most popular. This in itself is quite a broad question. How can we reduce it to a simple set of analyses? ◆ We might first remember that every Dig bowl involves four main choices—the base, the main, the first side, and the second side. So we might want to ask how popular each of the options in each of these categories are:

- What's the most popular main?
- What's the most popular base?
- What main is most popular with which base?
- How does this all relate to sides?

In addition, we might ask more general questions—for example, "are people who order salad as a base likely looking for healthier options?" If the answer is no (some people just like lettuce!), we might include options in our new menu with salad as a base, but less healthy sides to go with it. We will handle this specific question in section 9.8.

For now, however, let's simply identify which mains and bases are most popular, and which combinations work best. Pause a second and figure out how you'd do this (hint: we already began this at the end of section 7.9). ◆

First, let's look at the orders dataset. You will remember that in chapter 7, we had brought the name of each restaurant and of each item into that dataset (this, in itself, required using some joins): ◆

```
df_orders.head()
```

	ORDER_ID	DATETIME	RESTAURANT_ID	TYPE	DRINKS	COOKIES	M/
0	O1820060	2018-10-11 17:25:50	R10002	IN_STORE	1.0	2.0	N
1	O1011112	2018-05-31 11:35:00	R10003	IN_STORE	0.0	0.0	N
2	O752854	2018-04-21 18:12:57	R10001	DELIVERY	0.0	2.0	
3	O2076864	2018-11-17 12:50:52	R10005	PICKUP	1.0	0.0	

Next, let's see which mains and bases are most popular: ◆

```
df_orders.MAIN_NAME.value_counts().plot(kind='bar')
```

`<matplotlib.axes._subplots.AxesSubplot at 0x12314e490>`

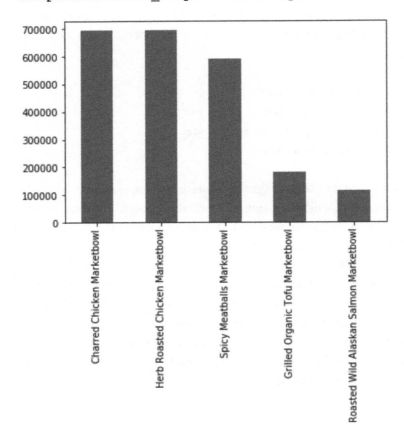

Clearly, chicken is popular, followed by meatballs. Tofu and salmon seem to get a little less love!

Let's look at bases:

```
df_orders.BASE_NAME.value_counts().plot(kind='bar')
```

```
<matplotlib.axes._subplots.AxesSubplot at 0x121d873d0>
```

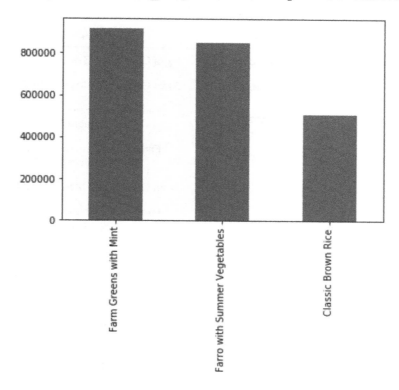

Looks like Dig's clientele is pretty healthy—salad has pride of place in this list of bases. The next most popular item seems to be farro, and finally rice.

Now let's move on to a slightly more difficult challenge. How do we figure out which sides are most popular with which mains? Pause a second and see if you can figure it out. ◆

One solution is simply to group the order data by MAIN_NAME *and* BASE_NAME, and count the number of times each combination occurs: ◆

```
( df_orders.groupby(['MAIN_NAME', 'BASE_NAME'])
        .size()
        .sort_values(ascending=False)
        .reset_index() )
```

	MAIN_NAME	BASE_NAME	0
0	Herb Roasted Chicken Marketbowl	Farm Greens with Mint	280243
1	Charred Chicken Marketbowl	Farm Greens with Mint	279591
2	Herb Roasted Chicken Marketbowl	Farro with Summer Vegetables	259056
3	Charred Chicken Marketbowl	Farro with Summer Vegetables	258945
4	Spicy Meatballs Marketbowl	Farm Greens with Mint	238509
5	Spicy Meatballs Marketbowl	Farro with Summer Vegetables	220116
6	Charred Chicken Marketbowl	Classic Brown Rice	155311
7	Herb Roasted Chicken Marketbowl	Classic Brown Rice	154203
8	Spicy Meatballs Marketbowl	Classic Brown Rice	132060
9	Grilled Organic Tofu Marketbowl	Farm Greens with Mint	73682
10	Grilled Organic Tofu Marketbowl	Farro with Summer Vegetables	68153
11	Roasted Wild Alaskan Salmon Marketbowl	Farm Greens with Mint	46052
12	Roasted Wild Alaskan Salmon Marketbowl	Farro with Summer Vegetables	42779
13	Grilled Organic Tofu Marketbowl	Classic Brown Rice	41323
14	Roasted Wild Alaskan Salmon Marketbowl	Classic Brown Rice	25616

The first line of code groups the DataFrame, the next finds the number of rows with each combination, the next sorts the result in descending order (most popular at the top), and the last line finally resets the index to put the result in a DataFrame.

Looks like chicken salad is a winner! This is all well and good, but this table is a little difficult to interpret. How might we visualize this information in a graph that actually shows the relative popularity of each side with each main? ◆ We can first use `unstack()` from section 8.3.2 to create a table in which each column corresponds to a base:

```
( df_orders.groupby(['MAIN_NAME', 'BASE_NAME'])
        .size()
        .unstack() )
```

BASE_NAME MAIN_NAME	Classic Brown Rice	Farm Greens with Mint	Farro with Summer Vegetables
Charred Chicken Marketbowl	155311	279591	258945
Grilled Organic Tofu Marketbowl	41323	73682	68153
Herb Roasted Chicken Marketbowl	154203	280243	259056
Roasted Wild Alaskan Salmon Marketbowl	25616	46052	42779
Spicy Meatballs Marketbowl	132060	238509	220116

Notice how the *second* column in the index (BASE_NAME) is converted into three columns. Finally, we can use `plot()` to plot each column side by side:

```
( df_orders.groupby(['MAIN_NAME', 'BASE_NAME'])
        .size()
        .unstack()
        .plot(kind='bar') )
```

<matplotlib.axes._subplots.AxesSubplot at 0x1236f84d0>

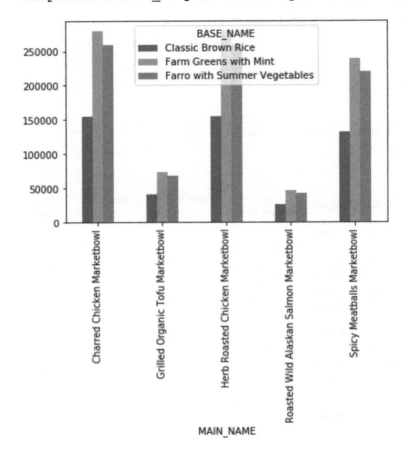

This graph is far more revealing, and makes it clear that the relative popularity of each side does not depend on the main in the bowl. This combined insight is useful—it implies that we don't need to worry too much about the exact combinations of sides with mains, and we can focus instead on which combinations are most appropriate for delivery.

For the sake of brevity, we won't perform similar analyses for sides, but you should give it a try. Later in this chapter, we will explore other questions pertaining to the design of Dig's new menu.

9.5 STAFFING FOR SUCCESS

Our next question is centered on staffing, one of the big challenges of any business in the foodservice industry. This challenge looms large in Asmat's description of Dig's move to being more data-driven. She refers to using data to support the professional development of Dig employees, as well as the difficulties that arise from storing various human resources (HR) data in separate systems. Dig's full staffing datasets lie beyond the scope of this book, but we still can address a specific aspect of this problem with the datasets that we *do* have. This is a more common situation than you might expect—we often *wish* we had access to certain datasets, but we have to manage with what we have on hand. Pause here for a second and try to brainstorm what aspect of this problem you might be able to handle with the data we do have. ◆

The problem we handle is one that Asmat mentions in our introduction to Dig, when she refers to "the supply of labor and shifting landscape of labor laws in the United States." Many considerations fall under this umbrella. For example, an increasing number of municipalities in the United States are passing laws to preclude employers from changing employee shifts at the last minute. This requires companies to release staffing schedules some time in advance, which can be quite difficult given the highly variable demand in foodservice. This task is even harder for Dig, because its commitment to cooking every item on site requires a minimum level of trained staff in the restaurants at all times.

How might we use our data to facilitate this process of schedule design? ◆ Our data will allow us to analyze the distribution of orders throughout the day at each restaurant. This would be a crucial first step to compiling a staffing schedule that will ensure that Dig is able to fulfill demand at each of its restaurants. For example, if we found that the Columbia restaurant is busiest around lunchtime, we would ensure that our long-term schedule allocates enough team members to that restaurant at that time. Before we jump in, you might want to ask yourself what you expect the results to be, so that you can compare your expectations with reality.

Begin by thinking of the kind of plot you would want to produce to investigate this. ◆ Perhaps the most obvious first step would be to produce a graph that—for each restaurant—shows how order volumes vary over the day. This can be accomplished in a number of ways, so take a few seconds to think about what approach you might take. ◆

We can do this easily using `groupby()` and `unstack()`. Let's begin by producing a DataFrame that—for each restaurant and each hour of the day—gives the total number of orders that occur during that hour over the entire year: ◆

```
( df_orders.groupby([df_orders.DATETIME.dt.hour,
                     df_orders.RESTAURANT_NAME])
        .size() )
```

```
DATETIME   RESTAURANT_NAME
9          Columbia               2
           Flatiron               2
           Midtown                3
           NYU                    5
           Upper East Side        1
                                ...
23         Midtown               97
           NYU                  149
           Upper East Side       94
           Upper West Side       96
           Williamsburg         107
Length: 118, dtype: int64
```

Notice that this groupby() statement uses every trick we studied in chapter 8:

- We aggregate over multiple columns, by passing a list to groupby() containing *two* things to group over.
- Instead of passing column names, we pass a series of values. This allows us to group over hour, even though it doesn't exist as a column in the DataFrame, and without creating a whole new column.

The result is a series that—for every restaurant and hour—gives the number of orders during that hour at that restaurant. How can we convert this into a Data-Frame that contains one column per restaurant, and one row per hour of the day? ♦ We simply use unstack():

```
( df_orders.groupby([df_orders.DATETIME.dt.hour,
                     df_orders.RESTAURANT_NAME])
        .size()
        .unstack() )
```

RESTAURANT_NAME	Bryant Park	Columbia	Flatiron	Midtown	NYU	Upper East Side
DATETIME						
9	NaN	2.0	2.0	3.0	5.0	1.0
10	5581.0	7035.0	6927.0	8106.0	3756.0	2306.0
11	22289.0	9698.0	27094.0	31643.0	35330.0	22564.0
12	31444.0	10008.0	37918.0	44244.0	56872.0	36402.0

Finally, all that's left is to plot the result:

```
( df_orders.groupby([df_orders.DATETIME.dt.hour,
                     df_orders.RESTAURANT_NAME])
         .size()
         .unstack()
         .plot() )
```

```
<matplotlib.axes._subplots.AxesSubplot at 0x122c76d90>
```

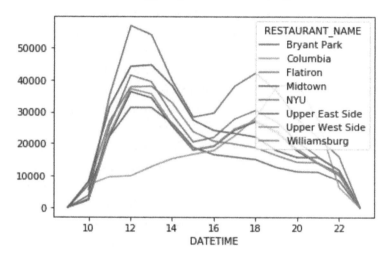

Let's look at the plot we've produced. Is it what you expected? Does anything stand out? What are some salient points you would make using these plots if you were to present these results to your boss? ◆ Following are a few points that stick out to us:

- Most restaurants are busiest around lunchtime, with a secondary peak around dinner. This would be a crucial piece of information in deciding how to staff each restaurant.
- The lunchtime peak is at roughly the same time for every restaurant, but the dinner peak seems to vary by restaurant.
- Some restaurants have strikingly different distributions. The Columbia restaurant, for example, has almost no volume over lunch but robust demand at dinner. This implies the staffing schedule at Columbia should be fundamentally different from those at other restaurants in the chain.

Do any others occur to you? This should give you a taste of how useful pandas can be in staff planning. We will return to this topic in section 9.9 when we analyze the relationship between order volume and weather.

9.6 DEMOCRATIZING DATA: THE SUMMARIZED ORDER DATASET

When we began our study of pandas in chapter 5, we loaded two datasets: the orders dataset, which listed each individual order in full granularity, and the summarized orders dataset, which summarized these orders by store and day.

To anyone who has worked closely with a data team, this will be all too familiar. Real datasets are always complex, often dirty, and rarely easily accessible; as a result, business intelligence teams within companies often have to process the company's datasets into formats that more readily lend themselves to analysis.

As discussed in the context of Dig, the inherent complexity of real datasets can arise for various reasons. In a smaller early stage company, it might not yet be clear how the data will be used. It is also unlikely that an early stage company would have a fully built-out data infrastructure that easily allows the extraction of specific views of the data. In a larger legacy company, the opposite problem might be true. Over many years, the company's data infrastructure might have mushroomed into a set of unwieldy disparate systems, each storing a specific kind of data that might not be particularly useful in isolation. It sometimes requires a tremendous amount of skill (not to mention political clout) to combine these datasets in a way that can lead to useful insights.

This can be problematic. In our experience, one of the most common reasons companies have trouble deriving insight using data is the onerous technical hurdles that fall between those who know the business well and need answers, and the data. The ability to massage the data into a form that business leaders can analyze is therefore one of the most useful skills we have seen in practice. We call this *democratizing data*—making it available to broader parts of the company for analysis.

Of course, with great power comes great responsibility. The risk of creating a more condensed view of key datasets is that if it is done wrong (e.g., through a coding mistake), erroneous conclusions might be drawn without any hope of debugging them. Democratizing data correctly is therefore one of the most important skills in a data analyst's toolkit, and we introduce this concept by creating the summarized_order dataset ourselves.

First, let's look at the orders dataset. You will remember that in chapter 7, we brought the name of each restaurant and of each item into that dataset (this required the use of some joins): ◆

```
df_orders.head()
```

	ORDER_ID	DATETIME	RESTAURANT_ID	TYPE	DRINKS	COOKIES	M/
0	O1820060	2018-10-11 17:25:50	R10002	IN_STORE	1.0	2.0	N
1	O1011112	2018-05-31 11:35:00	R10003	IN_STORE	0.0	0.0	N
2	O752854	2018-04-21 18:12:57	R10001	DELIVERY	0.0	2.0	

You will recall that the `summarized_order` dataset contained one row for every day at every restaurant and listed the number of orders at that restaurant on that day as well as the percentage of orders that were delivery orders.

To create this dataset, let's first create a DataFrame that gives the *number of orders* on each day at every restaurant. ♦ In case you're a little stuck, begin by setting the index to `DATETIME`, grouping by `RESTAURANT_NAME` and resampling by day. Then ask yourself which aggregating function from section 8.3.1 you would use to find the number of rows at each restaurant on each day. Finally, convert the result to a DataFrame with the correct column names. Here's how we do it: ♦

```
df_num_orders = ( df_orders.set_index('DATETIME')
                           .groupby('RESTAURANT_NAME')
                           .resample('D')
                           .size()
                           .reset_index()
                           .rename(columns={0:'NUM_ORDERS'}) )
print(len(df_num_orders))
df_num_orders.head()
```

2919

	RESTAURANT_NAME	DATETIME	NUM_ORDERS
0	Bryant Park	2018-01-01	373
1	Bryant Park	2018-01-02	789

The first line sets the index of our DataFrame to the DATETIME column to make it ready for a resample() operation (as described in section 8.5.2). We then group by the restaurant name, and resample by the index so that the output lists data for each restaurant by day. We then apply the size() operation to find the number of rows in each group. Finally, we reset the index to obtain two columns: one with the restaurant name and one with the day. As we saw earlier, when you use the size() function on entire groups rather than on one specific column, the resulting column name ends up being zero, so we need to rename that column to NUM_ORDERS to indicate that this is what this column contains.

The result is a DataFrame that contains one row for every day at every restaurant, and the number of orders on that day. Note that we also print the number of rows in the dataset—in this case, 2919; we will use this later.

Our second step will be to produce a DataFrame that contains the percentage of orders at each restaurant that are delivery orders. The easiest way to do this is as follows: ◆

```
df_orders['IS_DELIVERY'] = (df_orders.TYPE == 'DELIVERY')
df_pct_delivery = ( df_orders.set_index('DATETIME')
                    .groupby('RESTAURANT_NAME')
                    .resample('D')
                    .IS_DELIVERY
                    .mean()
                    .reset_index()
                    .rename(columns={'IS_DELIVERY':
                                     'PCT_DELIVERY'}) )
print(len(df_pct_delivery))
df_pct_delivery.head()
```

	RESTAURANT_NAME	DATETIME	PCT_DELIVERY
0	Bryant Park	2018-01-01	0.0
1	Bryant Park	2018-01-02	0.0
2	Bryant Park	2018-01-03	0.0
3	Bryant Park	2018-01-04	0.0
4	Bryant Park	2018-01-05	0.0

The first thing we do is create a column in our DataFrame in which each row contains a one if the order is a delivery order, and zero otherwise. Why do we do this? Simply because we then can find the average of that column to find the percentage of delivery orders. The rest of the code proceeds very much as the previous code does. Notice that—reassuringly—the number of rows in this DataFrame is the same as in the previous one.

Finally, we need to join these two datasets to produce the final summarized order dataset. ♦ If you're having trouble, start by asking yourself which column(s) in each of these datasets you should perform the join on. Then ask yourself what kind of join this should be—inner, outer, left, or right? Here's our solution: ♦

```
df_summarized_orders = (
        pd.merge(df_num_orders,
                df_pct_delivery,
                on=['RESTAURANT_NAME', 'DATETIME'],
                how='outer') )
print(len(df_summarized_orders))
df_summarized_orders.head()
```

2919

	RESTAURANT_NAME	DATETIME	NUM_ORDERS	PCT_DELIVERY
0	Bryant Park	2018-01-01	373	0.0
1	Bryant Park	2018-01-02	789	0.0
2	Bryant Park	2018-01-03	818	0.0
3	Bryant Park	2018-01-04	782	0.0
4	Bryant Park	2018-01-05	719	0.0

This is a straightforward merge as discussed in section 7.5, but a few things bear explaining. First, why do we do an outer join? As we saw earlier, the tables we are joining together have the same number of rows, and presumably, the restaurant names and dates will match exactly in those two tables. Why not, then, just do an inner join? Here's the key point—by doing an outer join, we get to check (for "free") whether the keys in the two tables do indeed match exactly. What would happen if some restaurant name and date combinations appeared in one table and not in the other? In that case, an outer join would create additional rows in the output. The fact that the result of an outer join contains the same number of rows as the original two tables implies that the keys do, indeed, match.

One last point: If you look at the original `summarized_orders` DataFrame we explored in chapter 5, you will notice it had 2,806 rows, whereas the DataFrame we created here has 2,919. Why the difference? The DataFrame from chapter 5 did not include days on which no orders were placed. If we filter down this Data-Frame to days on which there *were* orders, we get the same number of rows:

```
(df_summarized_orders.NUM_ORDERS > 0).sum()
```

```
2806
```

Let's take stock of what we've done. We've gone from a dataset with more than two million rows—impossible to open in Excel, and therefore unlikely to be of any use to a business analyst—to one with just under three thousand rows. As we saw in chapter 6, this smaller dataset contains enough data to derive powerful insights about each restaurant's performance, and it is small enough to be handled in Excel by someone with a deep understanding of the day-to-day functioning of the business. This exemplifies data democratization in action!

9.7 FINDING FERTILE GROUND FOR A NEW DELIVERY SERVICE

In section 9.4, we began discussing an exciting new phase in Dig's history—the move to create a delivery-first service to elevate the customer experience. We discussed how Dig might analyze its existing order patterns to create a new menu.

In this section, we shall consider this new service from a different angle. In our introduction to Dig, we read about how popular Dig's delivery service became at some of its restaurants, but in extending this service, we might want to know the restaurants at which deliveries are most popular. This might help us, for example, decide which restaurant to use as a pilot for the new program. This also touches on the staffing questions we discussed in section 9.5—the staffing needs for a delivery-heavy restaurant are likely to be different from those for a restaurant where most orders happen in-store.

Let's start by doing this on a restaurant-by-restaurant basis. How might we find, for example, the proportion of delivery orders at the Columbia restaurant? We could do this as follows: ◆

```
( df_orders[df_orders.RESTAURANT_NAME == 'Columbia']
        .TYPE.value_counts(normalize=True).reset_index() )
```

	index	TYPE
0	IN_STORE	0.728053
1	PICKUP	0.171285
2	DELIVERY	0.100662

(Recall that `normalize=True` in the code gives proportions that sum to one rather than counts.) This is helpful, but how can we do this for every restaurant, and more important, how can we visualize the results in a way that will be useful and actionable? Take a few seconds to think about this before you read on. What makes this task a little more difficult (and justifies this section's placement later in the chapter) is that it's not quite clear exactly how we might visualize the result. It's worth giving it a try yourself first. ◆

Our solution will first produce a table that looks something like this:

RESTAURANT_NAME	IN_STORE	DELIVERY	PICKUP
Bryant Park	0.754002	0.068645	0.177353
Columbia	0.728053	0.100662	0.171285
Flatiron	0.725600	0.102343	0.172056
Midtown	0.753170	0.068805	0.178024
NYU	0.730706	0.100520	0.168774
Upper East Side	0.656743	0.189381	0.153876
Upper West Side	0.656462	0.189686	0.153852
Williamsburg	0.729094	0.101127	0.169779

Each entry lists the proportion of that restaurant's orders filled using that kind of modality. For example, 10 percent of Columbia orders are delivery orders, as we saw in the individual calculation given previously.

How could we produce a table like this? We could use a number of methods based on the material we've already learned (and we provide an example in the *Jupyter Notebook* associated with this chapter), but let's use the opportunity to introduce a more elegant method that doesn't use any new techniques, but rather uses methods we've already seen in a new (and, dare I say it, exciting) way.

Let's first run the following code:

```
( df_orders.groupby('RESTAURANT_NAME')
        .TYPE
        .value_counts(normalize=True) )
```

We simply group by RESTAURANT_NAME, and then apply value_counts() to the TYPE column for every restaurant.

Why is this different from the aggregations we've done so far? Simply because the aggregating function we're using—value_counts()—doesn't return a single number but a full series. Let's break this down. Consider a statement like df_orders.groupby('RESTAURANT_NAME').DRINKS. mean(). For each RESTAURANT_NAME, we calculate the mean of the DRINKS column. This is a *single* number, which we can fit easily into a table with one row per restaurant.

When we aggregate using value_counts(), however, each restaurant gets a full series. How should pandas fit this result into a table with one row per restaurant? Let's try it out:

```
( df_orders.groupby('RESTAURANT_NAME')
        .TYPE
        .value_counts(normalize=True)
        .head(10) )
```

```
RESTAURANT_NAME   TYPE
Bryant Park       IN_STORE    0.754002
                  PICKUP      0.177353
                  DELIVERY    0.068645
Columbia          IN_STORE    0.728053
                  PICKUP      0.171285
                  DELIVERY    0.100662
Flatiron          IN_STORE    0.725600
                  PICKUP      0.172056
                  DELIVERY    0.102343
Midtown           IN_STORE    0.753170
Name: TYPE, dtype: float64
```

pandas does the smart thing! It takes the index of the `value_counts()` function's output, and *combines* it with the index from the `groupby()` to create a two-column index. Finally, we can use `unstack()` from section 8.3.2 to create the table we need:

```
( df_orders.groupby('RESTAURANT_NAME')
        .TYPE
        .value_counts(normalize=True)
        .unstack() )
```

TYPE	DELIVERY	IN_STORE	PICKUP
RESTAURANT_NAME			
Bryant Park	0.068645	0.754002	0.177353
Columbia	0.100662	0.728053	0.171285
Flatiron	0.102343	0.725600	0.172056
Midtown	0.068805	0.753170	0.178024
NYU	0.100520	0.730706	0.168774
Upper East Side	0.189381	0.656743	0.153876
Upper West Side	0.189686	0.656462	0.153852
Williamsburg	0.101127	0.729094	0.169779

The last step is to plot it (notice that we sort the restaurants in increasing order of delivery percentage, because the purpose of our analysis is to figure out where to launch the new delivery offering):

```
( df_orders.groupby('RESTAURANT_NAME')
        .TYPE
        .value_counts(normalize=True)
        .unstack()
        .sort_values('DELIVERY')
        .plot(kind='bar') )
```

`<matplotlib.axes._subplots.AxesSubplot at 0x1267251d0>`

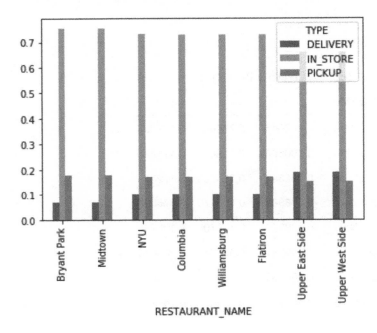

For each restaurant, we now have a plot that displays the proportion of each order type. We have one last step before we can interpret the plot: can you think of any way this plot could be more useful? ♦ The fact that these bars are side by side makes them a little difficult to compare—stacking them would allow us to compare them directly. We can do this easily by passing a simple extra argument to the plot() function—stacked=True:

```
( df_orders.groupby('RESTAURANT_NAME')
        .TYPE
        .value_counts(normalize=True)
        .unstack()
        .sort_values('DELIVERY')
        .plot(kind='bar', stacked=True) )
```

`<matplotlib.axes._subplots.AxesSubplot at 0x125f89110>`

This is a far easier plot to analyze, because now we can compare each proportion between restaurants. Notice also how using `normalize=True` in `value_counts()` means that every bar in the plot has the same height, even though some restaurants have far more sales than others. This makes it far easier to compare these proportions. Look at the graph: what insights can you derive from it? ◆ Following are our observations:

- Pickup volume seems to be roughly constant across all stores, at just under 20 percent.
- In-store and deliveries vary considerably across restaurants. They range from Bryant Park, with the fewest deliveries, to the Upper East Side and the Upper West Side, with the most. For those familiar with New York, this won't be surprising. The Upper East Side and Upper West Side are heavily residential neighborhoods, presumably more likely to order at-home deliveries. Bryant Park, by contrast, is near an area with many office buildings.

These insights would be an important part of Dig's thinking in regard to where they might launch their new delivery service.

9.8 UNDERSTANDING YOUR CUSTOMERS: ARE SALAD EATERS HEALTHIER?

In section 9.4, we discussed the design of new menus for Dig's delivery-first service, and we carried out some basic analytics on Dig's order patterns to help make this decision.

In this section, we consider the question from a different angle. As we read in our introduction to Dig, there are three possible bases in every Dig bowl, one of which is salad (the other two are farro and rice). We might initially assume that customers who choose a salad as a base are looking for healthier, lower-calorie options in their diet. But is this true, or do those people just happen to like lettuce?

This question is relevant because it allows us to know our customers better and, in turn, to design a delivery menu that serves them better. If we do indeed find that salad eaters gravitate toward healthier options, we would want to include a number of salad-based bowls with healthy sides and mains on our menu. Conversely, if we find little relationship between these options, we might instead focus on designing bowls that we think will be tastiest and travel best (e.g., mixing a salad with a healthy-but-piping-hot chicken entrée might result it in wilting).

Again, this question is ambiguous. How might we define a "healthy" customer? No column defines this. ♦ Two other columns, however, might act as proxies for this. First, the number of cookies in each order, and second, the sides that were ordered in the bowl (some, like mac and cheese and cauliflower with parmesan are cheesier, and perhaps less likely to be ordered by health-conscious customers).

Let us then rephrase our question as follows: first, do people who order bowls with salad bases tend to order fewer cookies; and, second, is the mix of sides different for those who order bowls with salad bases?

Let's consider the first question about cookies. ♦ Consider how salads are denoted in the dataset:

```
df_orders.BASE_NAME.value_counts()
```

```
Farm Greens with Mint          918077
Farro with Summer Vegetables   849049
Classic Brown Rice             508513
Name: BASE_NAME, dtype: int64
```

It looks like Farm Greens with Mint is the menu item we're looking for. Rather than retyping that string again and again, let's save it in a variable:

```
salad = 'Farm Greens with Mint'
```

Now let's address our question:

```
print(df_orders[df_orders.BASE_NAME != salad].COOKIES.mean())
print(df_orders[df_orders.BASE_NAME == salad].COOKIES.mean())
```

```
0.3664534590480054
0.08817561054247083
```

The first line filters down `df_orders` to orders in which the base was *not* a salad, and then it finds the mean number of cookies per order. The second line finds the same average when the base *was* a salad. As we suspected, we see that customers without salad order 0.37 cookies per order on average, whereas those *with* salad order 0.09 cookies on average.

Of course, you can get the same result using `groupby()`, as follows:

```
df_orders.groupby(df_orders.BASE_NAME == salad).COOKIES.mean()
```

```
BASE_NAME
False    0.366453
True     0.088176
Name: COOKIES, dtype: float64
```

Thankfully, the results are identical.

T-TESTS IN PYTHON

You might wonder, of course, whether this difference (0.37 cookies versus 0.09 cookies per order) is a significant difference or just a random variation. If you've taken an introductory statistics class, you know that the way to figure this out is to use a t-test. The theory of t-tests is beyond the scope of this book, but for those of you who are familiar with it, here's how it's done in Python (note that the first time you run this code, it might take a while for Python to make the **scipy** package ready to use):

```
from scipy import stats
stats.ttest_ind(df_orders[df_orders.BASE_NAME!=salad].COOKIES,
                df_orders[df_orders.BASE_NAME==salad].COOKIES)
```

```
Ttest_indResult(statistic=386.1313807565163, pvalue=0.0)
```

We first import the `stats` part of the `scipy` package. We then pass two lists to the `stats.ttset_ind()` function. The first is the list of number of cookies for orders *without* salad, the second is for orders *with* salad. The p-value of 0.0 in the output implies a statistically significant difference.

Let's now move on to the second part of the question: is the distribution of sides any different for bowls with salad bases compared with the others? Let's begin with bowls *with* salads, and plot the distribution of the *first* side for that bowl:

```
( df_orders[df_orders.BASE_NAME == salad]
        .SIDE_1_NAME
        .value_counts(normalize=True)
        .sort_index()
        .plot(kind='bar') )
```

```
<matplotlib.axes._subplots.AxesSubplot at 0x13023f2d0>
```

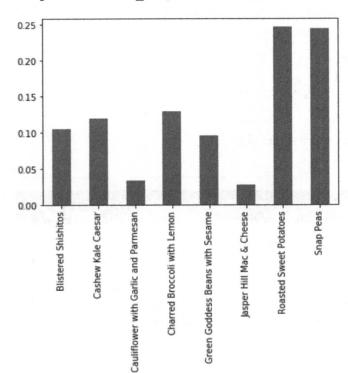

We are first filtering down our orders DataFrame to bowls with a salad base and then plotting a normalized distribution of the first side in those bowls (recall that using normalize=True ensures the bars all sum to one). Finally, we apply a sort_index() to show the results in alphabetical order. It looks like roasted sweet potatoes and snap peas are by far the two most popular sides.

Let's now see how non-salad eaters fare. How would you modify the previous code to produce the same plot for non-salad eaters? ◆ All you'd have to do is change the == in the first line to != to produce the plot for bases that are *not* salads. Rather than do this, however, can you think of a visualization that might be simpler than this graph? ◆ Ideally, we'd want a plot showing the proportions of each of the sides for salad eaters and non-salad eaters *side by side*. We've already done something similar in section 9.7. Go back and look and try to figure it out yourself before we show you. ◆

```
( df_orders
    .groupby( df_orders.BASE_NAME == salad )
    .SIDE_1_NAME
    .value_counts(normalize=True)
    .unstack(level=0)
    .plot(kind='bar') )
```

```
<matplotlib.axes._subplots.AxesSubplot at 0x1306f40d0>
```

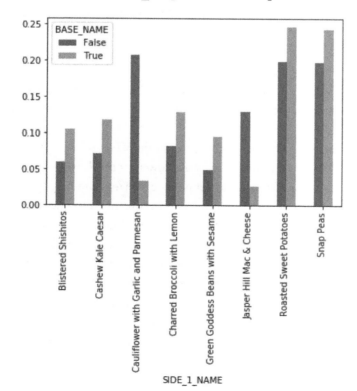

Let's understand each line (again, the numbers correspond to line numbers in the code):

2. We use groupby(), using a series, as discussed in section 8.5.1. All rows with greens as a base will be in one group, and all rows without greens as a base will be in the other group.
3. We then extract the name of the first side.
4. We find normalized value counts—at this point, the output will look something like this:

```
( df_orders
    .groupby( df_orders.BASE_NAME == salad )
    .SIDE_1_NAME
    .value_counts(normalize=True))
```

```
BASE_NAME   SIDE_1_NAME
False       Cauliflower with Garlic and Parmesan   0.208072
            Roasted Sweet Potatoes                 0.199584
            Snap Peas                              0.198432
            Jasper Hill Mac & Cheese               0.130618
            Charred Broccoli with Lemon            0.082552
            Cashew Kale Caesar                     0.072204
```

5. We take the second level of the index, and convert it to columns using unstack(), as discussed in section 8.3.2.
6. We plot the results.

Notice that the resulting plot's legend has two entries—True and False. These correspond to the values of the grouping series in line 2; True for those rows that had a salad as a base, and False otherwise.

The results are quite striking—we find that the proportion of bowls with mac and cheese and cauliflower and parmesan are significantly lower for bowls with salad as a base. Conversely, broccoli, snap peas, and sweet potatoes are much more popular. This shouldn't be the greatest surprise, but it does confirm that in our menu design efforts, we should ensure that salad-based options include healthier components.

One last point: these plots consider only the *first* side, in column SIDE_1. Customers, however, can order *two* sides, and the second side is contained in the column SIDE_2. Because there's nothing special about the "first" side versus the "second" (they're presumably entered at random by the cashier), we wouldn't expect this to make any difference. But, for peace of mind, we've included optional code in the *Jupyter Notebook* for this chapter that takes both sides into account. The results look very similar.

9.9 ORDERS AND WEATHER

Our final analysis brings together many of the topics we discussed in this chapter. In particular, we look at the relationship between various order patterns and the weather. This relationship could touch on many parts of Dig's operations, from food ordering, to staffing levels, to promotional efforts, to the company's new delivery service. Before we begin, take a few seconds to ask yourselves what questions the company might ask about this relationship, and how they might be useful. ◆

Many questions come to our minds, but among them, we consider the following:

- We might expect the proportion of delivery orders to depend pretty heavily on the weather. In particular, in the dead of winter, we might expect deliveries to be more prevalent. Is this true? This will strongly affect how we might plan staffing for those periods.
- Does the temperature outside affect the number of drinks customers order? This might affect our choice of when to launch the new drinks line we discussed in section 9.3, or perhaps help staff members decide when to display promotional posters for drinks in stores.

To answer any of these questions, we need a dataset containing weather data in New York City. Download the `weather.csv` dataset from the "raw data" folder on the book's website, load it into `pandas`, and convert the first column to a date. Then, have a look at the first few rows of the dataset: ◆

```
df_weather = pd.read_csv('raw data/weather.csv')
df_weather.DATETIME = pd.to_datetime(df_weather.DATETIME)
df_weather.head()
```

	DATETIME	TEMPERATURE	PRECIP
0	2018-01-01 00:00:00	9.66	0.0
1	2018-01-01 01:00:00	9.19	0.0
2	2018-01-01 02:00:00	9.04	0.0
3	2018-01-01 03:00:00	8.37	0.0
4	2018-01-01 04:00:00	8.14	0.0

Our next step will be to combine this dataset with our order dataset. This is difficult because the two datasets are on different time frequencies. Notice that in the weather dataset, we have data points for every hour of each day. Our order dataset, however, contains one line every time an order is placed. How are we to join these two datasets to carry out the analyses described previously? This is a tricky question, so take a few minutes to think about it. ♦

Our solution will be to simply resample the orders DataFrame using the methods we covered in section 8.5.2 to find a summary of orders for every hour. We then can join this new hourly table to our weather data. On the basis of the analyses we said we wanted to carry out, we need the following columns in our new hourly order table: ♦

- The number of orders in that hour
- The average number of drinks per order in that hour
- The percentage of orders in that hour that were deliveries

We will create three tables, each containing one of these columns, and then join them to obtain one final table.

Let's begin with a column that contains one row per hour, and gives the number of orders in that hour. We can generate it as follows: ♦

```
df_num_orders = ( df_orders.set_index('DATETIME')
                 .resample('H')
                 .size()
                 .reset_index()
                 .rename(columns={0: 'NUM_ORDERS'}) )
```

The first line sets the index of the DataFrame to the DATETIME column. We then resample the DataFrame by hour, and apply the size() function to find the number of rows in each hour and reset the index. At this point, we're left with a DataFrame with one column called DATETIME containing the hour the row refers to, and one column called 0 (you will recall this happens because we applied the size() function to the whole DataFrame rather than to a particular column). The last line renames that column to NUM_ORDERS. Try each part of this statement to ensure that you understand what it does.

Let's now produce a second DataFrame that gives the average number of drinks bought in every hour: ♦

```
df_av_drinks = ( df_orders.set_index('DATETIME')
                    .resample('H')
                    .DRINKS
                    .mean()
                    .reset_index() )
```

This works exactly like the previous code, except that we now use the mean() function on the DRINKS column, and therefore we do not need to rename anything at the end.

Finally, we need a third DataFrame that will list the average number of orders in that hour that were deliveries. This is only slightly more tricky; we can generate it as follows: ◆

```
df_orders['IS_DELIVERY'] = (df_orders.TYPE == 'DELIVERY')
df_pct_delivery = ( df_orders.set_index('DATETIME')
                    .resample('H')
                    .IS_DELIVERY
                    .mean()
                    .reset_index() )
```

We begin by creating a column equal to True if the order is a delivery order and equal to False otherwise. Why does this make sense? Because you will remember that when we sum or average a column of True/False values, True values are treated as one and False values are treated as zero. Thus, by finding the average of each column, we can find the percentage of orders that were deliveries, which we do in the next statement.

Finally, we need to take these three tables and combine them into one large table using pd.merge(). Pause for a second and ask yourself what the right way is to do that. What column should you join on? What kind of join should you use? And how can you deal with joining *three* tables instead of two? Here's our solution: ◆

```
df_combined = pd.merge(df_num_orders, df_av_drinks,
                    on='DATETIME', how='outer')
df_combined = pd.merge(df_combined, df_pct_delivery,
                    on='DATETIME', how='outer')
```

First, notice we are joining on the DATETIME column, which gives the hour for each table. Second, notice that we are doing an *outer* join. In theory, this should be the same as an inner join, because the resample() function should output every hour in the year in all three of the previous tables. But better safe than sorry—an outer join ensures that we don't inadvertently drop any rows. Finally, note that we handled the three tables problem quite simply, by doing two joins in a row.

Because resample() produces one row for every hour, this table also will contain rows that correspond to hours in which *no orders* were placed at all. Our last step will be to get rid of those rows by filtering our DataFrame: ♦

```
df_combined = df_combined[df_combined.NUM_ORDERS > 0]
```

Let's have a look at the fruits of our labor:

```
df_combined.head()
```

	DATETIME	NUM_ORDERS	DRINKS	IS_DELIVERY
0	2018-01-01 10:00:00	80	0.037500	0.175000
1	2018-01-01 11:00:00	359	0.083565	0.178273
2	2018-01-01 12:00:00	526	0.043726	0.188213

Exactly as we wanted.

Now that we have a DataFrame with orders *by hour*, all that remains is to join it to the weather DataFrame. What kind of join do we need here? We can do it as follows: ♦

```
df_combined = pd.merge(df_combined, df_weather,
                  on='DATETIME', how='left')
df_combined.head()
```

	DATETIME	NUM_ORDERS	DRINKS	IS_DELIVERY	TEMPERATURE	PRECIP
0	2018-01-01 10:00:00	80	0.037500	0.175000	11.14	0.0
1	2018-01-01 11:00:00	359	0.083565	0.178273	13.05	0.0
2	2018-01-01 12:00:00	526	0.043726	0.188213	14.41	0.0

The correct join is a *left* join because our "base" table is the orders table (df_combined), which will contain one row for every hour on which orders took place. For each of those hours, we want to bring in weather data. There will be plenty of hours in df_weather during which orders did *not* take place (e.g., times in the middle of the night), and we don't want to bother bringing in those times. Thus, a left join is appropriate.

We finally are ready to address our first question and determine whether the proportion of deliveries varies with temperature. How would you use df_combined to answer this question? Your first instinct might be to plot a graph with temperature on the *x*-axis, and the proportion of deliveries on the *y*-axis, with one point for every row in the DataFrame. We can do this as follows: ♦

```
df_combined.plot(x='TEMPERATURE', y='IS_DELIVERY',
                                kind='scatter')
```

`<matplotlib.axes._subplots.AxesSubplot at 0x1306d0bd0>`

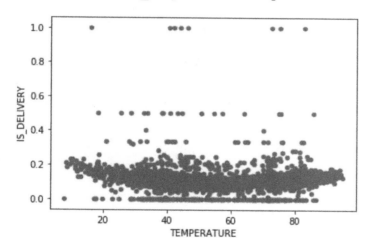

Unfortunately, this doesn't seem particularly helpful. The table contains almost nine thousand rows, so our plot contains nine thousand points. It's quite difficult to make out exactly what's going on in this mess of points.

A better approach might be to create "buckets" of temperature (say from 0°F to 10°F, 10°F to 20°F, and so on) and find the *average* delivery percentage in each of those buckets. This summarized result might be a little more insightful than this mass of points.

First, we need to figure out how to produce these buckets. pandas has some specialized functions to do this, but we can use a quick-and-dirty approach for now. All we need to do is divide each temperature number by 10, round it, and then multiply it by 10 again. For example, a temperature of 23°F would first be divided by 10 to get 2.3. This would then be rounded to 2. Finally, we would multiply it by 10 to get 20. Similarly, a temperature of 17°F would be divided by 10 to get 1.7, rounded to get 2, and multiplied by 10 to get 20. Thus, every temperature from 15°F to 25°F would be placed in the "20" bucket. Any temperature from 25°F to 35°F would be placed in the "30" bucket, and so on.

To carry out these operations in pandas, we can simply do this:

```
((df_combined.TEMPERATURE/10).round()*10).head()
```

```
0    10.0
1    10.0
2    10.0
3    20.0
4    20.0
Name: TEMPERATURE, dtype: float64
```

Interestingly, pandas also allows you to type df_combined.TEMPERATURE. round(-1) to do this in one step.

All that's left to do is to groupby() these buckets, and find the average delivery percentage per bucket. We could do this, of course, by creating a new column containing the buckets, or we could use the trick in section 8.5.1 to group by a series:

```
( df_combined
    .groupby((df_combined.TEMPERATURE/10).round()*10)
    .IS_DELIVERY
    .mean()
    .plot(kind='bar') )
```

```
<matplotlib.axes._subplots.AxesSubplot at 0x12844c0d0>
```

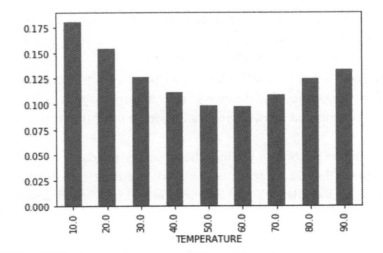

The results are exactly as we might expect. At very low temperatures, the percentage of delivery orders is through the roof, reaching almost 20 percent at the coldest temperatures. As things warm up, delivery gets less popular, until temperatures get *very* hot, at which point the proportion of deliveries ticks up a little again. This could be crucial information for Dig as it plans for a week that looks like it might be particularly cold.

We can do exactly the same using the DRINKS column to see how the number of drinks per order varies with temperature:

```
( df_combined
    .groupby((df_combined.TEMPERATURE/10).round()*10)
    .DRINKS
    .mean()
    .plot(kind='bar') )
```

```
<matplotlib.axes._subplots.AxesSubplot at 0x1284edfd0>
```

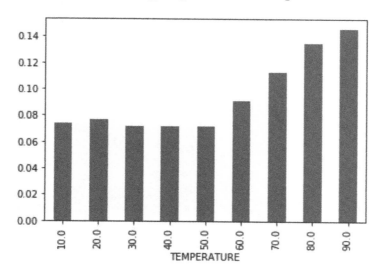

Again, the results are enlightening. When temperatures are moderate, the number of drinks per order seems to hover around eight drinks per hundred orders. As temperatures get very warm, the numbers tick up to a maximum of more than fourteen drinks per hundred orders. This could be invaluable information if Dig were looking for a good time to advertise a new drink offering.

Take a second to marvel at what we've done. We started with more than two million rows of data—a dataset that would have been far too large to open in Excel. Using almost every trick we have learned, we reduced it to a much smaller dataset that summarized these millions of orders on an hourly basis. Finally, we combined two distinct data sources together to produce valuable business insights that would have been difficult to obtain without the tools Python made available to us.

9.10 WRAPPING UP

This was the last chapter in this book. If you stuck with us the whole way, many congratulations! In this chapter, we hopefully showed you how versatile and powerful Python and pandas can be in analyzing real life-size datasets.

Believe or not, we have only scratched the surface. We haven't even touched on an enormous amount of functionality. Nevertheless, having learned the material in this book, you are now equipped with the tools you need to explore this programming world on your own. In the conclusion, we point you to various resources you can use to begin this journey and locate the tools you will need to make Python work for you.

WHAT'S NEXT?

IT'S TIME TO WRAP UP THIS BOOK. And what a long way we've come!

As Stephen Colbert says, "Welcome to the nerd zone, my friend." One of the things we love about coding is that once you've learned it, you can't *unsee* it. Meaning that once you've pulled back a layer and explored the hidden inner working of some of the tools we use every day, it's hard to see the world in the same way. One day soon, you may read something somewhere that has a coding joke and you'll stop and think, "Oh! I get it!"

So how did we get here? We started with the basics—using the command line, writing and running scripts in Python, and troubleshooting and debugging errors. We then moved on to variables, data types, and control structures—from if statements, to for loops. We closed off part 1 by discussing functions, a powerful way to encapsulate small bits of reusable code. In part 2, we then dove into the world of data—we discussed pandas, and using it to read, write, and modify datasets. We looked at how multiple datasets could be combined for analysis. Finally, we discussed aggregation, and used these techniques to answer a number of business questions from the Dig case.

Remember day one?

```
print("Winter is coming.")
```

This seems like so long ago. And something that seemed so complex, now seems so simple.

Of course, it's easy to feel overwhelmed at this point. To paraphrase Donald Rumsfeld, "there are known knowns, there are known unknowns, and then there are the unknown unknowns." It's possible you're feeling even more overwhelmed than when you started, because now you realize how much you still don't know about Python.

Remember that the goal of this book was not for you to finish feeling like you have mastered Python, but for you to learn enough to be able to continue exploring on your own, and not feel overwhelmed. The scope of Python is *huge*, and now you know a tiny bit of it (but hopefully it will come in handy).

It has been said that Albert Einstein once was asked what his phone number was. He proceeded to pull out a phone book.

His friend said, "What, you don't have your phone number memorized?"

To which Einstein reportedly responded, "Never memorize anything you can look up."

In this age of Google, know that you can always do a quick search in case you need to remember how to do something in Python.

So, sit back, relax, and remember that knowing Python makes you more valuable than 99 percent of other MBAs, managers, analysts, and so on.[1]

Where do you go from here? Remember those choose-your-own-adventure books in which you'd read up to a certain point, be faced with a decision about whether to open a door (turn to page 17) or go down a dark hallway (turn to page 48)? Learning to code is a little like that. We chose the topics in this book to introduce you to a number of different aspects of Python. You're now in a good position to understand whatever topic you want to explore next—what page you want to turn to.

If you're already hungry for more, we recommend these great follow-up books:

1. If you're interested in Python's ability to make your life easier by automating day-to-day tasks, look no further than *Automate the Boring Stuff with Python* by Al Sweigart. This book shows you how to do things with Python like send emails and text messages, read PDF documents, access Google Spreadsheets, and more.

2. If you're interested in studying the material in part 2 in greater depth, the *Python Data Science Handbook* by Jake VanderPlas is excellent. It covers all the material we discussed and much more.

3. If you are interested in machine learning and in how Python can help you build your own machine learning solutions, *Introduction to Machine Learning with Python*, by Andreas Müller and Sarah Guido, is a great resource.[2]

Fortunately, as of writing this, the first two of these books are available for free in their entirety online. Another great resource we'd recommend is HackerRank. com, where you can practice your Python skills with basic to advanced challenges. Companies have even started using sites like HackerRank as a way to evaluate coders during the hiring process.

One of the hardest parts of continuing your learning on your own is the troubleshooting process. What happens if you're on your own and you run into a problem that you can't figure out how to solve? Fortunately, Python has a large community for support. One of the best ways to learn is to go to a Python meetup and ask someone who knows more than you. If you happen to live in a major city in the United States, the website meetup.com has Python-related meetups most days of the week. But if you don't, plenty of online communities and forums still are available to you. The unofficial Python Slack community, called PySlackers, currently has more than twenty-five thousand members who often are friendly and willing to help a beginner (as long as you're nice).

We both want to take this opportunity to thank you for coming with us on this journey. We hope you had as much fun reading this book as we had writing it. If you're feeling grateful, or you have any questions or feedback, please reach out to us and stay in touch by emailing authors@pythonformbas.com. Good luck.

NOTES

1. GETTING STARTED WITH PYTHON

1. *Stack Overflow Developer Survey 2019*, Stack Overflow, 2019, https://insights.stackoverflow.com/survey/2019/.
2. "Number of Words in the English Language," Global Language Monitor, January 1, 2020, https://www.languagemonitor.com/global-english/no-of-words/.
3. Robert Lane Greene, "Lexical Facts," *The Economist*, May 29, 2013, https://www.economist.com/johnson/2013/05/29/lexical-facts.
4. Sergey Brin and Larry Page, "The Anatomy of a Large-Scale Hypertextual Web Search Engine" (Computer Science Department, Stanford University, Stanford, CA, 1998), http://infolab.stanford.edu/~backrub/google.html.
5. David Robinson, "The Incredible Growth of Python," *Stack Overflow* (blog), September 6, 2017, https://stackoverflow.blog/2017/09/06/incredible-growth-python/.
6. *Stack Overflow Developer Survey 2019*, Stack Overflow, 2019, https://insights.stackoverflow.com/survey/2019/.
7. Stephen Kurczy, "MBAs Who Code" (Ideas at Work, Columbia Business School, September 12, 2018), https://www8.gsb.columbia.edu/articles/ideas-work/mbas-who-code.
8. If this bothers you, you can actually turn off this feature by running the following code in your command line:

```
conda config --set changeps1 False
```

and then restarting the command line.

2. PYTHON BASICS, PART 1

1. Or Bing, DuckDuckGo, or whatever search engine you prefer.
2. Pearl Philip, "'Syntax Error: Invalid Syntax' For No Apparent Reason," Stack Overflow forum, June 16, 2014, https://stackoverflow.com/questions/24237111/syntax-error-invalid-syntax-for-no-apparent-reason.

3. "How Do I Ask a Good Question?" Stack Overflow, Help Center, https://stackoverflow .com/help/how-to-ask.

4. Guido van Rossum, Z Barry Warsaw, and Nick Coghlan, *PEP 8—Style Guide for Python Code* (Fredericksburg, VA: Python Software Foundation, 2018), https://www.python.org /dev/peps/pep-0008/#method-names-and-instance-variables.

5. Actually, this is only true in Python 3. In Python 2, you'd always get back an integer, but then running 1 / 2 would return 0, which as you can imagine, might get confusing. In Python 2, if you wanted to divide two numbers and get back a float, you'd have to specifi- cally tell it to do that. That's pretty counterintuitive, so they changed this in Python 3.

6. The origin of the word "string" for text actually goes back much further than Python. Strings are called "strings" because they are made up of a sequence, or string, of characters.

3. PYTHON BASICS, PART 2

1. Joel Spolsky, "Netscape Goes Bonkers," *Joel on Software* (blog), November 20, 2000, https:// www.joelonsoftware.com/2000/11/20/netscape-goes-bonkers/.

2. Technically, `range()` actually produces something called a range (not a list) in Python 3, but you can loop over it just like a list.

3. At the moment, the shortest solution to FizzBuzz on HackerRank is a full twenty characters shorter than the one we've included, and we honestly have no idea how they managed to do it (the solution itself isn't posted, just the score). We're pretty impressed.

4. It is also possible to label elements in dictionaries with numbers, but we'll say "strings" throughout this section to distinguish these dictionaries from lists.

4. PYTHON BASICS, PART 3

1. It's interesting to note that `if()` is a function in Excel but not in Python—that's just a decision made by the people who created Python. They could have made it a function, but they didn't.

2. There's actually a subtle difference between calling `split()` and `split(" ")`. Try it on the following string: `"Once more      unto the breach"` (notice the multiple spaces and make sure you type them in, although it doesn't matter if you copy the spacing exactly).

3. Other code smells include functions that are really long and have too many levels of indentation in Python, but there are many, many others.

4. "How many lines of code does Windows 10 contain?" Quora, https://www.quora.com/How -many-lines-of-code-does-Windows-10-contain.

5. It uses Python's extended slice syntax. We encourage you to explore this on your own if you're interested, but it's not worth including here.

6. Some slight technical differences exist in Python between packages, libraries, and modules, but for the purpose of this book, it's helpful to just consider them all the same thing.

7. Also note the lack of parentheses in `print "Hello, world!"`—a telltale sign this comic was written for Python 2.

8. You have other ways to install packages, and other package repositories are available, but most Python coders find that `pip` is by far the easiest to use.

5. INTRODUCTION TO DATA IN PYTHON

1. Linette Lopez, "How the London Whale Debacle Is Partly the Result of an Error Using Excel," *Business Insider*, February 12, 2013, https://www.businessinsider.com/excel-partly -to-blame-for-trading-loss-2013-2.

2. You can launch *Jupyter* in a number of ways. For example, you can launch an application called *Anaconda Navigator*, which exists on both PC and Mac, and launch *Jupyter Notebook* from there. We find the previous method to be the easiest.

3. For those of you who are curious, the book's website also contains the file `Orders.csv` that records every order in full, including all the noted complexities.

4. The other method is to call the relevant function with the argument `inplace=True`. We never use this method in this book, for various reasons, not least of which is the fact it might be removed in future versions of `pandas`; see https://github.com/pandas-dev/pan-das/issues/16529.

5. If you do this incorrectly, you'll get a `FileNotFound` error.

6. EXPLORING, PLOTTING, AND MODIFYING DATA IN PYTHON

1. When and if you learn more about plotting in Python, you'll discover that the main plot-ting library in Python is called `matplotlib`. Rather than introduce `matplotlib` syntax separately in this book, we rely on a shortcut that allows plots to be produced directly from `pandas`. All the options and features we discuss here are also available if you ever produce plots in `matplotlib` directly.

2. Of course, you might want to build different rules for each restaurant, which would require individually calculating means and standard deviations for each restaurant. We do not, unfortunately, have the tools to do this yet, but we will return to this problem in chapter 9.

3. These "continuous histograms" are generated using a method called a *kernel density estimator*; hence, the "kde" in the function's arguments.

4. We will return to these functions in section 8.3.1, when we also discuss how they handle missing values.

5. You might notice that the *x*-axis is somewhat scrunched up because there are many numbers to plot. Tweaking the appearance of a plot is an enormous topic that we won't have time to address in this book, but tweaking the size is actually quite simple—you sim-ply need to use the `figsize` argument with the `plot()` function. In this case, try passing `figsize=(10,5)`: the first number is the width, and the second is the height.

6. The more astute among you might have noticed that this statement compares a variable of type DateTime (`df_orders.DATETIME`) with a string (`'2018-06-01'`). Generally, this would be a problem, but in this specific instance, `pandas` is smart enough to make the comparison.

7. In fact, what makes this error especially infuriating is that this isn't *always* true. Sometimes, `pandas` will return a direct reference to the original DataFrame instead of a copy and this statement *will* work. Nevertheless, because this behavior is unpredictable, you should *never* use this method of editing specific cells in a DataFrame.

8. Note that we will cover far more efficient ways of doing this in chapter 9, and we will apply these methods to this problem in section 9.7. We use this example here as a way to get more practice with the concepts in this chapter.

7. BRINGING TOGETHER DATASETS

1. In theory, an outer join could work here as well, as long as there are no data errors—in particular, as long as there are no drivers in `df_driving` that also are not in `df_drivers`.

8. AGGREGATION

1. One downside of *not* using a specific column when applying `size()` is that the resulting series will not have a name. Thus, if you do `reset_index()` on the result, pandas will have nothing to call the column, and it will simply call it 0. To see this in action, try to do this: `df_orders.groupby('RESTAURANT_NAME').size().reset_index()`.
2. The parts of a multi-level index are called "levels", not "columns" in pandas. Since we do not go into multi-level indexes in any great detail in this book, we will refer to them as "columns" for simplicity.
3. If you're a glutton for punishment, you also could do each aggregation separately and then join the two tables; we give you code to do this in this chapter's notebook. We think this method is simpler, however!
4. At this point, we should note that there are many other ways to use `agg()`; we introduced only the one we find most useful and general, but we encourage you to explore the documentation and the other ways the function can be used.
5. In theory, you can use `resample()` with a column of the DataFrame, but as of the time we wrote this book, this functionality was a little buggy when used with `groupby()`, so you should avoid this (for those who are interested, see pandas issue #30057 on GitHub, reported by yours truly). If this improves in a later version, we will post a notice on the book's website.
5. "Offset Aliases," pandas User Guide, https://pandas.pydata.org/pandas-docs/stable/user _guide/timeseries.html#offset-aliases.

WHAT'S NEXT?

1. Okay that's a totally made-up statistic . . . sort of. The *Stack Overflow Developer Survey 2019* listed Python at the top of its "Most Wanted" programming languages for the third year in a row. *Stack Overflow Developer Survey 2019*, Stack Overflow, 2019, https://insights.stackoverflow .com/survey/2019/.
2. Al Sweigart, *Automate the Boring Stuff with Python*, https://automatetheboringstuff.com; Jake VanderPlas, *Python Data Science Handbook* (Sebastopol, CA: O'Reilly Media, 2017), https://jakevdp.github.io/PythonDataScienceHandbook; Andreas Müller and Sarah Guido, *Introduction to Machine Learning with Python* (Sebastopol, CA: O'Reilly Media, 2017).

INDEX

Mattan Griffel and Daniel Guetta teach two programs for professionals—Python for Managers—offered by Columbia Business School Executive Education in both synchronous and asynchronous formats. With a focus on practical business applications, the programs include opportunities to read and write scripts, work with simulated data from a case study, and execute a final project with real-world application. At the end of the programs, you will be able to organize, aggregate, and analyze large amounts of data using Python. For more information, visit Columbia.Business/python.

 **Columbia Business School** | EXECUTIVE EDUCATION
AT THE VERY CENTER OF BUSINESS™